Case Studies in
Applied Sport Psychology

An Educational Approach

Mark A. Thompson, Ph.D.
Inner Edge

Ralph A. Vernacchia, Ph.D.
Western Washington University

William E. Moore, Ph.D.
East Carolina University

KENDALL/HUNT PUBLISHING COMPANY
4050 Westmark Drive   Dubuque, Iowa 52002

This edition was printed directly from camera-ready copy.

Copyright © 1998 by Mark A. Thompson, Ralph A. Vernacchia and William E. Moore

ISBN 0-7872-5160-7

Printed in the United States of America
10 9 8 7 6 5 4 3 2 1

Dedication

This work is dedicated to Dr. David L. Cook for his vision of applied sport psychology and his commitment to making it a "Utopia" for all. Without his desire to foster a new way of sharing and learning, this book would not have been possible. Thanks, Dave.

To my wife, Deborah, and our children, Alex and Mallory - the sources of my drive, commitment, and inspiration.

- Mark

CONTENTS

Part III ~ Recommendations   245

14   The Value of Failure   247

Mark A. Thompson, Kenneth Ravizza

15   A Charge   257

Mark A. Thompson

Preface

Several years ago, after attending numerous professional conferences, a thought occurred to me that would transform my professional career. I noticed that at conference sites through the years, my greatest professional growth occurred in small groups around dinner, in the hotel lobby, or on the golf course. The experiences that were shared and the wisdom that emerged from the group in these settings were priceless. I believed that the interaction and information exchange in these settings far outweighed the benefits gained from sitting and listening to yet another lecture in the traditional conference format.

Around 1989, the "Utopian Think Tank" was conceived. The initial think tank was held in Utopia, Texas and was composed of twenty-one of the leading applied sport psychology professionals in the country. These were individuals who, across the years, had consistently gathered in informal settings to share case studies and experiences at national sport psychology conferences. A professional bond, respect, and trust had been established through the process.

The purpose of the think tank was to meet in an informal setting, share successful and unsuccessful case studies, and fellowship together through unique activities (hot-tubbing in the rain, tubing down a lazy river, having a campfire cookout with real "cowpoke" entertainment, shooting sporting clays). Utopia, Texas was chosen as the site due to its one-of-a-kind setting and proximity to my family's wildlife ranch. This ranch provided many opportunities for team-building activities among the group as well as serenity for self-reflection.

The effect of this and subsequent meetings through the years has had a profound impact on our lives. A new way of learning and communicating applied sport psychology was born which would affect each of our careers and the athletes and coaches for whom we worked. Over the better part of ten years, now, these get-togethers have taken place at varied locations, from the East Coast to the West Coast, and including return trips to Utopia. We have welcomed and benefited from the involvement of numerous sport psychology professionals, coaches, graduate students, and athletes. Each formal gathering has produced a unique environment that reinvigorates and breathes passion into the lives of both new and old "Utopians". The result has been an ever-expanding circle of colleagues/friends who are committed to developing and offering the best in applied sport psychology.

This book is an outgrowth of many of the case studies which were discussed in Utopia. It is our hope that the information within these pages will open new possibilities for your work with aspiring champions. We believe that sport psychology is an art and that case studies provide a powerful tool with which to transmit information across our profession. We are indebted to the lives of the athletes whom you will meet in the chapters that follow. They represent a new breed of champions who have approached our field trusting that we have information which will take them to the next level. Lets not let them down.

David L. Cook, *Mental Advantage, Inc.*

Acknowledgments

This book is truly a team effort. The contributing authors are only the tip of the iceberg. Others we would like to acknowledge include fellow professionals who contributed case studies, including: Glen Albaugh, Deidre Connelly, Dick Coop, Lew Curry, Will Freeman, Tom Hanson, Gary Howard, Phil Lowcock, Bob McGowan, John Muczko, Dave Templin, and Darla Wagner. Others deserving recognition for their feedback, encouragement, and belief in the value of case studies include: Don Dobson, Gary Mack, Craig Poole, Sue Reardon, Gary Schwartz, Glen Sefcik, and John Stevenson. The editors would also like to acknowledge David Pike and Paul Carty of Kendall/Hunt Publishing Company, for their patience and freedom in developing the book. Finally, and most importantly, we would like to acknowledge the athletes and coaches who have allowed us to enter their lives, given their trust, and believed with us in the performance and personal value of applied sport psychology.

Contributors

Mark A. Thompson is the founder of Inner Edge, a private consulting firm offering performance enhancement consultation to the sport, exercise, and business communities. Dr. Thompson is a Certified Consultant, AAASP, is a member of the USA Gymnastics National Health Care Referral Network, and is former Chair of the NASPE Sport Psychology Academy. His research has addressed mental training programs, aggression in sport, training in applied sport psychology, and sport participation dynamics. He has over 30 research presentations, one book chapter, and numerous invited presentations to his credit. Dr. Thompson was a university faculty member for seven years, teaching applied sport psychology and sport sociology courses, and working with the intercollegiate athletic department. He has consulted with recreational and professional athletes in golf, gymnastics, basketball, baseball, volleyball, swimming, body building, and track & field. His competition background includes participation in basketball, football, track & field, golf, and baseball. He currently enjoys coaching his children's basketball and soccer teams as well as participating in recreational golf, cycling, softball, and basketball.

Ralph A. Vernacchia is a professor of physical education in the department of physical education, health and recreation at Western Washington University where he directs the undergraduate and graduate programs in sport and exercise psychology. He is a co-author of Coaching Mental Excellence: It Does Matter Whether You Win or Lose!, and has presented extensively on a variety of sport psychology topics throughout the nation. He is a certified consultant (AAASP) and is currently the chair for AAHPERD's NASPE Sport Psychology Academy. His research interests include mental training, and the psychology of coaching and athletic performance. He serves as a performance consultant to the Western Washington University Athletic Department and is a co-chair for the sport psychology sub-committee of USA Track and Field. He has traveled internationally as a performance consultant with several US track and field teams and serves as sport psychology curriculum chair and an instructor for the USA Track and Field National Coaching Education Program. He was a cross country and track and field coach for twenty-two years and was inducted into the Western Washington University's Athletic Hall-of-Fame in 1993 in recognition of his coaching accomplishments.

William E. Moore is an assistant professor and Director of tennis at East Carolina University. He received his master's and doctorate degrees in Sport Psychology from the University of Virginia. Dr. Moore's research interests center around the interrelationships between psychology and motor control in understanding the performance status of skilled athletes. This research has translated into an understanding of the foundations of "trust" as it relates to athletic performance. His research has been published in both applied and research journals. Dr. Moore has consulted with athletes from a number of elite and professional organizations, including the: USOC, PGA, LPGA, USPTA, and USTA. He has also played and coached tennis at Junior, Collegiate, and Professional levels.

Gloria Balague is a Clinical Assistant Professor at the University of Illinois at Chicago and a consultant for USA Track & Field and USA Gymnastics. She was born and raised in Barcelona, Spain where she obtained her degree in psychology and worked at the National Sports Medicine Research Center. She has served as a sport psychologist for the US Junior National Team, the 1992 USA Olympic Track & Field team, the 1995 World Indoors, the Pan American Games, and the 1996 US Olympic Rhythmic Gymnastics team. Dr. Balague has been extensively involved in coaching education and has focused her research on achievement motivation. She served as the Vice-President of ISSP from 1989-1993. Dr. Balague has made hundreds of presentations world-wide, including the Intervention/Performance Enhancement Keynote at the 1997 AAASP conference in San Diego.

David L. Cook is president of Mental Advantage, Inc., a Fort Worth-based performance enhancement firm which serves both business and sport communities. He served as Director of Applied Sport and Performance Psychology at the University of Kansas for 12 years. He is a former chair of the NASPE Sport Psychology Academy and has authored two books. Dr. Cook is nationally known as one of the leading experts in the areas of individual and team performance enhancement training. He has been called upon by performers and teams from Fortune 500 companies, the NFL, NBA, MLB, Olympics, Collegiate National Champions, and over 100 professional golfers.

Richard D. Gordin has been a Professor and Chair of Graduate Studies at Utah State University for 20 years. He is currently consulting for USA Gymnastics, USA Track & Field, the United States Fencing Association and many professionals on the PGA Tour. He is the past Chair of the Certification Committee of AAASP and is a Charter Member of Division 47 of APA. He has been listed on the Sport Psychology Registry of the USOC since its inception in 1983. He has published over 60 papers and presented over 200 times in the area of applied sport psychology. His areas of expertise are performance enhancement and hypnosis in sport.

Keith P. Henschen is a professor in the Department of Exercise and Sport Science at the University of Utah, where he has been for 26 years, with an expertise in the psychosocial aspects of sports. Dr. Henschen's research interests include the psychology of performance, use of psychological interventions in sport, and sport psychology for special populations. He has published approximately 180 articles, 20 book chapters, 5 monographs, and co-authored three text books. He has directed 40 doctoral dissertations and 20 masters' theses. Dr. Henschen is a frequent research presenter and conference speaker with over 300 presentations to his credit. He has consulted with numerous world class, professional and elite level athletes as well as three National Governing Boards for the USOC. He has served as the sport psychology consultant for the US Gymnastics Federation, US Biathlon Association, and the US Association of Track & Field. Dr. Henschen also works with numerous college and professional teams in a variety of sports.

Richard T. McGuire is a graduate professor in sport psychology and the Head Track & Field Coach at the University of Missouri. He also serves as the Chairman of Sport Psychology for USA Track & Field. Dr. McGuire served on the staff of the 1992 and 1996 US Olympics Track & Field teams. Other sport psychology consultation includes work with Major League Baseball, the Canadian National Basketball team, and member of the PGA. Dr. McGuire is also co-founder of Turning Point, Int'l. which provides education and encouragement for athletes, coaches, teachers, and the business community.

Kenneth Ravizza is a professor in the Department of Health, Physical Education, and Recreation at California State University at Fullerton. He is a Certified Consultant, AAASP, and has served as Chair of the NASPE Sport Psychology Academy. Dr. Ravizza has worked extensively with collegiate, Olympic, and professional athletes. His work has included consultation with Olympic water polo, baseball, women's field hockey, figure skating, and equestrian. He has also worked with professional baseball and football teams. Dr. Ravizza's research has examined the nature of peak performance in sport and assisted in his development of stress management programs for varied populations.

James P. Reardon is Director of Columbus Traumatic Stress Center in Columbus, Ohio where he is a consulting psychologist with over twenty years of clinical experience. In his clinical work, Dr. Reardon specializes in diagnosis and treatment of post-traumatic stress, anxiety, dissociative, and personality disorders. He is a Certified Consultant, AAASP and is a member of the USOC Sport Psychology Registry. His national and international sport psychology experience is extensive, including serving as a sport psychology consultant for numerous elite and Olympic athletes, including: USA Track & Field, USA/Visa "Gold Medal Decathlon Program", Basketball Canada, the 1990 Goodwill Games, numerous World Championships, and the 1996 Olympic Games.

Wesley E. Sime is a health psychologist and sport psychologist. He has advanced degrees in both exercise physiology and counseling psychology. He is a licensed psychologist and is certified by AAASP with USOC registry membership. Dr. Sime provides consultation to several university teams in addition to individual work with professional athletes and health psychology clients struggling with symptoms of headache, ulcers, anxiety, depression, etc. Wes is certified in two adjunctive areas (Stress Management Education and in Clinical Biofeedback) which helps in his work with athletes and other clients. He has recently completed training in EMDR and finds this to be an interesting new technique potentially effective for athletes, especially those who have suffered severe traumatic injury and are attempting to return to sport competition.

Jeff Simons is Director of Sport Psychology Services in the Centre for Rehabilitation, Exercise and Sport Science at Victoria University, Melbourne, Australia. He is a registered sport psychologist in Australia and a Certified Consultant, AAASP. Dr. Simons spends the majority of his time as a consultant sport psychologist for state and national sport governing bodies. He was a staff member on the 1996 Australian Olympic Team and serves on several national sport science committees. Dr. Simons received his Ph.D. from University of Illinois and taught at University of Southern California, UCLA and University of Colorado prior to Victoria University. He specializes in psycho-motor performance enhancement and has worked extensively with elite athletes and coaches in more than 25 sports.

Jodi Yambor is a professor of psychology in the Department of Human Services at Thomas College in Thomasville, Georgia. She is also a private consultant with Performance Enhancement Enterprises of Tallahassee, Florida. Dr. Yambor is a Certified Consultant, AAASP, is a member of the USOC sport psychology registry, and works with USA Track & Field. She was the first sport psychology consultant hired full-time by an athletic department at the University of Miami. Dr. Yambor has participated in numerous clinics and conferences internationally for coaches, athletes, and parents. Dr. Yambor has six years of college coaching experience, was a 15 time All-American swimmer, is a former American record holder, and was recently inducted into the University of Miami Sports Hall of Fame.

David P. Yukelson is an applied sport psychology practitioner with the Academic Support Center for Student-Athletes at Pennsylvania State University. In this role, he provides counseling and support for coaches and athletes in the areas of mental skills training, motivation, self-confidence, stress management, and responsible decision making. Dr. Yukelson is a Fellow and Certified Consultant, AAASP, has served as Chair of the NASPE Sport Psychology Academy, and has worked extensively with the US Men's and Women's National and Junior Elite Racewalking Teams. He is a national faculty member with the American Coaching Effectiveness Program and has written and presented extensively on the topic of "Communication". Dr. Yukelson's research has included mental skills training, individual and group sport motivation, life skill development for student-athletes, and the psychology of injury.

PART I

Introduction to the
Case Study Method

In Part I, the focus is on laying the philosophical, historical, and practical foundation for the book. A philosophy of applied sport psychology is outlined to provide the reader with an understanding of the perspective of the contributing authors and practitioners who supplied the case studies. An in-depth discussion of the case study method and recommendations for its use are provided to serve as the "how to" guide for application of the book material. This includes an understanding of the history and role of the case study in applied sport psychology. Finally, Dr. Keith Henschen provides a fresh, honest, insightful perspective on understanding issues that lie beneath surface issues in applied sport psychology.

CHAPTER 1

~ A Philosophy of Applied Sport Psychology ~

Mark A. Thompson, Inner Edge

A philosophy serves as a set of guiding principles for those who subscribe to the philosophy. Applied sport psychology is defined by a general philosophical approach to intervention and performance enhancement for sport. Williams and Straub (1993) define **applied sport psychology** as, "...identifying and understanding psychological theories and techniques that can be applied to sport and exercise to enhance the performance and personal growth of athletes...". This general definition is made operational by the authors of the following chapters to develop a consistent working philosophy of applied sport psychology. This is not to say that all contributors are of one mindset, but they do share common beliefs about an approach to applied sport psychology. The following should provide some insight into these common beliefs.

Emphases of Applied Sport Psychology

During a discussion of philosophy of applied sport psychology, one might hear the statement, "You don't have to be sick to get better.". Though a simplistic statement, it possesses deep meaning and significant ramifications for the applied sport psychology professional. It also meshes with the authors' common philosophy. The *applied* orientation is distinct from a medical model approach which focuses on the elimination of sickness and/or abnormality. *Clinical* sport psychology has roots in the medical model, addressing issues that are beyond the breadth of "normal" performance issues. These issues, indeed, have significant impact on athletic performance, but, by the nature of the issues, fall outside the boundaries of the *educational* sport psychology professional. According to Weinberg and Gould (1995), clinical sport psychologists, by training, are capable of detecting and treating those who experience clinical emotional disorders (e.g., eating disorders, clinical depression). The clinical orientation may vary according to the training of the psychologist. These orientations may include, but not be limited to socio-behavioral, psychodynamic, or cognitive-affective perspectives.

The clinical orientation is essential to the field of sport psychology and sport, in general, but may not encompass other essential elements of sport performance. These elements are addressed by, depending on one's terminology, *educational* sport psychology or *applied* sport psychology. Educational/applied sport psychologists may be thought of as "mental coaches" (Weinberg & Gould, 1995). As a mental coach, the applied sport psychology professional facilitates the athlete's learning about the psychological dynamics that influence performance (e.g., confidence, motivation, concentration/attentional focus, arousal, anxiety, communication, etc.) and techniques or strategies that can aid in the achievement of greater performance (e.g., goal-setting, arousal management, positive self-talk, thought-stopping, etc.).

An applied orientation is akin to assessing an athlete's current status (Point A) and focusing on how to assist the athlete in achieving his/her goal (Point B). Reflecting the statement at the beginning of the section, an assumption is made that the athlete is "normal" and the focus is on performance issues. Intervention/mental training serves to build the bridge between Point A and Point B. However, if the professional identifies abnormal or dysfunctional tendencies or behaviors, referral to qualified fellow professionals is warranted. Since the practitioner must be able to identify abnormal behavior, the applied professional benefits from training in clinical and/or counseling psychology.

Athletic Excellence

An *applied* orientation may appear to be too narrow of a focus, whereby the athlete is overlooked as a whole, multi-faceted individual, and treated as a uni-dimensional entity similar to how one might view a great racehorse. The applied sport psychology professional must recognize that the "athlete" is only one component of the unique individual with whom he or she is working. An athlete does not exist in a vacuum. Indeed, the sport psychology professional must understand that an athlete's performance may reflect dynamics in other areas of the athlete's life. It is imperative for the applied practitioner to become familiar with the athlete as a person and, possibly, facilitate the athlete's recognition of this multi-faceted existence. Consequently, the applied sport psychology professional and the athlete are involved in a mutual journey of discovery, with the destination being the achievement of the athlete's goals. For many athletes, the goal is excellence; a level of performance determined by the individual.

Vernacchia, McGuire, and Cook (1992) share the following perspective on excellence:

> "Excellence! To strive toward excellence, where excellence is measured only against oneself, and never against another individual or against some predetermined standard or record. Literally, to strive to become the very best that one can become."

Consequently, excellence is individually defined and will result only from an athlete possessing a desire to strive for distinction and demonstrating a commitment to work diligently toward that goal. The applied sport psychology professional's responsibility is to assist the athlete in self-discovery and aiding in the acquisition of psychological/mental performance tools that can lead to enhanced performance.

To understand excellence in sport, one must begin with a recognition that excellence is not normal. Athletes strive for distinction by performing outside the parameters within which most athletes perform. Consequently, excellence, by definition, is abnormal; but not the type of abnormality that should be eliminated. In fact, the applied sport psychology professional should assist the athlete and coach in attaining such abnormality on a consistent basis.

The means by which this "consistent abnormality" is achieved lies at the root of the applied sport psychology professional's philosophy. In the case studies to follow, the reader should recognize the tendency of the practitioner to progress through a series of steps:

- familiarization with the individual and the situation
- ascertaining the goals of the individual
- identifying the "psychological" strengths and weaknesses of the individual
- facilitation of an understanding of what "works" with the individual
- educating the individual on skills and techniques to enhance his/her performance
- monitoring the progress of the individual towards the stated goals

In short, the athlete determines the direction of the intervention, rather than the applied sport psychology professional supplanting his/her intervention strategy onto the situation.

Personal Growth

In keeping with the Williams & Straub (1993) definition of applied sport psychology, a concurrent goal of the applied sport psychology professional should be facilitation of the athlete's personal growth. The debate rages on as to whether sport builds character or if character emerges via sport participation. Similarly, many contend that participation in sport aids one's personal growth; teaching cooperation, unselfishness, unity, responsibility, goal-directedness, respect for authority, and many other socially redeeming characteristics. However, many others contend that sport participation either stunts personal growth or facilitates such unsavory characteristics as: arrogance, perfectionism, antagonism, defiance of authority, irresponsibility, selfishness, and an ultra-competitive nature, among others.

Regardless of perspective on the preceding argument, the philosophy outlined here proposes that personal growth can be facilitated through the same skills and training that enhance performance. In other words, the authors of this text believe that mental training that addresses goal-setting, coping skills, communication, visual imagery, positive self-talk, arousal management, etc. can be generalized to other areas of the athlete's life. Such generalization can aid athletes in their personal relationships, educational pursuits, occupational demands, and a multitude of other roles.

The steps addressed earlier focus on the progression of how the applied sport psychology professional is recommended to work with an individual. The term *individual* was used to acknowledge that when an applied professional is working with an athlete or coach, they recognize the athlete's multi-faceted nature. The sport psychology professional would be doing a disservice if he or she simply focused on the sport aspect of the individual. This situation is highlighted in the *Issue Behind the Issue* chapter. Also, in the *Value of Failure* chapter, this narrowed-vision approach will be outlined as a mistake some professionals are likely to encounter.

Summary

To demonstrate foundational tenets of this philosophy of applied sport psychology, two quotes and one book excerpt are offered:

> **"Think you can, think you can't;**
> **either way you'll be right."**
> - Henry Ford

> **"Man does not simply exist,**
> **but always decides what his existence will be,**
> **what he will become in the next moment."**
> - Viktor Frankl

> **"The power of one is above all things the power to believe in yourself, often well beyond any latent ability you may have previously demonstrated. The mind is the athlete; the body is simply the means it uses to run faster or longer, jump higher, shoot straighter, kick better, swim harder, hit further, or box better. 'First with the head, then with the heart' is more than simply mixing brains with guts. It means thinking well beyond the powers of normal concentration and then daring your courage to follow your thoughts."**
> - Bryce Courtenay, *The Power of One*

The ultimate arbiter between two physically and technically equal competitors is their mental skills. The competitors are ultimately responsible for their thoughts, perspectives, and responses to situational dynamics. This is, at one time, a wonderful, yet challenging and scary position to hold, but it is one that millions of individuals devote their lives to filling. The responsibility of the applied sport psychology professional is to assist athletes and coaches in finding their own excellence.

References

Courtenay, B. (1989). The power of one (pp. 423). New York: Random House.

Vernacchia, R.A., McGuire, R.T., & Cook, D.L. (1992). Coaching mental excellence: "It does matter whether you win or lose...". Dubuque, IA: Brown & Benchmark.

Weinberg, R.S. and Gould, D. (1995). Foundations of sport and exercise psychology. Champaign, IL: Human Kinetics.

Williams, J.M. and Straub, W.F. (1993). Sport psychology: Past, present, future. In J.M. Williams (Ed.), Applied sport psychology: Personal growth to peak performance (pp. 1-10). Mountain View, CA: Mayfield Publishing.

CHAPTER 2

~ Making the Case for Case Study Research ~

Ralph A. Vernacchia, Western Washington University

One of the accepted tenets of applied sport psychology is the belief that thought precedes and influences athletic performance (Bunker, Williams, & Zinsser, 1993). The very nature of the term applied sport psychology suggests the application of logical and rational "ways of thinking" to sport, hence the term, *psycho-logic*. Therefore, if we believe that thought precedes action, then it is important that prior to and during performance athletes and coaches engage in ways of thinking and feeling which will facilitate performance. As simple as this process sounds, it is difficult to realize since the stress of athletic competition can often distract both athletes and coaches from executing their skills with confidence. Doubt, fear, and worry may creep into pre-performance thoughts and can soon create distorted thinking patterns which are counterproductive to effective performances (Bunker, Williams, & Zinsser, 1993; Williams & Leffingwell, 1996).

Applied sport psychology is directed toward normalizing our ways of thinking when we are asked to perform in the demanding arena of competitive athletics. Consequently, applied sport psychology practitioners advocate the use of a variety of cognitive strategies (i.e., self-talk, thought stoppage, etc.) which can serve to enhance athletic performance. If, in fact, the field of applied sport psychology is concerned with improving performance effectiveness through effective thinking and decision-making then it is imperative that we understand and explore the diverse ways that athletes think before, during, and after they have performed in the athletic environment. It is both apparent and logical that academics and practitioners in the field of applied sport psychology would ask research questions of athletes which would assess the cognitive styles of effective and ineffective athletic performers. To this end case study research is directed.

This chapter will provide a historical overview and applied perspective of the development and appropriateness of case methodologies, such as the case study and interview, as viable and effective tools for understanding athletic behavior. It is the purpose of this chapter to provide a framework of references for students and professionals who are interested in utilizing case studies/reports, case interviews, and single-subject research designs in their research.

Historical Perspective and Overview of the Case Method

Bruce Ogilvie and Thomas Tutko (1966), both clinical psychologists, popularized and initiated a renewed interest in sport psychology with the publication of their book, *Problem Athletes and How to Handle Them*. In their book, Ogilvie and Tutko identified several types of athletes who were difficult to coach, including the athlete who resists coaching, the con man, the hyper-anxious or "psyched out" athlete, the injury-prone athlete, the withdrawn athlete, the depression-prone athlete, and the athlete who is susceptible to "success phobia". Case studies which illustrated the "problems" of each type of athlete were presented as well as coaching suggestions for "handling" each of the various types of athletes described in their text.

Arnold Beissner (1967), a psychiatrist and former champion amateur tennis player, explored, described, and analyzed the problems of individual athletes he had treated. His book, *The Madness in Sport* utilized the case histories to provide an in-depth view of the psychological and emotional impact athletic participation had upon athletes who participated in a variety of sports including basketball, football, golf, tennis, and weight lifting. Individual case histories were also related to psychological theories about play and work as well as the psychosocial meanings of sport. While the two previously mentioned texts dealt with athletes who had psychological and emotional "problems" as a result of their participation in sport, the text *Psychology and the Superior Athlete* written by Miroslav Vanek and Bryant Cratty (1970) presented performance-oriented case narratives of the Czechoslovakian Olympic team which described the performance characteristics, motivational profile, personality traits, psychological preparation for competition, and performance effectiveness of each athlete. These case studies were an attempt to classify and discuss categories of athletes' problems rather than an attempt to outline specific ways of remediating "special hang-ups" of elite athletes.

Largely due to the visible efforts of Ogilvie and Tutko in the late 1960's sport psychology gained popularity and acceptance among athletic coaches who recognized that personality played an important role in an athlete's performance. It was during this period that psychometric inventories were utilized by sport psychologists and researchers to identify and describe the personality traits of successful elite athletes (Ogilvie, 1968; Vealey, 1992; Wiggins, 1984; Williams & Straub, 1993).

During the 1970's sport psychology academics were becoming less involved in the descriptive orientation of psychometric testing and more involved with understanding the underlying personality dynamics and interactions which affected an athlete's performance (Williams & Straub, 1993). As a result of the psychometric approach to research, personality traits appeared to be well defined and described, but little explanation was given for the underlying causes which affected athletic behavior. Furthermore, this led to a circular dilemma for the sport psychology researcher and practitioner who was limited to describing an athlete's personality as a score on a personality test or inventory, and then round out this logic by describing the test scores as representative of an athlete's personality (Vernacchia, 1973, 1977).

The limitation of psychometric research orientations in the field of sport psychology led to the utilization of case study methodologies which appeared to be a more viable avenue for assessing and understanding the motives and thinking patterns of athletes (Vernacchia, 1973, 1977). While psychometric research approaches stress inductive analysis of data, hypothetical constructs, operational validity, a nomothetic framework, and predictive validity, case study methodologies were directed at discovering and understanding the various personality dynamics which influenced athletic behavior. Case study methodologies stressed a natural process research approach which was characterized by several basic assumptions (Vernacchia, 1973, 1977):

1. Although data were gathered inductively, the case study approach to research is deductive in that it constructs a theory by logically fitting together pieces of behavior;
2. The case study approach is molar in nature and thus stresses the totality of an athlete's behavior;
3. The case study approach stresses hypothetical constructs which cannot be directly measured and can be used to tie together theoretical elements of a theory;
4. The case study approach stresses construct validity by logically joining theoretical elements;
5. The case study approach is ideographic in that it recognizes the uniqueness of the individual athlete as reflected by his or her individual differences and thus small groups or individuals are studied.

Rainer Martens (1979) recognized the need for sport psychology researchers to conduct applied or field studies in his article, *About Smocks and Jocks.* In the article Martens expressed his disenchantment with laboratory research and "logical positivism" and identified the negative biases related to applied research which exist in academia (Martens, 1979). Martens plea, "To get at the complexities of human behavior in sport, much of our field research will need to be large-scale, long-term, and multivariate" (Martens, 1979, p. 98) gained more acceptability for case study research which stressed a phenomenological and ideographic approach to assessing human behavior.

The 1980's were characterized by a coming of age of applied sport psychology as evidenced by the formation of the Association for the Advancement of Applied Sport Psychology (AAASP) in 1985 (Williams & Straub, 1993). Once again Rainer Martens (1987) addressed the need for more applied or field research in his article, *Science, Knowledge, and Sport Psychology* which was a keynote address at the initial AAASP national convention held at Jekyll Island, Georgia in the fall of 1986. In his address he once again made his case for "practicing sport psychology" by stating:

> With regard to human behavior, I believe most events are determined or caused, but I also believe some events are random and thus unpredictable. What this means to me is that the study of human behavior cannot be an exact science; at best we will be able only to understand and predict behavior imperfectly (Martens, 1987, p. 34).

In his AAASP address, Martens also promoted a heuristic research paradigm which emphasized the value of experiential knowledge. He felt such a paradigm, which stresses ideographic research approaches, introspection, and field studies, could best investigate the relationship of cognitive processes and human behavior (Martens, 1987). Case study research could be a integral part of a heuristic research paradigm especially when one considers the information such a research paradigm could provide for applied sport psychology practitioners. Martens addressed these implications when he stated:

Applied knowledge, in contrast to applied research, involves sifting through all the research available on a problem, using one's tacit knowledge regarding the problem, and developing creative programs for how to solve it. Applied research alone often does not directly reveal how the research can be used to help solve a problem. The process of synthesizing research and developing knowledge that can be directly applied to solving problems requires enormous intellectual skill and considerable creativity (Martens, 1987, p. 54).

The formation of AAASP created a need for information and instruction regarding the practice of applied sport psychology. Case studies thus became a very viable avenue to gain a better understanding of the application and effectiveness of performance enhancement and intervention strategies. *The Sport Psychologist*, an applied journal first published in 1987, often utilizes case studies to illustrate the efficacy of a variety of applied sport psychology educational programs and interventions including: assertiveness training (Connelly, 1988; Connelly & Rotella, 1991); ethics (Biddle, Bull, & Seheult, 1992); mental retardation (Travis & Sachs, 1991); provision of sport psychology consulting services (Botterill, 1990; Bull, 1989; Collins, Doherty, & Talbot, 1993; Dorfman, 1990; Halliwell, 1990; Rotella & Newburg, 1989; Van Mele, Vanden, Auweele, & Rzewnicki, 1995).

Journals such as the *Journal of Applied Sport Psychology, Contemporary Thought on Performance Enhancement, Journal of Performance Education, Journal of Applied Research in Coaching and Athletics,* and the *International Journal of Sport Psychology* have published research which utilized case studies (Anshel, 1989; Asken & Goodling, 1986; Davis, 1991; Gerdes, 1996; Hanson, 1996; Newberg & Perrin, 1993; Vernacchia & Cook, 1993; Zimmerman, Protinsky, & Zimmerman, 1994). Several textbooks include chapters which utilize case studies as teaching tools to illustrate concepts and applications in the field of applied sport and exercise psychology (Heil, 1993; Henschen & Straub, 1995; May & Asken, 1987; Morris & Summers, 1995; Murphy, 1995; Orlick, Partington, & Salmela, 1983; Straub, 1980; Straub & Williams, 1984; Williams, 1986, 1993).

During the 1980's applied sport psychology researchers had primarily utilized the case interview to study and report athletes' mental approach to competition, especially at the elite levels (Carlson & Fogerty, 1987; Hemery, 1986; Gould, Eklund, & Jackson, 1993; Orlick & Partington, 1986, 1988; Ungerleider & Golding 1992). It was during the 1980's and 1990's that sport psychology researchers utilized single-subject research methodologies and designs to establish the efficacy of sport-related performance enhancement and intervention strategies (Allison & Ayllon, 1980; Buzas & Ayllon, 1981; Cohn, Rotella & Lloyd, 1990; Gray, Haring & Banks, 1985; Hall & Erffmeyer, 1983; Hamilton & Fremouw, 1985; Hume, Martin, Gonzales, Cracklen & Genthon, 1985; Kendall, Hrycaiko, Martin & Kendall, 1990; Prapavessis, Grove, McNair & Cable, 1992; Templin & Vernacchia, 1995; Ziegler, 1987).

The late 1980's and 1990's reflected an acceptance and utilization among sport psychology professionals of qualitative research methods which included variations of three main approaches: (1) the case study (Smith, 1988), (2) the case interview (Scanlan, Ravizza, & Stein, 1989; Scanlan, Stein, & Ravizza, 1989), and (3) single-subject research design (Bryan, 1987; Kazdin, 1982). Case study methodology is currently an effective research and educational tool utilized by contemporary applied sport psychology professionals. In many ways qualitative research methods such as the case study, case report, and case interview will allow sport psychology professionals to critically research, analyze and re-evaluate core disciplinary issues in applied sport psychology. The current and future vitality of applied sport psychology is dependent upon the ability of researchers and practitioners to jointly recognize the value and usefulness of both quantitative and qualitative research methodologies in formulating an accurate and representative knowledge of sport behavior (Dewar & Horn, 1992).

Variations of Case Methodology and Research Design

Sport psychology may learn a great deal about the motives and behaviors of athletes and coaches who live in a pressure-packed and competitive world through historical narratives and biographies. These informal avenues for accessing and assessing athletic behavior can provide applied sport psychology professionals with a better understanding of the culture, politics, and mentality of sport.

Biographies and historical narratives of former outstanding athletic performers can be very valuable to the applied sport professional who strives to formulate a perspective regarding the psychology of athletic performance. Autobiographies, such as Roger Bannister's (1955), vividly describe the emotional and mental states of an athlete who broke the "psychological barrier of the centuryî - the four minute mile. The enduring athletic feats, thoughts, and feelings of such great athletes as Jesse Owens and "Babe" Didrikson Zaharias are retrospectively presented and analyzed by highly respected academics (Baker, 1986; Cayleff, 1995). Similarly, Carlson and Fogerty (1987) have presented oral histories of 58 former Olympic gold medal winners (1912-1984) in a variety of sports which provide invaluable insights into the quest and attainment of athletic excellence.

Case Study and Case Reports

Case studies or case reports can vary in terms of the scope of information which they present (Kazdin, 1982) but, in general, they consist of an investigation of an athlete's mental states as they relate to his or her performance effectiveness. Case studies and reports can also provide the sport psychology professional with valuable insights into the appropriateness and effectiveness regarding the influence of performance intervention and enhancement techniques or strategies.

As a result of the inherent threats to internal validity it is desirable to approach case studies/reports in a systematic manner, especially if inferences regarding performance outcomes are to be proposed (Kazdin, 1982). A comprehensive and systematic description of the various factors which influence an athlete's behavior can be extremely helpful in understanding the "why" of his or her actions and can include: (1) personal history, (2) performance evaluations, (3) psychometric test results, (4) physiological test results, and (5) personal interviews (Vernacchia, 1977).

An athlete's personal history can be obtained through the administration of a questionnaire which elicits background information about an athlete's family, educational, employment, and athletic history. Performance evaluations can be obtained through statistical information which describes the past and current effectiveness of his or her performance as well as by the subjective evaluations of the athlete's coach(es). Most importantly, performance evaluations should clearly describe the situational characteristics in which an athlete's behavior and performance occur as well as and effectiveness and outcomes of specific performance enhancement or intervention strategies.

Psychological profiling through the use of appropriate tests and measures can also contribute to a better understanding of an athlete's behavior, motivations, and performance tendencies. A variety of psychometric inventories (Anshel, 1987; Ostrow, 1996) are available to the sport psychology professional who desires to compile a profile of an athlete's personality or to evaluate an athlete's mental skills effectiveness. Commonly employed personality and mental skills inventories (Vealey, 1992) include: Profile of Mood State (POMS), State-Trait Anxiety Inventory (STAI), Test of Attentional and Interpersonal Style (TAIS), Sport Competition Anxiety Test (SCAT), Competitive State Anxiety Inventory-2, State Sport -Confidence Inventory, Psychological Skills Inventory for Sport (PSIS), Intrinsic Motivation Inventory, and the Causal Dimension Scale.

One of the most overlooked aspects of the case study or report is the inclusion of physiological test results or parameters which may provide critical information regarding an athlete's performance. This is particularly true if we find that an athlete has a sound attitude and mental skills approach to his or her performance. An athlete may not have the physiological capacities as a result of genetics, maturation or training to meet the performance demands and requirements of certain situations. Training background can render them ineffective in performance setting because of unlearned or underdeveloped motor skills.

The key component of the case study or report is the personal interview phase which allows the athlete to reflect upon and describe his or her performance behaviors and outcomes. It is during this phase that the applied sport psychology professional probes the athlete with a series of pre-determined questions in an effort to gain insights into the perceived reasons and causes for effective and ineffective performances.

Smith (1988) presents a comprehensive overview of case study research methodology and its role in bridging the gap between research and professional practice in sport psychology in his article, *The Logic and Design of Case Study Research.* Reflecting on the work of Martens (1987), Smith (1988) concludes that, "High quality case studies can play an integral role in the accumulation of knowledge about psychological principles in the athletic environment, and can promote the development of intervention strategies for enhancing performance, health, and psychological well-being" (p. 11). His article reviews a variety of qualitative research designs, including single-subject experimental approaches, and salient perspectives regarding the validity and reliability of case study designs (Smith, 1988).

Smith (1988) also recommends the following guidelines for planning and reporting case studies: (1) a case study protocol which contains a series of research questions; (2) the introduction should present the theoretical significance of the case study; (3) a detailed description of the subject(s); (4) a fair and unbiased reporting of the findings; and (5) agreement by the participants that supports, clarifies, and validates the accuracy of the case study.

Case Interviews

The case interview has recently received more attention as a separate research tool in the field of applied sport psychology especially in the light of the use of content analysis research methodologies (Gould, et. al., 1993; Jackson, 1992, 1995, 1996; Scanlan, Ravizza, & Stein, 1989; Scanlan, Stein, & Ravizza, 1989). Case interviews which employ systematic content analysis of athlete responses to probing questions allow researchers to gain a better understanding of how athletes think and behave in a variety of situations related to athletic performance. The case interview is not as comprehensive as a case study and focuses primarily on the interview phase of case study methodology.

Content analysis research methodologies allow researchers to study and categorize emergent themes or cognitive commonalties which exist among a group of athletic performers. These commonalties can include mental and physical strategies employed by athletes to prepare for competition, manage the "pressures" of competition, cope with the media, respond to adversity, coping with success and failure, or particular theoretical concepts such as flow in sport (Jackson, 1992, 1995, 1996).

At the heart of the case interview are the questions which are used to probe an athlete's thoughts and feelings regarding the various aspects of his or her development, training, and performance. Interview questions are developed in relation to the areas or content categories researchers are investigating. Prior to interviewing a particular group of athletes, researchers identify the research focus of their study and develop questions which will be representative of their research focus. For example, in 1993, the mental skills and attributes of Olympic track and field athletes were studied by utilizing a series of questions which explored the athletes' dreams, development, reaction to adversity, mental preparation, as well as the mental and physical qualities responsible for their success (Vernacchia, 1994, 1995). The specific interview questions utilized in the study and their representative content categories were:

- **DREAMS:** When did you first start dreaming about being an Olympian?

- **DEVELOPMENT:** What were some of the most important factors in your development?

- **ADVERSITY:** What are some of the obstacles you've had to overcome in your development? How did you do it?

- **MENTAL PREPARATION:** How do you mentally prepare yourself for major competitions?

- **MENTAL AND PHYSICAL QUALITIES:** What mental and physical qualities do you think have been the most important in your development?

As well as responses which are related to each content category, the case interview method also examines the frequencies of the responses regarding each research question and groups them into overall emergent themes which represent the commonalties of the athletes interviewed. For example, in the above mentioned study of Olympic athletes, the themes that emerged from the research questions were organized into the four following categories:

1. **Psychological:** **Attitude and Mental Attributes and Skills** which included: emphasis on fun and enjoyment; patience; perseverance and persistence; mental imagery and visualization; confidence; and dreams.

2. **Developmental: Training and Performance Related** which included: physical preparation and work ethic; coaching influence; injuries; and early participation in a variety of sports.

3. **Socio-economic** which included: family and social support and parental attitudes; scholarship attainment; and financial support and concerns.

4. **Spiritual and Religious** which included spiritual and religious factors and the influence of prayer.

The real value of the case interview method is that it allows researchers to retrospectively probe the attitudes, thoughts, perceptions, and behaviors of elite athletes particularly as these cognitive state behaviors relate to athletic performance. The case interview method can provide valuable information regarding salient sport-specific cognitive and behavioral strategies which can be learned through mental skills training.

Summary

Qualitative research methodologies in sport psychology have been utilized since the re-birth of the discipline in the mid-1960's to provide insight into sport behavior and athletic performance. While sport psychology professionals have informally assessed the mental states of athletes through observation, biographies, historical narratives, media interviews, popular magazine articles, and books, case methodology in the form of case studies and interviews can provide sport psychology professionals with reliable and valid information regarding the psychology of athletic performance.

The late 1980's and 1990's have witnessed an acceptance and increased utilization of research studies which employ case methodology and single-subject designs as viable avenues to study human behavior in sport, athletics and exercise settings. Continued use of quantitative and qualitative research methodologies will allow applied sport psychology professionals to design and implement relevant enhancement and intervention programs with their clients - coaches, athletes, parents, and recreational sport and fitness participants.

References

Allison, M.G., & Ayllon, T. (1980). Behavioral coaching in the development of skills in football, gymnastics, and tennis. Journal of Applied Behavior Analysis, 13, 291-314.

Anshel, M. (1987). Psychological inventories used in sport psychology research. The Sport Psychologist, 1, 331-349.

Anshel, M. (1989). Examination of a college football coach's receptivity to sport psychology consulting: A three year case study. Journal of Applied Research in Coaching and Athletics, 4, 139-149.

Asken, M.J., & Goodling, M.D. (1986). The use of sport psychology techniques in rehabilitation medicine: A pilot study - case report . International Journal of Sport Psychology, 17, 156-161.

Baker, W.J. (1986). Jesse Owens: An American life. New York: The Free Press.

Bannister, R. (1955). The four minute mile. New York: Dodd, Mead & Co.

Beisser, A. (1967). The madness in sport. New York: Appleton-Century-Crofts.

Biddle, S.J.H., Bull, S.J, & Seheult, C.L. (1992). Ethical and professional issues in contemporary British sport psychology. The Sport Psychologist, 6, 66-76.

Botterill, C. (1990). Sport psychology and professional hockey. The Sport Psychologist, 4, 358-368.

Bryan, A.J. (1987). Single-subject designs for evaluation of sport psychology interventions. The Sport Psychologist, 1, 283-292.

Bull, S.J. (1989). The role of the sport psychology consultant: A case study of ultra-distance running. The Sport Psychologist, 3, 254-264

Bunker, L., Williams, J.M., & Zinsser, N. (1993). Cognitive techniques for improving performance and building confidence. In J. Williams (Ed.), Applied sport psychology: Personal growth to peak performance (2nd Edition) (pp. 225-242) Mountain View, CA: Mayfield Publishing Co.

Buzas, H.P., & Ayllon, T. (1981). Differential reinforcement in coaching tennis skills. Behavior Modification, 5, 372-385.

Carlson, L., & Fogerty, J. (1987). Tales of gold. Chicago, IL: Contemporary Books.

Cayleff, S.E. (1995). Babe: The life and legend of Babe Didrikson Zaharias. Urbana, IL: University of Illinois Press.

Cohn, P.J., Rotella, R.J., & Lloyd, J. (1990). Effects of a cognitive-behavioral intervention on the pre-shot routine and performance in golf. The Sport Psychologist, 4, 33-47.

Collins, D., Doherty, M., & Talbot, S. (1993). Performance enhancement in motocross: a case study of the sport science team in action. The Sport Psychologist, 7, 290-297.

Connelly, D. (1988). Increasing intensity of play of nonassertive athletes. The Sport Psychologist, 2, 255-265.

Connelly, D., & Rotella, R.J. (1991). The social psychology of assertive communication: Issues in teaching assertiveness skills to athletes. The Sport Psychologist, 5, 73-87.

Davis, K. (1991). Performance enhancement program for a college tennis player. International Journal of Sport Psychology, 22, 140-153.

Dewer, A., & Horn, T. (1992). A critical analysis of knowledge construction in sport psychology. In T.S. Horn (Ed.), Advances in sport psychology (pp. 13-22). Champaign, IL: Human Kinetics.

Dorfman, H.A. (1990). Reflections on providing personal and performance enhancement consulting services in professional baseball. The Sport Psychologist, 4, 341-346.

Gerdes, D.A. (1996). Morality, leadership, and excellence: A case study of basketball coach Roy Williams. Journal of Performance Education, 1, 131-143.

Gould, D., Eklund, R.C., & Jackson, S.A. (1993). Coping strategies used by U.S. Olympic wrestlers. Research Quarterly for Exercise and Sport, 64, 83-93.

Gray, J.J., Haring, M.J., & Banks, N.M. (1985). Mental rehearsal for sport performance: Exploring the relaxation-imagery paradigm. Journal of Sport Behavior, 7, 68-78.

Hall, E.G., & Erffmeyer, E.S. (1983). Effect of visuo-motor behavior rehearsal with videotaped modeling on free throw accuracy of intercollegiate female basketball players. Journal of Sport Psychology, 5, 343-346.

Halliwell, W.(1990).Providing sport psychology consulting services in professional hockey. The Sport Psychologist,4, 369-377.

Hamilton, S.A., & Fremouw, W.J. (1985). Cognitive-behavioral training for college basketball free-throw performance. Cognitive Therapy and Research, 9, 479-483.

Hemery, D. (1986). The pursuit of sporting excellence: A study of sport's highest achievers. Champaign, IL: Human Kinetics.

Hanson, T. (1996). the mental aspects of hitting in baseball: A case study of Hank Aaron. Journal of Performance Education, 1, 57-76.

Heil, J. (1993). Psychology of sport injury. Champaign, IL: Human Kinetics.

Henschen, K.P., & Straub, W.F. (Eds.) (1995). Sport psychology: An analysis of athlete behavior (3rd Ed.). Ithaca, NY: Mouvement Publications.

Hume, K.M., Martin, G.L., Gonzales, C., Cracklen, C., & Genthon, S. (1985). A self-monitoring feedback package for improving freestyle figure skating practice. Journal of Sport Psychology, 7, 333-345.

Jackson, S.A. (1992). Athletes in flow: A qualitative investigation of flow states in elite figure skaters. Journal of Applied Sport Psychology, 4, 161-180.

Jackson, S.A. (1995). Factors influencing the occurrence of flow state in elite athletes. Journal of Applied Sport Psychology, 2, 138-166.

Jackson, S.A. (1996). Toward a conceptual understanding or the flow experience in elite athletes. Research Quarterly for Exercise and Sport, 67, 76-90.

Kazdin, A.E. (1982). Single-case research designs: Methods for clinical and applied settings. New York: Oxford University Press.

Kendall, G., Hrycaiko, D., Martin, G.L., & Kendall, T. (1990). The effects of an imagery rehearsal, relaxation, and self-talk package on basketball game performance. Journal of Sport and Exercise Psychology, 12, 157-166.

Mahoney, M., Gabriel, T., & Perkins, T. (1987). Psychological skills and exceptional athletic performance. The Sport Psychologist, 1, 181-199.

Martens, R. (1979). About smocks and jocks. Journal of Sport Psychology, 1, 94-99.

Martens, R. (1987). Science, knowledge, and sport psychology. The Sport Psychologist, 1, 29-55.

May, J.R., & Asken, M.J. (Eds.) (1987). Sport psychology: The psychological health of the athlete. New York: PMA Publishing Corporation.

Morris, T., & Summers, J. (Eds.) (1995). Sport psychology : Theory, applications and issues. Brisbane, Australia: John Wiley.

Murphy, S.M. (1995). Sport psychology interventions. Champaign, IL: Human Kinetics.

Newburg, D., & Perrin, T. (1993). Mental strategies of successful role players in basketball. Contemporary Thought on Performance Enhancement, 2, 92-109.

Ogilvie, B., & Tutko, T.A, (1966). Problem athletes and how to handle them. London: Pelham Books.

Ogilvie, B. (1968). Psychological consistencies among high level competitors. Journal of the American Medical Association, 205, 156-162.

Orlick, T., & Partington J.T., (1986). Psyched: Inner views of winning. Ottawa, Canada: Coaching Association of Canada.

Orlick, T., & Partington, J.T., (1988). Mental links to excellence. The Sport Psychologist, 2, 105-130.

Orlick, T., Partington, J.T., & Salmela, J.H. (Eds.) (1983), Mental training for coaches & athletes. Ottawa, Canada: Coaching Association of Canada.

Ostrow, A. (1996). Directory of psychological tests in the sport and exercise sciences. Morgantown, WV: Fitness Information Technology, Inc., Publishers.

Prapavesis, H., Grove, J.R., McNair, P.J., & Cable, N.T. (1992). Self-regulation training, state anxiety, and sport performance: A psychophysiological case study. The Sport Psychologist, 6, 213-229.

Rotella, R.J., & Newburg, D.S. (1989). The social psychology of the benchwarmer. The Sport Psychologist, 3, 48-62.

Scanlan, T.K., Ravizza, K., & Stein, G.L. (1989). An in-depth study of former elite figure skaters: I. Introduction to the project. Journal of Sport and Exercise Psychology, 11, 54-64.

Scanlan, T.K., Stein, G.L., & Ravizza, K. (1989). An in-depth study of former elite figure skaters: II. Sources of enjoyment. Journal of Sport and Exercise Psychology, 11, 54-64.

Smith, R.E. (1988). The logic and design of case study research. The Sport Psychologist, 2, 1-12.

Straub, W.F. (Ed.) (1980). Sport psychology: An analysis of athlete behavior (2nd Ed.). Ithaca, NY: Mouvement Publications.

Straub, W.F., & Williams, J.M. (Eds.) (1980), Cognitive sport psychology. Lansing, NY: Sport Science Associates.

Templin, D.P., & Vernacchia, R.A. (1995). The effect of highlight music videotapes upon the game performance of intercollegiate basketball players. The Sport Psychologist, 9, 41-50.

Travis, C.A., & Sachs, M.L. (1991). Applied sport psychology and persons with mental retardation. The Sport Psychologist, 5, 382-391.

Ungerleider, S., & Golding, J.M. (1992). Beyond strength: Psychological profiles of Olympic athletes. Dubuque, IA: Wm. C. Brown Publishers.

Van Mele, V., Vanden Auweele, Y., & Rzewnicki, R. (1995). An integrative procedure for the diagnosis of an elite athlete: A case study. The Sport Psychologist, 9, 130-147.

Vanek, M., & Cratty, B.J. (1970). Psychology and the superior athlete. London: The Macmillan Company.

Vealey, R. (1992). Personality and sport: A comprehensive view. In T. S. Horn (Ed.), Advances in sport psychology (pp. 25-59). Champaign, IL: Human Kinetics.

Vernacchia, R.A. (1973). Case profiles of track athletes. An unpublished doctoral dissertation, University of Utah.

Vernacchia, R.A. (1977). Humanistic research for the sport psychologist: The case profile approach. Canadian Journal of Applied Sport Sciences, 2, 105-108.

Vernacchia, R.A. (1994). Psychological profiles of Olympic track and field athletes. An unpublished manuscript, Western Washington University, Bellingham, WA.

Vernacchia, R.A. (1995, October). Mental skills and attitudes of Olympic track and field athletes Paper presented at the annual meeting of the Association for the Advancement of Applied Sport Psychology (AAASP), New Orleans, LA.

Vernacchia, R.A., & Cook, D. (1993). The influence of a mental training technique on the performance of selected intercollegiate basketball players. Applied Research in Coaching and Athletics Annual, 188-176.

Wiggins, D.K. (1983). The history of sport psychology in North America. In J.M. Silva, III & R.S. Weinberg (Eds.), Psychological foundations of sport, (pp. 9-22). Champaign, IL: Human Kinetics.

Williams, J.M. (Ed.) (1986). Applied sport psychology: Personal growth to peak performance. Mountain View, CA: Mayfield Publishing Company.

Williams, J.M. (Ed.) (1993). Applied sport psychology: Personal growth to peak performance (2nd ed.). Mountain View, CA: Mayfield Publishing Company.

Williams, J., & Leffingwell, T. (1996). Cognitive strategies in sport and exercise psychology. In J.L. Van Raalte & B.W. Brewer (Eds.), Exploring sport and exercise psychology, (pp. 51-73). Washington, DC: American Psychological Association.

Williams, J.M., & Straub, W.F. (1993). Sport psychology: Past, present, future. In J.M. Williams (Ed.), Applied sport psychology: Personal growth to peak performance (2nd ed., pp. 1-10) Mountain View, CA: Mayfield Publishing Co.

Zeigler, S.G. (1987). Effects of stimulus cueing on the acquisition of groundstrokes by beginning tennis players. Journal of Applied Behavior Analysis, 20, 405-411.

Zimmerman, T.S., Protinsky, H.O., & Zimmerman, C.S. (1994). Family systems consultation with an athletic team: a case study of themes. Journal of Applied Sport Psychology, 6, 101-115.

CHAPTER 3

~ Use of the Casebook in Applied Sport Psychology ~

Ralph A. Vernacchia, Western Washington University

A casebook can be an invaluable educational resource for sport psychology students and professionals who wish to explore the application effectiveness of various sport psychology theories, mental training strategies and interventions. The use of a casebook in various educational settings can create an awareness of the ideographic nature of sport psychology as well as the effectiveness or ineffectiveness of performance enhancing and interventionist strategies. The casebook approach to sport psychology can help coaches, athletes and sport psychology consultants formulate cognitive-behavioral strategies aimed at generating effective athletic performances.

This casebook has several educational functions, namely:

1) to describe human behavior in sport settings
2) to provide a description and evaluation of sport psychology interventions and performance enhancement mental strategies
3) to develop the analytical skill of prospective sport psychology consultants
4) to increase the confidence and competence levels of prospective sport psychology consultants
5) to provide professional development opportunities for sport psychology consultants through continuing education about their discipline

More specifically, this chapter will describe and discuss the use of an applied sport psychology casebook as an educational tool which can prepare students and professionals for the "real world" of sport psychology consulting.

The Casebook in Educational Settings

The Value of a Casebook for the Undergraduate Student

During the initial stages of their education, sport psychology undergraduate students can benefit greatly from the application information that a casebook can provide. Casebooks comprised of case studies, reports, profiles, and interviews can serve to illustrate the research, theoretical, and applied foundations of sport psychology. Most importantly, undergraduate sport psychology classes and programs can provide students with an understanding of human behavior in the sport environment.

The following case study (Vernacchia, 1977) is an example of a case which is appropriate for entry level sport psychology students since it provides a global view of an athlete's behaviors as well as the underlying motivational dynamics which drive his performances. The case presents the athlete's family and athletic history, his coach-athlete relationship, performance enhancement strategies used in competitive situations, and the athlete's attitude toward his sport. The "Case of Bill" is not a problem oriented exercise for students, it merely provides the student with an understanding of a highly successful athlete's motivations, attitudes, as well as, personal and performance behaviors which have influenced his performance. In essence it is not a case of "let's fix it" but of "let's fine tune it" so the athlete can continue to perform effectively as personal, academic, athletic, and professional changes take place in his life. The "Case of Bill" may be useful in helping entry level sport psychology students gain an understanding of the nature and motivational dynamics of human behavior in sport:

"The Case of Bill"

Bill, a 24-year old senior, has experienced a highly successful collegiate athletic career to the extent that he was rated a superior athlete. He has been a three time NCAA All-American in cross country and track, had won numerous conference titles in cross country and track, and holds school records in a variety of distance running events. He has also participated in international track and field competitions as a member of a USA national team.

Bill is the youngest member of his family, he has two older brothers, and is engaged to be married. Bill's father has attended all his races and displayed a keen interest in how he performs. Although he did not feel extremely close to his father, Bill did feel secure when he was around his father. His relationship with his mother, up until her death just over a year ago, was very close as Bill found it easy to talk, confide, and discuss his feelings with her.

Bill is a sensitive person who was well aware of how he projected himself to others and was constantly looking for ways to improve his image with others. He describes this image as follows:

> "I feel like I come across like I'm someone who is nice, not too intelligent, somebody who doesn't really have the backbone he should, but I guess I do feel like people think I'm a nice person. The one quality I want to project, I know I don't project is confidence...I think I kind of project that I'm somewhat aloof...I think part of my problem is I kind of look at almost everybody I know as better than myself...I think most people have better qualities than myself."

Although Bill recognized a need for change in the image he projected to other persons, he expressed that he was content with his present lifestyle. Bill did described himself as a "big self-doubter" who did need support and encouragement especially from those persons he respected.

Athletically, Bill is intrinsically motivated and an extremely dedicated distance runner. For example, he was required to attend National Guard meetings once a month and in order to fit his training into this schedule, he ran 17 miles a 3:30 am before leaving to fulfill his military obligation. Perhaps the importance of running in his life can be best described by Bill himself:

"…Running is something I feel a personal obligation to do and I just don't feel right when I miss it…It's such a beautiful time of the to run (morning) even when it's dark there's just no one out there and all you can hear is yourself breathing and you feet hitting the ground. You just kind of wrestle with yourself on some of the problems you have or just maybe your attitude…Running is just an emotional time for me…I just try to get things in the right perspective. It's just kind of a special time…It's almost like I'm addicted to it (running). I just feel like I can face things easier and the world looks better when I can run…Track has touched everything in my life…It (running) gives me a better attitude about myself and I like myself better when I'm running…There's just something about it that gives you a real inner sense of satisfaction."

Bill is very independent in regards to his training methods. He seldom trained with other members of the team as he felt he benefited more from his workouts by running alone. Due to Bill's experience and maturity, Bill's coach had been more of an advisor, and , consequently, Bill has functioned well as an independent, self-motivated, and self-reliant athlete. Bill felt that the "subtle" or "fireside manner" in which his coach had conveyed ideas and suggestions came across personally, which in turn, encouraged Bill to place confidence and trust in his coach.

Goal setting was an important aspect of the coach-athlete relationship for Bill. Performance goals were mutually agreed upon by Bill and his coach and discussing his goals helped Bill erase any self doubts he may have had regarding his capabilities. This also helped him reconfirm and/or readjust his initial thoughts regarding his goals depending upon how realistically they had been formulated.

Although Bill may have lacked confidence in social situations, he was extremely confident and assertive in competitive settings. He prepared himself for competition by trying to become "inwardly aggressive" which he defined as the willingness to take a chance. He felt and believed that if he was aggressive, he could handle competitive situations by "making things happen" in a race. In line with such beliefs, Bill felt most comfortable as a front runner and pace setter. He felt that by leading races he could control and force the pace. By setting an early fast pace in distance races, which was Bill's usual racing tactic, he felt he could make his opponents feel tired early in the race so that they doubted their ability, became scared, and "dropped off" of the pace.

Another dimension of Bill's competitive attitudes revealed that he didn't like an aggressive attitude towards his opponents when he entered a race and , more specifically, he did not like to "key" on a individual. He has discovered through past experience that being too competitive sometimes brought out the worst in him. Bill felt that such an aggressive attitude towards other competitors took the beauty out of running.

Bill described his motivation and reasons for participating in track as stemming from the recognition he had received because of his success in track. Track has enabled him to make new friends, and very simply, to see what he was capable of as an athlete. He also felt that his transition from national to world class competition had developed at the appropriate time in his life—he felt emotionally capable to handle the pressures and responsibility such a transition will demand.

Overview

The case of Bill is an example of the ability of case studies to provide a descriptive overview of an elite athletes' world. This is an important educational issue in sport psychology since entry level students in the field want to "leapfrog" into intervention approaches without gaining a sound understanding of the foundations of human behavior in sport, especially socialization influences (i.e. family upbringing, socio-economic factors, educational background, etc.) which ultimately effect athletic motivation and performance. Once a general understanding of the dynamics of athletic behavior is introduced, case studies, interviews, and reports can continue to be effective teaching tools which can provide useful examples and illustrations of mental skills training programs and interventions.

The Value of a Casebook for the Graduate Student

The casebook is most appropriate for graduate education in applied sport psychology. The descriptive nature of the casebook materials will enable students to draw inferences regarding human behavior in sport as they utilize and develop their analytical abilities. Students can in effect learn to make decisions by making decisions about the application of mental skills or cognitive-behavioral strategies they would utilize in a variety of unique "real world" settings.

The casebook approach will allow prospective sport psychology professionals who are engaged in graduate education to build their confidence by developing their analytical and decision-making abilities. In its most basic educational form, a casebook is a process and product approach to evaluating the efficacy of particular performance enhancement or intervention strategies. Case studies and reports provide the springboard for students to retrospectively analyze, evaluate and discuss the appropriateness and effectiveness of mental skills training programs and performance enhancement intervention strategies. This process can help students create a template which can be reviewed and possibly selected for application in similar cases which they may face in their future professional endeavors.

As mentioned in the previous chapter, one of the basic tenants of sport psychology is that thought precedes and influences athletic performance. Another basic tenant of sport psychology is that behavior is situation specific, hence the need for students to understand the influence socialization has upon athletic performers and performance. Seminars directed toward the psychosocial inspection and analysis of situation specific sport behaviors, via case studies and reports, are an essential component of any graduate program in sport psychology.

A casebook text can be a valuable educational tool to aid students in developing their ability to analyze and enhance athletic performance. Case studies can be incorporated in graduate classes, or appear as a separate class, especially in doctoral programs, as an integral part of graduate training in sport psychology.

In regards to teaching methodology, cases can be presented to students which provide a background regarding the various factors that are effecting an athlete's ability to perform effectively. Such a problem-solving approach challenges students to draw upon both their theoretical and experiential knowledge of sport psychology in order to arrive at appropriate performance enhancing strategies.

In a seminar setting graduate students can be presented with the situational characteristics of a particular case and asked to review the case and present, in writing, their solution or suggestions to the problems or issues which the case presents. At the next seminar meeting the case can be discussed in a group setting under the guidance of an instructor who has experience as a sport psychology consultant. The instructor can add information to the case as the class discussion unfolds or can provide the students with the actual outcomes of the case once various intervention and enhancement strategies have been discussed. Students are asked to review the situation presented and answer three basic questions:

1. Who's the client?
2. What's the issue and the "real" issue?
3. How do I resolve or address the issues?

These are the basic questions addressed and answered in the various chapters and cases which are contained in this text. Cases presented in this text have been presented in a format which stresses that the sport psychology professional develop an approach to performance enhancement or intervention which (1) normalizes the athlete's thinking (cognitive intervention), (2) provides cognitive-behavioral strategies which can be utilized by an athlete in the "heat of the battle", and (3) provides an evaluation process for selected strategies which evaluate their effectiveness, thus leading to the modification, refinement, and elimination of selected strategies. Each case in this book is to be evaluated as to its cognitive, cognitive-behavioral, and performance outcomes.

The following case study (Vernacchia, 1992) of an athlete, who was a member of a U. S. international track and field team, illustrates the cognitive, cognitive-behavioral, and performance outcome phases depicted throughout this text:

"The Case of John"

Situation: John was a 19 year-old 400 meter runner who was a member of the USA 4 x 400 meter relay team which competed at the World Junior Track and Field Championships. John had run poorly in the qualifying heats of the 4 x 400 meter relay heats, especially in the final 80 meters of the his race. During this stage of his race he "faded" badly in the stretch and lost the lead the two previous runners had given him. The USA team did, however, qualify for the final.

Cognitive Intervention: On the day of the final John's teammates approached the team's sport psychology consultant and asked him to speak with John since John appeared very "nervous" about the upcoming final race. After speaking with John it became apparent that he was confident but over aroused regarding his upcoming race. He told the sport psychology consultant that it was difficult for him to control the energy which he had "bottled" up inside himself prior to and during the early stages of his races.

The sport psychology consultant had an opportunity to listen to John's thoughts, attitudes, and feelings regarding his situation and it became apparent that John was "overthinking" and "overfeeling" about his upcoming race.

The sport psychology consultant felt it was important for John to focus his thoughts and feelings on the formulation of a specific emotional/physical race plan which he could implement in the final event.

John was asked to visualize and describe his best race ever. This exercise served to help John regain a positive preoccupation with his upcoming performance.

Cognitive-Behavioral Strategies: The following suggestions were made to John regarding his situation:

* John was encouraged to take a walk rather than sit in his room "thinking" constantly about his race. This would help him to relax himself and he would benefit more if he could walk with a friend and discuss topics which were unrelated to his upcoming race;

* The sport psychology consultant worked with John to establish an emotional race plan by breaking the race down in sections and associating a number with each section. The number represented his arousal level during that particular section of the race. Numbers ranged from 1 (low) to 10 (high) and were applied to each 100 meters of the overall 400 meter race. He decided to associate the number 7 with the first 100 meters, the number 8 with the second 100 meters, the number 9 with the third 100 meters, and the number 10 with the final 100 meters of the race.

This strategy was utilized so that John would not expend all his emotional and physical energies in the first 300 meters of the race as a result of disregarding his most effective race pace early in the race. The goal here was to help him control his arousal or *excite-ability* during the race.

Performance Outcome: John ran well in the final race. Even though he faded slightly in the final 50 meters of the race, he passed the baton off in first place and the USA won the race. At the closing ceremonies, which were held after the relay, John was extremely happy about his performance and the team's success.

Overview

The case of John illustrates the "real world" intervention issues students will face as consultants. Sometimes performance enhancement mental strategies will need to be adapted to an individual's situation and personality characteristics immediately prior to an impending performance. This case addresses the issue of composure, other cases found in this text may address issues of concentration, confidence, etc., but in any case the consultant must deal with the issues and "real" issues in a timely fashion. If not dealt with in a timely fashion these issues can undermine effective athletic performances.

The case method approach would also be employed in conjunction with a graduate student's internship experience in sport psychology. As graduate students confront the "real life" cases of their internship experience they can reflect on similar cases presented in class seminars in order to select appropriate strategies and approaches they may be considering. A casebook can also provide a frame of reference for a variety of performance blocks and problems. This text has organized case studies in to a variety of mental skills categories, such as, composure, confidence, concentration, coach-athlete conflict, team issues, parent-athlete issues, injury and career termination, etc. *Anticipation is an important aspect of successful consulting and students can be trained to anticipate and prepare for the possible consequences of their suggested interventions by reviewing the outcomes of cases similar to the ones they are encountering in their internship experience.*

The Value of a Casebook for Professionals

Once removed from graduate school, sport psychology professionals can soon become isolated in their work or workplace. They no longer have colleagues available to discuss professional issues and cases they are encountering. In order to compensate for this reality, professionals subscribe to sport psychology journals, and attend annual meetings of their respective professional organizations. Continuing education in sport psychology provides professionals with the means and opportunity to keep pace with current trends and practices in their field.

Unfortunately national conferences involve large group meetings which make it difficult to engage in a very extensive or in-depth treatment of specific concerns individual professionals may have. While workshops are available at national conferences, it soon becomes evident that professionals would benefit from the intimate learning environment which had been so important for their professional development while they were in graduate school.

Small group meetings comprised of applied sport psychology professionals, who have similar or diverse interests, philosophies, or consulting styles and practices, can be a very stimulating and effective venue to address professional concerns and problems, as well as, innovative ideas and strategies. Such meetings can serve as "retreats" or reflective times of professional fellowship which can rejuvenate one's professional zest for his or her discipline.

It is recommended that these meetings have no more than 15 participants in order to retain the group intimacy and to stimulate group interaction and communication. Participants are asked to review both successful and unsuccessful cases they have encountered in their work. Group members react to each case and provide feedback and suggestions based on their experiences with similar cases or performance issues. Discussions stemming from case presentations provide a clearer understanding of the culture, politics, and mentality of sport specific interventions. Other pertinent perspectives may come from an educational, as well as, a clinical approach to sport psychology consulting.

There is much to be gained and learned from colleagues with diverse practices and educational backgrounds, but most importantly, group participants will form a professional network that will be available to them once the group seminar has ended. Professionals should now feel free to contact one another if feedback is needed regarding cases which might arise during one's consulting endeavors. A professional network is an invaluable asset for effective sport psychology consulting.

Summary

A case method or casebook approach to mastering the art and science of sport psychology can be an invaluable educational asset for professors, students, and sport psychology consultants. The casebook can bring the "real world" issues of sport psychology consulting to academic and professional settings in a very relevant and meaningful way.

A casebook can provide "concrete" or operational examples of the various professional issues and enhancement/intervention situations consultants face. The interactive atmosphere surrounding the use of an applied sport psychology casebook can serve to enhance the professional development and performance of students and consultants by increasing their analytical and decision making capabilities, and ultimately their confidence.

In the final analysis, a casebook can provide "real world" examples which illustrate the threefold role and function of the sport psychology consultant, that is, *to know people* (human behavior), *to know sport* (its culture, politics, and mentality), and *to enhance performance* through sport specific mental skills training.

References

Vernacchia, R. A. (1992). Applied sport psychology services for track and field coach and athlete. Track and Field Quarterly Review, 92, 1-4.

Vernacchia, R. A. (1977). Humanistic research for the sport psychologist: The case profile approach. Canadian Journal of Applied Sport Sciences, 2, 105-108.

CHAPTER 4

~ The Issue Behind the Issue ~

Keith P. Henschen, University of Utah

As an applied sport psychology practitioner I have been continually reminded in my consulting that "what you see is not always what you get." In fact, in more cases than not, what athletes, parents, and coaches initially request is not what the sport psychology consultant eventually provides. Most lay people are able to detect symptoms of a more underlying problem and misconstrue these symptoms as the critical issue to be resolved. What you, as the trained professional, must do is to identify the real issues instead of the readily apparent superficial manifestations.

This chapter will be organized to discuss performance issues according to the athletes, coaches, and parents. Also, the dynamics affecting the sport psychology professional's interpretation and assessment of the issues will be presented. Finally, guidelines for the sport psychology professional will be presented for working with athletes, coaches, parents, and for working through oneself.

When the Whole Truth is Anything But

Issues According to Athletes

In the vast majority of cases, athletes at almost all ages can easily identify the problems which they are experiencing in the performance arena. Normally, these issues are symptoms or consequences of more deep seated problems or issues. An example is the following scenario:

> Tanya is a young gymnast (11 yrs. old) who has enjoyed considerable success in her sport for the past three years. She just recently has started feeling a lot of stress, anxiety, and fear prior to competitions and during performances on certain apparati (balance beam). Tanya also is a good student and finds herself constantly worrying about her grades, but has trouble on tests. She studies hard and seems to know the material, but has "brain cramps" during the tests. She comes to you, as a sport psychology professional, to help her improve her gymnastics performances and to help her deal with her fear.

Tanya is not at all unusual. She knows how she feels, thinks she understands her gymnastic performance problem (fear and anxiety), and wants to improve. Initially, as the sport psychology professional counsels with this athlete, it becomes obvious that gymnastic performance is not the real issue; but rather, how Tanya is responding to pre-pubescence and growing up. If you, as the professional, succumb to the obvious, then you have actually provided a disservice to this athlete by just "fixing" fear or anxiety control for gymnastics. In reality, Tanya does not understand why she feels a certain way, she just knows something is not right. Her representation of the issue is limited by her maturity, peer pressure, her feelings, and her desire to compete. In other words her objectivity is tainted by her subjectivity and lack of self confidence.

Physical vs. Mental

Athletes want performance issues mended immediately. They have the "credit card syndrome" - I want it now and I'll pay for it later. Following this same logic, it seems that all Americans have been conditioned by societal norms to be impatient. We want things immediately and we want broken things fixed as quickly as possible. Athletes view psychological issues the same way as they do physical skills. Since most athletes are meteorically above average, physical skills are relatively easily repaired, relearned, or learned initially. But psychological issues are not so easily remedied. Trying harder in the psychological area does not produce the same results as trying harder on the physical side. Athletes are also limited by what they hear or perceive from their peers. Performance issues are peer accepted if they are physical (poor shooting, not hitting, etc.) but peers can be unmerciful on psychological issues. Nobody wants to visit the "shrink." There is still a negative connotation to having something "wrong with you head" compared to having a pulled muscle or a broken arm. The real problem is that you can not see psychological problems heal, but physical ailments are more visually apparent. So the dynamics affecting the athlete's representation of the issue is multifaceted. Their perceptions are formed from input by numerous sources - significant others, peers, society in general, and their own personal stereotypes. Your challenge, as the sport psychology professional, is to cut to the chase and identify the source issue(s) which will eventually mitigate or alleviate all of the readily apparent superficial issues.

Issues According to Coaches

Coaches are an interesting phenomenon. Some are excellent, some are good, a few are poor; but all, except the excellent ones, seem to be a little confused concerning the psychology of performance. Coaches are master teachers where physical skills and techniques are paramount, but many have yet to figure out the relationship between practice and actual competition. Contrary to popular belief, *very few athletes are capable of performing as they have practiced*. The reason that athletes have trouble performing well in competitions is that their perceptions change during competition. They often feel stress and pressure during competition because they perceive additional importance unlike in practice situations. So coaches, in general, spend a lot of time on skills techniques; but sparse time on the mental aspects of competition, believing that mental skills are developed through physical drills and practice. A sad but true fact is that the mental aspects become just as crucial as the physical aspects of performance in most competitive situations. This is the real issue behind the issue where coaches are concerned.

When performances deteriorate from obvious psychological reasons, coaches have three recourses:

(1) try a quick fix approach
(2) resort to more physical practice
(3) involve a sport psychology professional.

To most of you reading this chapter, the obvious solution would be number 3; but this unfortunately is frequently the last instead of the first choice. This is another issue -- coaches waiting too long to employ psychological services.

Currently, athletics in general and coaches specifically are in a transitional state. The old guard does not understand nor appreciate the importance of psychological skills training. On the other hand, young coaches and today's athletes are well versed in the importance of psychological skills training and are demanding its inclusion as a performance segment. Older coaches are reluctant to utilize the services of a sport psychology professional, while newly trained coaches readily refer their athletes for psychological consultation.

The dynamics of the issues behind coaches include:

- the proliferation of new information in the area of sport psychology
- coaches limitations
- coaches assuming dual roles
- the fact that winning is still paramount

In the last two decades, new information, techniques, and methods have burst upon the scene of coaching. It is unreasonable to expect coaches to know all of theses innovations and that is where sport psychology fits in. Changes and discoveries in sport psychology have occurred so rapidly even trained sport psychologists sometimes are outdated (i.e. new theories, new counseling techniques and refined intervention methods). Secondly, there is the issue that coaches can only do so much. Conditioning, strength training, nutrition, sport psychology, strategy, and skills development are all areas of the competition puzzle. Psychology of performance is an area where coaches should tread lightly. Because psychological principles are involved, a mistake by a well meaning coach could easily have long lasting effects on an athlete.

The most crucial issue for coaches involved in sport psychology is that it forces them into a dual role situation- that of coach and that of counselor. These roles are mutually exclusive and should remain that way. Coaching is a part of the helping professions the same as teaching, but it is not analogous to counseling and should be. Sport psychology is more a form of counseling than coaching; and due to evident potential role conflicts, coaches should refrain from playing sport psychologist. Finally, the dynamics of winning should never be ignored nor underestimated. The nature of competition is winning and coaches are employed to do just that. Most referrals from coaches are because of performance issues, but performance is more than just winning. Sadly the issue is not the development of the whole person instead of regaining a winning perspective for many coaches. The bottom line is that coaches and sport psychology professionals are many times only superficially attacking the same problems- performance.

Issues According to Parents

Parents, as well meaning as they are, do not understand the real issues concerning their offspring and performance. Most parents are truly deeply concerned about their children's well being. The overwhelming basic issue with parents and sport psychology is that parents (most of them) are unable to evaluate the situation without bias. Parents are strongly emotionally involved with their children and therefore struggle to be objective.

Parents are both part of the solution and part of the problem when it comes to their children's sporting life. They are part of the solution because they can be a valuable resource for the athlete; but they can be part of the problem if they are unable to separate their emotionally for their child (the athlete). Another issue that frequently clouds the issue with parents is that they attempt to be the "mouth piece" for the young performer. This not only establishes another layer between the sport psychology professional and the athlete, but also provides additional filtering of important information. Parents must be taught to allow the sport psychology professional to do his/her work through directly communicating with the actual performer. Most young athletes, out of respect to their parents, will allow the parents to do most of the talking. This is dangerous because in the infinite wisdom of the parent, they already know the problem as well as the solution of their child's dilemma. The issues of parents treating their athletes as young children, or the parents wanting to impress the sport psychology professional with their diagnosis are also common phenomenon. Parents can be very helpful to the sport psychology professional if he/she knows how to receive their input, but keep them out of the actual counseling sessions. Parents should be considered as another source of valuable information concerning the athletes performance situation.

The dynamics affecting the parents' representation of the issues are multifaceted. Some parents are too involved in their athletes' lives; while most parents just want their young performers to be happy, and yet there are few parents who could care less. The sport psychology professional should first determine the involvement level of the parents with their children's athletic career, and then ask the athlete their perceptions concerning their parents involvement. These two areas are potential causes of conflict, resentment, etc. within the athlete. Another situation which frequently occurs is parents living vicariously through their children's sports endeavors. When overly aggressive parents are identified they need to be properly counseled on the appropriate level of involvement. One question I frequently ask of such zealots is- "Why don't you just bronze the little sucker and place him/her on the mantel and parade the neighbors through?" Needless to say, this subtle reminder is an eye opener.

The vast majority of parents really do care about allowing their child to have a good experience in the sporting world. Parents have the best intentions but are prone to quickly slip into a role of accomplice instead of a distant facilitator where sports are concerned. As a professional, your challenge is to simultaneously help the young athlete as you counsel the parents.

Issues According to the Sport Psychology Professional

The sport psychology professional must be astute enough to weigh all the information provided by the athlete, the coach, and the parents; and then triangulate the data to reach an effective individualized program for possible solutions. Bear in mind that frequently none of the actual participants (athletes, coaches, parents) really understand all of the performance issues in most situations. It is up to the professional to identify the source of the issues and to help provide direction to rectify them. Underlying causal issues are rarely quickly identifiable and are difficult to solve. Yet, it is the professional's responsibility to identify the problem and provide help for a solution. Common techniques for the sport psychology professional to utilize are psychometric assessments, interviews, and observations of practices and performances.

Guidelines for the Sport Psychology Professional

The remainder of this chapter will be devoted to presenting guidelines for the professional when working with athletes, coaches, parents, and oneself. Consider these guidelines as suggestions which you can accept or reject at your own discretion.

Working With Athletes

1. Listen carefully to input from the athlete.
2. Do not discount the athletes feelings or emotions.
3. After hearing the input from the athlete, verify the validity through other sources (practices, competitions, etc.)
4. Talk the language of the athlete. Provide examples within the context of the sport the athlete is involved in. The athlete needs to know that the professional really understands the context in which the issue is manifested.
5. Be open concerning you own personal beliefs, but do not be judgmental.
6. Educate the athlete as you are working with them. Let them know why you are doing certain interventions.
7. To be truly effective, the sport psychology professional must understand how age differences affect perceptions and how to provide treatments appropriate to where the athlete is currently regarding emotional and mental abilities.
8. Have a buffet of psychological interventions available for the athlete from which they can select.
9. Develop an individualized program (instead of doing the same thing with everyone).

Example:

Sherry is an 18 year old freshman in college at a large University in the western part of the United States. In her second semester (about half way through) she voluntarily comes to your office and asks to speak with you. Her sport is track and field and she was a excellent high jumper in high school (about 64") but is now having difficulty clearing 60" at indoor meets. She complains that she has no energy and seems to lose concentration very easily. She indicates to you that she has many friends and dates a lot and has trouble finding time to study enough, although her grades are pretty good (between a B+ and A- on average).

After listening carefully to Sherry's story you decide to give her a few psychometric tests   (i.e. POMS, short form of TAIS, TSCS) to help get to know her. You also visit one of her practices and the next indoor competition. The tests indicate that she is definitely fatigued, perfectionistic, and has poor concentration skills. By chance, you have Sherry's roommate in class and you ask her one day "How is Sherry doing". She laughs and says - "She's killing herself". Pursuing this comment, you find out that Sherry has a date almost every night and then studies (after the dates) for a couple of hours.

During the next meeting with Sherry you explain that you can help her performance only if she will do certain things. First she must balance her life between academics, training, rest, and social life. All of these are important and must receive equal weight. She needs to learn some time management skills which you will teach her. Also, you explain a number of concentration exercises that will help her in the performance area. You explain that it will take a number of weeks to accomplish these ends. She agrees to start this program.

Working With the Coach

1. Determine exactly what they expect and then decide if it is within your capabilities. (If the desired action is beyond your abilities, say so.)
2. Make no guarantees. Remember, you are working with people (athletes) so guarantees are not possible.
3. Listen carefully to their perception of the problems or issues.
4. Educate and keep them informed as you go along.
5. Establish open communication with the coach. Let them know the parameters within which you operate (ethics).
6. Mitigate their fears as to your actually being involved in coaching.
7. Be open, candid, and honest in your interactions.
8. Inform the coach as to the time line you expect when working with their athletes.

Example:

"Coach Big Time" comes to you and asks if you would work with her high school tennis team in the area of group dynamics. She indicates that she has a very good team but the girls are very individualistic and selfish when it comes to a team attitude. You listen carefully and indicate that you would be happy to work with the team and the coach. You explain to the coach how you will work with the team and also what you expect from her the coach. You explain to her that you will tell her what you perceive and not necessarily what she may want to hear. Your stress that yours and hers must be an open line of communication. You also explain that you will work with her team all this year but you can not guarantee the outcome; but you will do your best to develop "chemistry". Coach Big Time is excited to get started.

Working With Parents

1. Be empathetic to the situation they are experiencing.
2. Tell them what you think, not necessarily what they want to hear.
3. They should understand that even though they are employing you, you are obligated to be forthright and present all of your findings; even if it means that they (the parents) need to change their approach to their athlete.
4. Keep them informed of your progress without betraying any confidentiality with the athlete.
5. Encourage them to be a **guest** in the athletic lives of their children.

Example:

The parents of a very promising high school basketball player (sophomore - 6'10") call you and ask that you start to work with them and their son on mental skills training. You indicate that you have room in your private practice for another client and ask them to meet with you and to bring their son. During this initial meeting you talk to both parents and the athlete in a very forthright manner. You explain what you do an what you don't do. You explain to the parents that you understand that it is not easy to parent an elite athlete and that some of the advice you will give will not be easy for them to follow. The father is a bank president and seems to be very authoritative, demanding, and deeply involved in his son's athletic life. You explain to the parents that if you decide to work with them and their son that you will always tell them what you think, not necessarily what they want to hear. You also explain your ethics covering confidentiality and their son. Lastly, you discuss your philosophy that parents should be a guest in the athletic life of their son. The young man is excited to get started but you sense the father is a little hesitant. You ask the family to go home and discuss your employment and let you know in a few days.

Working Through Oneself

Maybe the most challenging or difficult aspect of any counseling situation is that of the sport psychology professional not letting their personal idiosyncrasies interfere with the situation. The good sport psychology consultants realize that they are not capable of effectively reaching everyone. They have a great referral system and do not allow their egos to override their common sense. Your personality does not permit you to be effective with all people, so don't take it personal; and just move on. All helping professionals will face this problem a few times in their careers. There will be some clients with whom, for whatever reasons, you are incompatible- so be it. These situations are not a slap at your competency, but rather a test of it. This factor of 'incompatibility' is identified, clarified, and addressed in greater depth in Chapter 14, *The Value of Failure*.

Working through oneself also involves such ethical issues as transference, countertransference, dependence, and father/mother fixations to name a few. There are possible pitfalls in any relationship, and the wise professional will anticipate such situations. Remember, one of the most crucial behind the scenes issues is your ethical standards.

Summary

Each client brings uniqueness to the situation and it is your responsibility (the sport psychology professional) to not only recognize this uniqueness; but to also treat the issues behind the symptomatic issues. Athletes, coaches, and parents all provide valuable perceptions, but you are the expert who ties them together and provides possible solutions. The real issues with respect to a performance problem may be different from problems identified in an initial interview, psychometric testing, or observation because the root causes are rarely discovered during the initial exploration process. Generally, the causes of performance decrements are complex and multiple in nature. As a result, finding out what is really going on may dramatically shorten and/or strengthen the services provided. The previously provided guidelines should alert you to many of the considerations available. But by far, the most crucial issue is you (the professional), and how perceptive you are concerning your own limitations and the cues being provided by the issues.

The great philosopher Pogo once said:

"We have found the enemy and it is us."

PART II

Case Studies in
Mental Skills Training

In Part II, nine chapters address some of the most common issues faced by athletes and their coaches. Each chapter begins with an overview of the central issue to provide the reader an understanding of the most prevalent dynamics to be found in the case studies. These introductory overviews are written from each author's unique perspective from their education and practical experiences. The authors were asked to write from their hearts and their heads to provide the reader with an insightful look into the approaches and perspectives of some of the elite applied sport psychology professionals of today.

The case studies are compilations of experiences of the contributing authors as well as a number of other applied sport psychology professionals. The cases vary in the amount of introductory information, details of intervention strategies, and outcome specifics. However, this is by design. The cases are intended to represent the reality of working in applied sport psychology; sometimes with limited information, a narrow time frame, an inability for follow-up, etc. Most cases are formatted according to three sections: *Introduction, Intervention,* and *Outcome*. Other cases are prospective and do not involve an intervention while others do not provide an outcome. In these cases, an *Overview* section is included. Mini-descriptions of each case study with accompanying page numbers are found in the **Case Studies Index** at the end of the book.

CHAPTER 5

~ Composure: Arousal and Anxiety Dynamics ~

Richard D. Gordin, Utah State University

Worry gives a small thing a big shadow.
-Swedish proverb

Composure and arousal control is one of the fundamental skills required of great performance. In my 20 years of consulting as an applied sport psychology consultant, I cannot think of one successful athlete who did not possess this important mental skill. The ability to control emotion on the playing field is a fundamental skill that must be mastered just as the ability to shoot, to jump, to block or to serve has to be mastered. The arousal-performance relationship has been one of the foundational issues studied in the field of applied sport psychology. For decades , sport psychologists have studied the arousal-performance relationship without definitive conclusion. From Spence and Spence's (1966) early work utilizing the drive theory to Hanin's (1986) recent development of the individual zones of optimal functioning theory, researchers have tried to explain this complex relationship. How does the physiological and psychological arousal manifested by performers enhance or detract from optimal performance? Why do athlete's fluctuate in performance outcome so dramatically in the space of a two hour game? Why do athletes play well in practice yet have such difficulty carrying this great performance to game day? As coaches and sport psychologists what can we do for an athlete with too much arousal on game day? These questions and many more are driving the search for the definitive answers to the arousal-performance relationship. Several theories and hypotheses have been proffered by researchers to explain this relationship including; the drive theory, the inverted-u hypothesis, the zones of optimal functioning theory, multidimensional anxiety theory, catastrophe theory and reversal theory. A brief discussion of each will follow.

Theories, Hypotheses, and Predictive Models

Drive Theory and Inverted -U Hypothesis

One of the earliest theories designed to explain the arousal-performance relationship was the drive theory. As an individual's arousal level increased so did his or her performance level. However, if you ask any performer, she can tell you of an occasion when the arousal level was either too high or too low and performance suffered as a consequence. Very little scholarly support exists to support this theory. Others (Martens, Vealey & Bump, 1990) have suggested that the relationship may indeed hold true to a moderate level of arousal and then performance decrements will occur. Additionally, arousal and anxiety are multidimensional concepts that include both somatic and cognitive characteristics. That is, the relationship between anxiety, arousal and stress is very complex and multifaceted rather than simplistic and uni-dimensional. The inverted-u explanation has intuitive appeal to athletes and coaches as both have tacitly experienced both under arousal and over arousal in competition. Unfortunately, many years of research and investigation has yet to support this hypothesis completely and the scientific and applied psychology community has abandoned support of this explanation. Alternative explanations have been offered that either expand upon or refute the inverted-u hypothesis.

Catastrophe Theory and Reversal Theory

Lew Hardy (1990) expanded the inverted-u hypothesis by contending that the multidimensional nature of perceived anxiety is very important to the consequences of the performance. If the athlete is overly worried or anxious cognitively, the inverted -u model holds for somatic anxiety only up to a point and then a catastrophe occurs and performance deteriorates dramatically and rapidly. This theory has received some initial support. However, Kerr (1985) has suggested that an athlete's interpretation of his or her arousal level is the key to performance not the level in and of itself. If an athlete interprets arousal or anxiety in a positive fashion then a positive performance might result , however, if arousal is interpreted in a negative fashion then a poor performance can be expected. An athlete might shift or reverse her interpretation many times during the course of the game. Therefore, it becomes paramount for the coach to assist in interpreting anxiety in a positive way.

Individual Zones of Optimal Functioning

Yuri Hanin (1980; 1989) has conducted considerable work studying the relationship between state anxiety and performance. A predictive model has been developed based upon multiple measures of an athlete's state anxiety level, prior to performance, retroactively reflecting on past performance and predicting future performances. Considerable research has supported Hanin's theory and this theory has considerable appeal ,however, the theory has not been supported in a number of research studies.

Theoretical Overview

Weinberg and Gould (1995) have summarized the research in the following way. Arousal is multidimensional and complex ,therefore, an athlete must find an optimal mix of emotion to facilitate good performance. Arousal and state anxiety do not automatically affect performance negatively. The interpretation of the anxious feelings is crucial. Self-confidence and preparation are also important to the outcome. Some optimal level of arousal is a necessity for great performance , however, it is very difficult to determine exact levels for each athlete. Both catastrophe theory and reversal theory suggest an interaction between somatic anxiety and perceived levels of anxiety by the athlete. Some athletes perform better when highly aroused and some perform better when more relaxed. Worry is not necessarily a negative thing however, *excessive* worry may be associated with decrements in performance.

Turning Anxiety and Worry into Positive Action

Worry is the most natural and spontaneous of all human emotions. Some worry is not necessarily bad and , in fact, athletes will never get rid of fear and doubt in competitive environments. It is necessary for athletes to be
afraid before they can be courageous. What an athlete does with the worry, doubt and fear is more important than the worry itself. The true champion is the one who faces his fear and conquers it in the heat of the battle. In my many years of consulting, I have never advised an athlete to be fearless. Instead , I have advised him to confront those fears and carefully plan a method of dealing with them. One of the characteristics of outstanding performers is the ability to bounce back from adversity. Competition by its very nature is unpredictable. A true champion prepares for every contingency and pledges to react in a decisive , positive way to any occurrence on the field.

The terms arousal, stress and anxiety have often be used interchangeably in the literature. Although these terms are related they do have distinguishing characteristics. Arousal is an activation of the organism ranging from coma to panic. Anxiety is a general sense of foreboding, fear and worry that can be distinguished by " right now" type feelings which is defined as state anxiety to a more enduring feeling or disposition to feel nervous which is defined as trait anxiety.

Stress has been defined as a general environmental demand on the body that lasts from birth to death. Some stresses are inevitable and can be construed as either good stress (exercise) or bad stress (a death in the family). Stress and anxiety are normal occurrences in the life of an athlete. For instance, the normal university athlete can experience social stresses such as team membership, pecking order demands , role conflicts and coach-athlete disputes. Other forms of stress occur such as time constraints, academic problems and general expectations from others that may exceed the capabilities of the athlete to meet these demands. The more important the event or game the more stress that might occur. There is a complex interaction of personal characteristics of the athlete (trait anxiety level) and the demand of the situation (championship game) that lead to pre-game state anxiety levels. The coach is often a poor judge of pre-game anxiety level in his athletes partly because he is dealing with his own anxiety level. Oftentimes, the pre-game speech is given as the byproduct of a need by the coach to ventilate his feelings and not to meet the need of the athlete to psyche-up for the competition. The pre-game speech can often be detrimental to the overly anxious athlete.

The fact that some athletes perform better at extreme levels of performance anxiety and some athletes are destroyed by becoming hyper -aroused forces us to alter our view point from traditional thinking. There is a complex interaction with the enduring dispositions of the individual, the type of task , the skill level of the athlete, the perceived ego threat, the perceived difference in demand and ability to meet the demand and the preference style of activation, to name only a few extenuating variables. Mahoney and Meyers (1989) have reported that skilled athletes tend to use their anxiety more effectively than their less experienced peers. The more skilled athletes tend to view their anxiety, at worst, as a nuisance and , at best, as an ally to better performance. These highly skilled competitors also tend to pace themselves in their pre-event moments more effectively and are less focused on their anxiety and more focused on momentary task demands during their performance. These findings are indicative of the need to assess and then devise individual interventions for each athlete. The first step is to learn to recognize anxiety in athletes.

Recognizing Anxiety in Athletes

Over the years I have been an advocate of psychological assessment. This has not been a popular view with most of my colleagues. I have persisted in my use of these assessments to meet my need to know the exact requirements of each person. I have utilized this information to design individual mental training programs for coaches and athletes. I have used a number of these tools to obtain information about an athlete's anxiety level including ; the State-Trait Anxiety Inventory (STAI) (Spielberger, 1983) , the Sport Competition Anxiety Test (SCAT) (Martens, 1977) , the Competitive State Anxiety Inventory-2 (CSAI-2) (Martens, Vealey, & Burton (1990) and most recently, the Competitive Styles Profile (CSP) (Ogilvie, Greene & Baillie (1997). I have never used these inventories to select personnel nor make personnel decisions.

Some the case studies in this chapter will illustrate the use of these inventories. No matter what inventory you administer , the information provided by the athlete must be validated from the view point of the athlete. Valuable time can be saved in determining anxiety level , while still honoring the privacy and idiosyncrasies of each individual. In addition to administering these inventories, it is imperative to spend time observing the behavior of each performer in practice and in game situations. No two athletes are alike with respect to anxiety and arousal. Poise under pressure consists of an individual' s predominant characteristics regarding preference to perform in a more nervous or psyched-up condition or in a more relaxed and calm condition. Some athletes have difficulty in deactivating if under extreme pressure. Some athletes often feel sabotaged in a pressure situation which can interact and trigger feelings including the fear of failure or fear of success. All of these tendencies are important considerations when designing appropriate interventions. The appropriate identification of competitive tendencies is crucial when working with athletes. These competitive tendencies can be identified quickly and accurately be utilizing psychological inventories and questionnaires. When combined with consensual validation with the performer, observation of the athlete in practice and competition, a very accurate assessment can lead to appropriate intervention plans.

What to Do Now? Appropriate Interventions

In the field of applied sport psychology many different interventions have been utilized for performance anxiety. I will explain and illustrate several of the most common interventions and then you can observe , in the case studies presented, how these interventions were utilized in each case. I feel a need to state my intervention philosophies in a straight forward fashion. First, anxiety is not a dirty word. Stress, arousal and anxiety can be used in a positive way by the experienced and prepared athlete. All athletes will experience anxiety while performing; therefore, it is not my intention to get rid of anxiety. My intention is to identify and utilize these perceived feelings to facilitate good performance. This is a vast departure from interpreting anxiety as psychopathological. The applied consultant must be ready to teach the athlete on his or her terms as you are the invited guest into the life of the athlete. It is not my intent to force my agenda on every athlete. The athlete brings a great deal of experience and talent into the relationship with the applied consultant. It is my suggestion that you utilize this expertise and respect the unique individual in each relationship with an athlete. Your job is to assess, interpret, listen, and suggest while at all times realizing the potential exists within each athlete to solve her own dilemmas. As a consultant , you bring your unique experience to the table and are employed to work with and for the athlete.

Most interventions for performance anxiety include some type of cognitive-behavioral component. If an athlete manifests a significant amount of somatic anxiety , some type of relaxation training may be indicated. Cognitive anxiety can also be ameliorated to some degree by learning to relax as well. Once again, each treatment intervention must be individualized and based upon the specific needs of the athlete. However, it has been my experience , in learning that most athletes need more help to calm down or deactivate in competitive environments than to energize. Remember that each athlete has a unique zone of optimal functioning. It is the consultant' s job to define that optimal zone for each athlete and then teach him or her to enter that zone upon demand. Some athletes perform better in a highly aroused state and some perform better in a lower emotional state. Most athletes know how to "psyche-up" and the situation will induce arousal for them without having to do additional exercises. However, many athletes do not know how to calm down when overly aroused.

Relaxation Strategies for Athletes

The most well known and utilized method for relaxing is Jacobson's (1938) Progressive Muscular Relaxation. Jacobson proposed that muscular tension and physiological activation are incompatible states with muscular relaxation. In order to relax, one must first recognize muscular tension in the body. His technique involves progressively tensing and relaxing all major muscle groups within the body in a systematic way. The athlete learns to recognize too much muscular tension, especially in the antagonist muscular groups, and can then utilize the agonist muscular groups more efficiently. When an athlete does not learn to recognize inappropriate levels of muscular tension a "double pull" phenomenon called bracing might occur and hinder peak performance. When combining progressive relaxation with Wolpe's (1969) systematic desensitization an athlete might learn to master a given anxiety provoking situation without experiencing the unpleasant sensations that accompany extreme anxiety and threat.

The relaxation response first discussed by Benson (1975) is another method used to relax. This response can be learned in a relatively short amount of time and requires little formal training. Benson's method applies the basic elements of meditation without emphasizing the religious undertones. This method requires four distinct elements that include; a quiet environment, a comfortable position, a mental device such as a cue word or phrase and a passive attitude. Another important component of this method is breathing. An athlete can exhibit effective breathing patterns that emanate from the diaphragm and almost immediately feel a calming effect during competition. In fact, many athletes utilize this deep belly breath automatically without a conscious effort to do so. Actual exercises can be taught to athletes experiencing difficulty breathing correctly. Williams and Harris (1998) describe a number of these muscle-to-mind exercises including; the complete breath, sighing with exhalation rhythmic breathing and concentration breathing. Breathing skills can be incorporated and taught in training sessions during stretching exercises or these skills can be honed outside the practice arena. An athlete should allow for 20-30 minute training sessions.

Jencks and Krenz (1984) developed a Modified Autogenic Training for Athletes (MAT) program of self-hypnosis that has been utilized for the last 15 years. This program is an adaptation of Schultz's standard autogenic training program. The following is a brief description of the program: During the first week of practice the athlete sits or lies in a comfortable position with eyes closed and repeats "Comfortably heavy" during each of seven exhalations for the (a) preferred arm, (b) the non preferred arm, (c) both arms, (d) the preferred leg, (e) the non preferred leg, (f) both legs, and finally (g) both arms and both legs. The entire sequence is repeated three times. The procedure takes about 10 minutes and is repeated three times per day for seven days. Each day you decrease the repetitions by one until at the end of the week when you are capable of achieving heaviness with one repetition. During week two, the athlete first repeats "arms and legs are comfortably heavy" and then follows the same procedure as heaviness except she substitutes "comfortably warm" instead of the heaviness formula. Subsequent practice takes the athlete through "heartbeat calm and regular" , "breathing, it calms me", "body center comfortably warm" and finally " forehead pleasantly cool". This self-hypnotic procedure can be learned by the athlete in a seven week period and then utilized whenever necessary in one or two breaths to elicit the proper level of tension during competition. The formulae should always be silently repeated with an exhalation.

My experience over the years has allowed me to make several recommendations when teaching relaxation training to athletes. First, always conduct sessions at the end of practice or after practice. If you conduct sessions prior to practice the athletes will be sluggish for several minutes after deep relaxation training. Second, I prefer individual practice and self-practice to group or heterohypnotic work. My reason for this preference involves my belief that for any method to truly become effective the athlete needs to control the outcome of the session. Third, I have found that most athletes do not prefer progressive muscular relaxation. I believe that a more direct relaxation procedure is preferable in most instances. Finally, it is wise to expect some initial skepticism when initially presenting any form of relaxation training to athletes. Do not fight this skepticism but be patient and allow the athlete to come to you on his or her own terms. In most cases, they will eventually ask for the training especially when they see the positive results from other teammates.

Cognitive-Behavioral Components of Anxiety Management

Any intervention for performance anxiety with athletes will and should include some type of cognitive-behavioral component in the treatment. This treatment may take the form of learning new coping skills, refinement of self-talk to appraise the personal meaning attached to the anxiety, concentration or focus training or model training. I will conclude this introduction to the following case studies by speaking to each of these cognitive-behavioral components separately.

Coping skills can be taught to an athlete to allow him or her to learn to focus on the competitive environment more positively. It is paramount to teach them to learn to control the environment rather than letting the environment control them. A detailed competition plan should be formulated and discussed focusing on only the controllable aspects of the competition. Plans should be outlined for plausible conditions that might occur. The athlete should always be reminded that mistakes will occur in competition and changes may occur to game plans in the middle of the event. The athlete has no control over these occurrences. However, the athlete has complete control on how he or she reacts to these circumstances.

Self-talk is crucial to great performance and learning to cope with performance anxiety. The most important conversation an athlete will ever have will be with himself. Self-talk should be positive and constructive both during and after competition. Self-talk can be practiced and planned. Affirmations are also important components to inner dialogue. Most critical self-talk originates with past events and with other people's expectations ,therefore , athletes must be taught to stop allowing others to think for them and to start to take control of their own actions. Recognizing critical self-talk, determining when it has the tendency to occur and then setting a plan to combat the negative talk are the important steps to helping competitors to gain control.

Concentration training is helpful in several ways to help combat excessive arousal and anxiety. Focusing on the process of performing rather than the outcome of performing allows a competitive athlete to attend to only the cues that are important to completing the task efficiently and successfully. This type of focus allows the athlete to insulate herself from extraneous and superfluous demands and concerns and focus solely on the competition plan of action. Many of the qualities of peak performance for example; feeling in a cocoon, being highly focused, sensing a feeling of power, experiencing a sense of time distortion and noting an absence of pain are associated with this type of intense concentration. The skill of focusing can be learned and should be incorporated into any stress management program.

Finally, *simulation training* or *model training* is often very useful in preparing the athlete for the inevitable first signs of fear and doubt that emerge in any significant challenge. As I stated earlier, it is never my intention to completely inoculate the athlete from these significant emotions associated with competition. Moreover, the ability to bounce back from adversity and respond to significant challenges will only serve to strengthen and develop psychological hardiness in the serious competitor. The athlete who masters the ability to face fears and doubt and emerge from them will be stronger, possess a sense of control and face difficulties with resolve and courage. Helping athletes practice responding to difficulties in the competitive venue is the definition of model training. This method originated in the former Eastern Block nations and has been utilized in North American sport psychological training for almost 25 years. I am an advocate of its use and often help the athlete and coach incorporate model training into the training program for highly skilled athletes.

In summary, arousal and anxiety are normal facets of the competitive environment. Elite performers learn to cope with stress and ultimately develop a propensity to seek challenging situations. The high achievers in sport look at stress, arousal and anxiety as the natural component of a day's work. All athletes can be taught the necessary skills to face their fears and turn them into avenues for growth. It is my wish that all applied sport psychologists continue to become excited when encountering the opportunities to help athletes and coaches overcome their fears. As Friedrich Nietzsche stated,   "That which does not kill you will make you stronger". Please enjoy the following case studies involving the stress of competition.

Case Studies of Composure

#1: College Swim Teams

Introduction:

In February of this year, the captains of both the men's and women's swim teams at my college met with me with a request for a program to help the athletes deal with some of the problems that they were facing in the competitive environment. With very little time to the target meets of the season (6 weeks to conference and only 8 weeks to the NCAA meet), the project took on more of a "fix-it" approach than an educational approach that I would have liked.

Intervention:

A "trouble-shooting" meeting was set up so that the athletes could help me to prioritize their concerns, thus helping me best utilize the short time we had.   A simple strengths/weaknesses chart was filled out by each swimmer. From this list a list of perceived weaknesses were used to develop the focus of the program. The most frequently occurring weakness responses were:

      a.   Lack of Confidence
      b.   Fear of Failure
      c.   Inability to Relax

Following the initial meeting, an impromptu meeting was scheduled to help the athletes put their perceived weaknesses into perspective. At this time, the progressive implementation strategy was explained. The strategies were implemented every Sunday evening until the target meets (with each athlete received a paper fully explaining the strategy at each session). The strategy meetings consisted of:

1. Troubleshooting Meeting
2. Self-led Relaxation
3. Visualizing Success
4. Affirmation
5. Mastery Rehearsal and Mastery/Coping Tapes

Each session lasted from 1-1½ hours and were well attended. After completion of the Conference Swim Championships, the athletes evaluated their performances and the effectiveness of the program on their performances. Eleven participants completed a survey asking for responses based on a Likert scale. We also asked for responses to open-ended questions and for comments on each section.

Overview:

Troubleshooting: The Likert scale indicated a very strong positive response to the troubleshooting section. Most respondents agreed with the question regarding whether this portion aided in identifying weaknesses and focusing, with only one person disagreeing.

Relaxation: The relaxation portion showed similar positive responses. The athletes found the guided exercise to be the most helpful, but seven athletes were able to successfully utilize this strategy independently two or more times each week. The athletes had the most difficulty implementing the relaxation strategy during the meet situation.

Imagery: Responses were also favorable for the imagery portion of the project, illustrating to the athletes and us that we all have the ability to visualize. The guided exercise was once again the most helpful section. The response to the independent usage was moderate. Visualization requires practice, and the time was limited for implementation, therefore, we assumed that the swimmers did not feel as comfortable using this strategy on their own. We inquired about the type of situation the athletes visualized. Ten respondents visualized their event at race pace. Many also used a combination of visualizing different speeds and particular points of their event as well as the total performance. Seven athletes visualized one or more times each week. Five utilized imagery daily or nearly every day.

Affirmation: The respondents felt that this section was very important. The written exercise to identify low confidence areas appeared to have been very helpful. Affirmation is a very personal tool and, as a result, is very subjective. The Likert scale indicated a positive response overall. However, the athletes felt that setting their own strategies was more helpful than the written exercise we provided. All respondents felt the affirmation exercises had a positive effect outside of swimming. The methods of positive affirmation most commonly used were talking to oneself and signs and notes in visible places. One respondent also commented that "Believing" was an important aspect of affirmation.

Mental Rehearsal and Coping Scripts: Most respondents felt that the guidelines we provided were helpful, although there were three requests for more detailed instructions and possibly samples of tapes and scripts. The responses to questions based on the Likert scale were more widely distributed than those for the other sections. It is our belief that the more moderate positive feedback is due to the lack of time necessary to become comfortable with the tapes.

The athletes concentrated on the areas of imagery most frequently. Affirmation and relaxation were commonly combined with imagery or used alone. One comment identifies an important feature of mental arousal, "And I was nervous, but was 'OK' about it." Arousal is necessary for performance as long as it is under control. Mental Rehearsal and Coping tapes help build the confidence necessary to attain this control.

Nine respondents answered affirmatively when asked whether our method of mental training was effective in helping to achieve their goals. One respondent answered negatively, and one was unsure. One swimmer responded that simply making the script and tape had a strong effect on her concentration level and performance, even though she only listened to the tape two or three times.

We also inquired as to how each respondent felt the program was effective. Relaxation, focus, and positive feelings helped the respondents believe they were capable. The aspects of the program found to be most helpful were the affirmation and relaxation phases. One respondent found the affirmation "extremely helpful." One respondent felt that the troubleshooting session was useless, but the overall response to this was positive.

When we asked if the athletes would recommend the program to another coach or athlete, eight participants responded positively. Comments included the assertion that the athlete must wholeheartedly believe in the method of it to work. Another felt that "even with limited involvement the method works." Five felt the program would be beneficial to sports other than swimming, cross-country and baseball specifically. Other comments included feelings of being rushed throughout the whole process, with which we fully agree. The program should be initiated during the first weeks of the season. Another respondent had difficulty with every aspect of the program and didn't feel it was especially helpful other than making him slightly more relaxed.

Overall, the responses to the program were positive. Very few respondents did not agree that the methods helped to some extent. The comments and open responses were positive and helpful. The comments expressing problems with the athlete or the program were enlightening and were taken into consideration when recommending changes for future use of the program.

#2: Female College Swimmer

Introduction:

Fran was a 21 year old senior female swimmer. She had mono her sophomore year, and had not PR'ed since she was 16. Fran wants to get strong both mentally and physically, become more confident, and maintain a sense of balance (i.e. personally, academically, athletically, and socially) in her life as a student-athlete.

Intervention:

I met with Fran, individually, 14 times (Sept.-April) mainly in the office; sometimes taking walks. The Mental Skills Training Program was individualized based on her needs at the time. Sessions dealt with a variety of issues such as developing mental plans for competition; goal setting strategies and log keeping; goal assessments; stress management; interpersonal relations; finding and maintaining a sense of balance between athletics, academics, and her own personal life; helping her deal effectively with personal problems; life after athletics, etc.

In addition, I met with Fran's team 12 times for either formal educational sport psychology meetings (i.e. goal setting, mental skills training, relaxation and stress management, visualization, communication and team harmony) or informally to assess how things are going as a team. I also logged numerous hours making myself available either before/after practices or during competitive meets.

I have found Orlick's Competition Reflections form to be quite helpful along with individualized goal setting programs that focus on a person's personal and athletic strengths as well as weaknesses. In this case, the weaknesses to be addressed were: technique work, speed work, pace work, strength and conditioning, mental skills training, etc.). I have used a relaxation tape by Ken Ravizza that the athletes enjoy ("Point of Balance") along with the visualization video from the Canadian Coaching Association as an introduction to visualization and mental skills training that the athletes respond well to.

Outcome:

Fran was a pleasure to work with. She was conscientious, a hard worker, and committed to the process of mental skills training. We worked on goals, relaxation and concentration, self-awareness, communication skills, and helping her reconcile her role as both a student and an athlete while at the same time learning to balance her athletic, academic, personal and social needs/demands more effectively. By the end of the year, she achieved a personal best in one of her events, reports being more confident and in control of herself both in and out of the pool, and focused throughout the year. At the final event of the year, she came up to me elated and thanked me for all of my help. I told her "You were the one who took control of the mental side of your life; all I did was provide direction and a little support."

#3: Women's Field Hockey Team

Introduction:

The women's field hockey team has a history of consistently qualifying for the NCAA playoffs. Prior to the season, the coach was interested in achieving three objectives: a) improved interpersonal communications and team harmony (i.e. athlete-athlete and coach-athlete); b) winning the conference tournament and qualifying for the NCAA tournament; c) getting individuals to become self-motivated, accountable, and responsible for their own actions.

Intervention:

I met with the team 17 times throughout the year and the coaches at least 14 times (not including numerous informal meetings in the hallway or on the telephone to serve as a sounding board or discuss various issues that arose within the team). Based on initial conversations with the coaching staff, 5 educational sport psychology workshops were designed and implemented:

- Goal Setting and What it Takes to be a Champion
- Communication and Team Building
- Mental Plans for Training and Competition
- Visualization, Concentration and Refocusing Techniques
- Self-Esteem and Self-Confidence

As the season progressed, we met fairly consistently to assess how things were going (i.e. individual goals, team goals, performance assessments, interpersonal communications, team issues, student-athlete issues, etc.). The dynamics of the team changed as the season progressed. The team was very young to begin with, then one individual was lost to the team due to a severe knee injury, another was suspended for the season for violating a team rule, personal problems, family problems, leadership problems (only one senior on the team who was constantly in the coaches doghouse), control issues, etc.

Outcome:

The team started poorly but finished strong at the end of the year to finish .500 and failed to make the NCAA playoffs for the first time in 8 years. However, the team was an extremely close knit team and accomplished their number one goal of improved interpersonal team harmony. The team matured as the season progressed, overcame one personal problem after the next, has high expectations about things to come for the next couple of years. The team was a pleasure to work with, I had tremendous support from the players and coaches, and they made me feel like a valued member of their "family." As for next year, they would like to learn how to play more relaxed, work on refocusing skills, and continue to work in the area of coach-athlete communications (in particular, as it relates to control issues).

#4: Female College Basketball Player

Introduction:

Amanda was a 20 year old female basketball player. She could be described as being a sensitive, conscientious, nice girl from an upper middle class Mormon family. Amanda was highly anxious and definitely stressed out (i.e. parents going through a divorce, asthmatic, migraines, reacting poorly to criticism, difficult time switching gears form the classroom into practice). She is the type that feels like she has to have everything under control and never wants to admit to herself that there is anything wrong.

Amanda was referred to me at the beginning of the year by the coach and trainer to help her deal with migraines and to become mentally tougher. I was told that she was an extremist whose headaches are probably stress related, was never challenged in high school and was not prepared mentally for collegiate competition.

Intervention:

I initially met with Amanda to teach her relaxation skills and identify her sources of stress. I then met with her on 16 different occasions to work on issues such as developing mental plans for competition, arousal regulation, stress management, concentration skills, and dealing with personal problems. Her way of dealing with migraines was to lock herself in a cold dark room and sit there until they passed. The team physician felt that her asthma was stress induced as well. After working with her on various relaxation and stress management techniques, a fluke visit to the dentist revealed that her migraines were caused by impacted wisdom teeth (even the team doctors missed this one).

As for dealing with her parents' divorce, I found myself teaching her assertiveness skills so she would learn how to communicate her feelings to her parents more effectively (A divorce in a Mormon family is almost unheard of!) and to become more aware of her feelings. From this perspective, I felt like we accomplished a lot.

I was very frustrated due to Amanda's season-long inconsistency. Based on her competition reflections questionnaire, mental preparation was a hit or miss thing. She relied on a short nap (more like restful meditation) in the locker room an hour before warm-ups to get herself ready to play. She had difficulty managing her arousal levels both prior to and during the game itself (sometimes too hyped, often times unfocused). I had her write out a game plan (a checklist) of the routine she wanted to follow to prepare for each game (i.e. physically, cognitively, emotionally). We worked on cue controlled concentration techniques (that focused on the feeling she wanted to generate), imagery prior to the game, goals and mental plans for competition so she could learn to engineer the environment to feel more confident and in control of what she wanted to accomplish.

She seemed to play well when she took the time to focus on those things that she wanted to accomplish, her body would exude confidence and she would play with controlled intensity. Other games she looked completely out of it. One game in particular, she did not get her nap, got herself too pumped up and was out of control (the coach could have killed her). We had talked in the past about this possibility occurring and what she might do to get herself ready if she didn't get her nap.

Outcome:

As mentioned earlier, Amanda was easily distracted, always looking for excuses, had a difficult time admitting to herself that anything was wrong, and would fluctuate in the way she would go about getting herself mentally ready to perform each game. I was frustrated, the coaching staff was frustrated with her erratic play, and she got frustrated when the coaches began to get on her case. Obviously, she needs to learn to control the way she chooses to respond to symptoms and sources of stress in her life, but how do you get someone to change if they feel they have everything under control or are not ready to internalize all that is being taught?

#5: Male College Swimmer

Introduction:

Ross, a sophomore male swimmer, came to my office looking for help dealing with a history of competition anxiety. A very gifted student-athlete (GPA of 3.6+ at a very demanding school), he was one of the top swimmers on our college team that had won 10 of the past 11 conference team titles.

The initial meeting with Ross was done informally over coffee. The main points gleaned from this meeting were:

1. He has very high expectations of himself.
2. He is very good at sabotaging himself before meets.
3. He has an external focus up to and during races.
4. His self-talk dialogue is virtually all negative.

After talking this over with him (and he recognized all of it), we set up a plan to help him change his behaviors prior to competition. It should be noted that his coach told me that Ross' practice behavior, while not to the self-defeating level of his meet behavior, is on the "high-strung" side.

Intervention:

The intervention was two-fold. The first component involved counseling Ross to help him understand how he was sabotaging himself before meets. Effort was also made to foster insight into how Ross' self-dialogue was inhibiting his performance. Another factor cognitively addressed was how his focus prior to meets was inhibiting his concentration. A final point that was stressed to Ross was how perfectionism keeps one just out of reach of the brass ring.

The second step was mental skills training that included training on the use of relaxation techniques and visualization of him performing in a relaxed, optimal state. He was also exposed to strategies to mentally remove himself from the immediate pool environment when he began feeling overwhelmed by the stress. To serve as a catalyst for these skills and coping strategies, we made a coping tape utilizing thought stoppage.

Outcome:

Ross placed second in his specialties at the conference meet. While this is very good by most people's standards, his times were not as fast as times that he swam in January during a heavy loading period. He told me after the meet that his anxiety was "off the chart" during the meet and that every strategy he tried to control the anxiety levels failed. I would hope that the lack of mental training time may have impacted the lack of success in this case. My recommendation to him for the off-season was for him to read through a list of articles given to him and to further practice the skills.

#6: College Baseball Player

Introduction:

Howard was a college baseball player I worked with during his junior and senior seasons. He came to me and presented the following issues that he wished to work on: nervousness during games, focus on trying to impress others, inability to get along with the coach, susceptibility to slumps, desire to develop his concentration skills, and long-term goal of playing pro ball.

Intervention:

I used Orlick's Competition Reflections form to help differentiate peak from poor performances. We assessed Howard's personal and athletic strengths and weaknesses as well as developed a goal setting program based on things he could control in the batter's box (i.e. routine, awareness and concentration, comfort in batter's box, one at bat at a time strive to hit ball hard consistently, rhythm, relaxation, and mental focus at plate). As sessions went on, we worked on visualization and script writing, positive affirmations, training logs, and I gave him some readings (he had a thirst for knowledge).

The fourth session, Howard came to realize that he had been overly critical of himself, putting too much pressure on himself. He also realized that stress is self-induced, and was trying to live up to unrealistic expectations (impress coach, teammates, etc.) rather than being more self-accepting and feeling good about himself as a person and as an athlete. Consequently, his performance started to improve, he became less self-critical, and more relaxed and comfortable at the plate. He focused on strengths in the strike zone, being more patient and making the count work for him, and striving to hit the ball hard each time at bat.

Howard's batting average raised to .400 most of the season, confidence in himself rose with his success. He also learned how to deal with his coach more effectively (not allow him to be a distraction). The last day of season, he went 0-3 and dropped his average to under .400 (it meant so much for him to hit .400, when the carrot was dangled in front of him, and the pressure was on, he reverted to old habits).

His senior season, he stopped by to chat in January. He had hoped to land a job teaching, but since that didn't work out, he returned to use his last year of eligibility. Howard hoped to improve on his .390 average in hopes of getting drafted (ultimate goal)!

We went back over the basics of the Mental Training Program we had discussed during his junior year and I gave him a book to read, "Mental Book of Baseball" which he loved. Howard came in to my office weekly to fine tune his program, and started the season like gang busters, hitting at a .600 clip. He then got injured on a trip to Florida, pulling a muscle in his rib case. Consequently, he had to sit out two weeks, resurrecting the anxiety, frustrations, self doubts, and uncertainties he had experienced in the past. An overriding issue was how the injury would affect his chances of getting drafted.

The doctor said he would have to learn to deal with the pain. He made some adjustments, but couldn't get around on inside pitches as well. We talked about mental discipline at the plate. The injury forced him to hone in on his concentration skills; result - he went on a tear (16 game hitting streak, 21-30 hitting, second leading hitter in the country, scouts coming to see him, carrot dangled in front of him). Howard began having difficulty dealing with the distractions, behaviorally. He started to overswing and get impatient, go after pitches out of the strike zone, trying to impress the scouts and hit for power instead of doing the things that got him there in the first place.

We talked about being aggressive but selective, developing the sense of invincibility he demonstrated most of the year. We worked on visualization and the basics of what we talked about in the past but no matter what it was we talked about, he could not turn things around. His average plummeted to .420 (which is better than last year but very disappointing when he was hitting about .540 before his slump) and he again seemed to revert to old habits when the pressure got turned up and the carrot was dangling in front of him.

Outcome:

Howard eventually got drafted in the 28th round and is currently playing rookie ball. He calls occasionally for some advice and encouragement. He is completely dedicated to his sport and mental training. Even though he experienced a slump at the end of the season, he has come a long way toward being more self accepting. Mental skills require constant attention and refinement. Along his journey, he has called on me for friendship and guidance. To me he was a pleasure to work with because he was inquisitive, conscientious, and committed to do all he could do to be the best he could possibly be. As he learns to trust himself in situations that matter the most, his success as an athlete and person will grow accordingly.

#7: Female High School Swimmer

Introduction:

Paula was a 17 year old high school senior who had enjoyed tremendous success as a swimmer. As a junior, she twice broke a National High School record. This success did not come without some complications, however.

Paula had a history of competing extremely well at major competitions, however, before and sometimes afterwards, she physically paid the price for her nervousness and anxiety. Prior to last year's State Meet, Paula was "sick" nearly the entire week. Symptoms included nausea, diarrhea, achy muscles, fatigue, etc. At the time, she appeared to have the flu; in retrospect, she was probably manifesting acute anxiety symptoms. She reported similar experiences before other "big meets" and also occasionally prior to exams and college entrance tests. She is an excellent student, maintaining a 3.8 grade point average.

The after effects of this anxiety also included an inability to recover physically and psychologically for several weeks. Last year, Paula had a disappointing performance at the United States Swimming Short Course National Championships, finishing fifth in one race and failing to qualify for the final in another.

Intervention:

Because she was one of the most highly sought swimming recruits in the country, this year was much more hectic for Paula than the previous year. Recruiting trips disrupted training and concentration, while repeated phone calls at home in the evening from various coaches and alumni disrupted studying and private time. Paula expressed a desire to learn some techniques to not only enhance performance, but also to diminish anxiety and nervousness. The PSIS-5 was administered in November last year. Not surprisingly, Paula scored very well on Motivation (86th percentile) and Confidence (83rd percentile), while scores on Concentration (58th percentile) and ,especially, Anxiety (55th percentile) were significantly lower.

In addition to the team interventions, Paula was seen individually on a monthly basis. Cognitive reprogramming, aided by hypnotic reinforcement, was used to help her integrate a more relaxed attitude toward competition and focus on "letting it happen," rather than trying to make it happen. Paula, who plans to major in psychology with the goal of becoming a sports psychologist, was very adept at utilizing hypnotic/imagery techniques. She was encouraged to practice on a daily basis and to utilize relaxation suggestions whenever she noticed herself becoming anxious.

Outcome:

At this year's High School Championships, Paula won the 100 Backstroke, breaking her own National Record. She had previously finished first in the 200 Freestyle with a personal best time. Less than twenty minutes after winning the backstroke, Paula anchored the State Champion 400 Freestyle relay, locking up the State Team Championship. Her relay was also a personal best.

Perhaps more significant than her performance was the fact that she was able to handle the "pressure" with no apparent anxiety/somatic symptoms or discomfort She was able to enjoy the process, not just survive it. As further evidence that she had not burned herself out, she swam a personal best 200 Backstroke at Time Trials the day after the State Championships.

Several weeks later, Paula competed in the United States Swimming Short Course Championship where she placed second in the 100 Backstroke, beating several leading swimmers including one who had placed fourth at the Olympics. She also made the Championship final in 200 Backstroke, dropping more than two seconds from her previous best time.

An examination of Paula's PSIS-5 post-test results reveal improvements across all of the scales, but most significantly Anxiety (55% to 75%) and Confidence (83% to 92%). The mental skills that she has learned and is able to utilize will continue to help her in swimming, but also in her day to day life.

Paula is presently training for an international meet in the Soviet Union in early June. She reports some nervousness and anticipation about her first international competition representing the United States, but also is confident about her ability to manage her emotions and enjoy the experience.

#8: Female Junior National Race Walker

Introduction:

Lila was an eighteen year old female race walker on the USA Junior National Track and Field Team which was competing at the world Championships. I was asked by the head trainer to help him with Lila who was both ill and emotionally upset about her future performance in her event.

Evidently she had not been able to adjust to the local diet and was not eating properly. Consequently, she became ill and weak and unable to train and prepare for her event. On the day before her event, Lila was unable to complete her workout, came to the training room and complained of an upset stomach and cramps. While on the training table she began to hyperventilate. She was worried about how she would do the next day in her event.

Intervention:

As I approached Lila she was trying to regain a normal breathing pattern. She repeatedly spoke about how poorly she felt and how she was unable to train and prepare properly for her race. She was very concerned about what her father would think of her if she performed poorly.

I encouraged her to relax and focus on her breathing and to concentrate on slowing it down by taking long deep breaths. I held her hand while I talked to her. In about a minute she calmed down and regained her normal breathing pattern and appeared much more relaxed. I stayed with her and encouraged her to rest. She fell asleep on the training table for about 30 minutes after this incident.

Both the trainers and I continued to reassure Lila that she would be fine for the next day's competition if she would get the sleep and rest she needed. I attempted to help her focus her concentration on preparing to give her best performance effort possible during the race. She reviewed her race plan again with her coach and began to pay attention and focus on the race pace lap times.

She was going to compete in the race. It was important for her to "listen to her body" during the race so she didn't walk too fast a pace in the beginning of the race.

We checked with her after dinner and during the evening to make sure she was recovering properly and would indeed be ready for the next day's competition. She slept soundly that night and felt rested for her race.

Outcome:

I accompanied her to the stadium and provided social and emotional support for her prior to, during, and after the race. Lila performed well considering her illness and apprehension prior to her race. Her performance was relatively comparable to her previous races and, all things considered, she felt good about her competitive effort at the world championships.

#9: Male Junior National Sprinter

Introduction:

Nick was a 19 year-old 400 meter runner who was a member of the USA4 x 400 meter relay team which competed at the World Junior Track and Field Championships.

Nick had run poorly in the qualifying heats of the 4 x 400 meter relay heats, especially in the final 80 meters of the race. During this stage of his race he "faded" badly in the stretch and lost the lead the two previous runners had given him. The USA team did however qualify for the final.

On the day of the final Nick's teammates approached me and asked me to speak with him since he appeared very "nervous" about the upcoming final race. After speaking with Nick it became apparent that he was confident but over-aroused regarding his upcoming race. He related to me that it was difficult for him to control the energy which he had "bottled" up inside himself prior to and during the early stages of his races.

Intervention:

I had an opportunity to listen to Nick's thoughts, attitudes, and feelings regarding his situation and it became apparent to me that he was "over-thinking" and "over-feeling" about his upcoming race. I felt it was important for Nick to focus his thoughts and feelings on the formulation of a specific emotional/physical race plan which he would implement in the final event. I also asked Nick to visualize and describe his best race ever.

I made the following suggestions to Nick regarding his situation:

- ◆ Take a walk rather than sit in his room "thinking" constantly about his race. This would help him to relax himself and it would be even more beneficial if he could walk with a friend and discuss topics which were unrelated to his upcoming race.
- ◆ Establish an emotional race plan by breaking the race down in sections and associating a number with each section which represented his arousal level during that particular section of the race. These numbers ranged from 1 (low) to 10 (high)

and were applied to each 100 meters of the overall 400 meter race. He decided to associate the number 7 with the first 100 meters, the number 8 with the second 100 meters, the number 9 with the third 100 meters, and the number 10 with the final 100 meters of the race.

This strategy was utilized so Nick would not expend all his emotional and physical energies in the first 300 meters of the race as a result of disregarding his most effective race pace early in the race. The goal here was to help him control his arousal or excitability during the race.

Outcome:

Nick ran well in the final race. Even though he faded slightly in the final 50 meters of the race, he passed the baton off in first place and the USA won the race. I saw him at the closing ceremonies, which were held after the relay, and he was extremely happy about his performance and the team's success.

#10: Elite Male Diver

Introduction:

Michael is a 29 year old male diver who has won numerous national and international titles. He competed in one Olympic games (finishing 5th) and was a leading contender for another Olympic competition.

Intervention:

Michael received biofeedback sessions as part of his mental skills training regimen, which emphasized acquisition, utilization, and automation of Moore's Concentration, Composure, and Confidence abilities. Feedback stimuli was visual and included measures of muscle tension, skin temperature, electrodermal responsivity (skin conductance), and heart rate.

Changes were made during intervention sessions between biofeedback sessions. In specific, feedback variables focused upon and interventions (i.e. autogenic phrases, video tapes, mental imagery etc.) were modified based on physiological outcomes and learning preference. Pre and post session self report ratings of perceived stress were obtained.

The results indicated that in two of the four physiological measures, larger changes were observed when the subject viewed videotapes of the most recent Olympic Diving trials. Specifically, observable changes were a decrease in skin temperature (8.5 degrees) and an increase in skin conductance (doubled) when watching this tape. Other competition tapes and/or recall did not produce this effect. The observed changes are consistent with autonomic arousal. Muscle tension and heart rate were relatively stable within and between sessions.

Interruption of video viewing and use of cognitive and composure-imagery interventions appeared to be more effective in regaining baseline measures than did terminating viewing or terminating viewing and using autogenic techniques. Physiological changes did not appear to be particularly related to pre-post stress self report ratings.

During eight sessions, the subject was able to more quickly regain physiological composure (return readings to baseline). At the end of the intervention, the subject was able to view a twenty (20) minute tape of the Olympic Trials without interruption and with less than a one (1) degree drop in skin temperature. Skin conductance was not significantly increased during the same session.

These findings suggest that skin temperature and skin conductance may be more useful than heart rate and muscle tension in biofeedback training for self-regulation. This is particularly true because of the activity inherent in athletic events, in which elevated heart rate and muscle tension are somewhat unavoidable. In this case the combination of cognitive and composure imagery interventions was more effective than autogenic techniques.

Outcome:
Within days of the final biofeedback session where autonomic arousal control was demonstrated, the subject competed in the first major competition involving the awarding of prize money for a diving meet. He won his event and $2,000. His self-report indicated that he felt that the composure self-regulation was an integral part of his success.

Further research is needed to determine how these variables relate to actual performance for other athletes and sports.

#11: Female Junior National Field Athlete

Introduction:
Monica was a 19 year old high school senior shot putter and discus thrower. She represented the USA at the World Junior Track and Field Championships. Monica approached me after she had performed poorly in the qualifying rounds of the shot put during which she failed to qualify for the finals. This was difficult for Monica since she felt that the shot put was her best event and she felt she should have easily qualified for the final. She was apprehensive about her performance in the upcoming qualifying rounds of the discus. She displayed a "Training mind-set" during her performances, that is, she was focusing on technique rather than effort and thus her performances were very mechanical. She wanted to meet with me to discuss mental strategies she could use to help her relax and avoid "pressing" during competition.

Intervention:
Monica and I met the day before the qualifying rounds of the discus to discuss her situation, thoughts, feelings, and attitudes. After listening to her concerns I asked her to reflect on a statement I had discussed in a team meeting regarding mental preparation for competition (attuning) namely, "You've got to try less on the most important day of your life." She admitted she was very "tight" physically and mentally prior to competition.

I asked her to picture the word "pressure" in her mind and then to erase the last three letters. She was trying too hard or "pressing" by focusing on failure rather than success. I also explained the stress-performance relationship to her, especially how increased muscle tension can impede the fluent execution of motor skills.

Most importantly, I asked Monica to visualize and describe her best possible performance ever in the discus. She vividly described every aspect of the performance and appeared to relive the joy and excitement she experienced from this past performance. This process appeared to help her "feel" the success of a past performance and helped her to begin looking forward to being successful in her event.

Monica was very open to suggestions which would help her to perform effectively in the qualifying round of the discus and I suggested the following cognitive/behavioral strategies:

- An audio-cassette tape of a relaxation exercise for her to use prior to competition.
- Self-monitor and control her breathing immediately before and during competition in order to help her relax physically and mentally;
- Be "effort" conscious.
- Adhere to her self-identified pre-competitive and pre-throw routines.
- Mentally rehearse a plan of action for the day of competition.
- Visualize and "feel" her former best performance ever prior to and at certain times during the competition (i.e. immediately prior to beginning her pre-throw routine).

Outcome:

Monica qualified for the final on her first throw, felt relaxed and went on to place 8th in the final. She felt good about her performance and thanked me for the suggestions I had provided.

#12: Elite Female Cyclist

Introduction:

Yvette was an international caliber cyclist who won the world road cycling championship five years prior to the intervention. She sought help because she no longer felt competitive in criterium racing, her strongest event. In fact, despite superior physical conditioning and a well-deserved reputation as an excellent strategist, Yvette rarely placed in races anymore. She attributed the tremendous drop in performance to her increasing fear of racing in a tight field of riders. This fear was due to several bad falls she had experienced over the last couple of years. Whenever she found herself surrounded by the pack, Yvette experienced a racing heart, shallow and very rapid breathing, and sensations of losing control of her bike. Her only defense for these episodes was to drop off to the side or to the back of the pack, much to the decrement of her performance.

Yvette was turned off by a classic systematic desensitization procedure because she felt it was inappropriate for the reality of the competitive situation. She felt that learning to not react would reduce her competitiveness. In addition, she was afraid of losing the fear for safety reasons.

Intervention:

We took a positive, action-oriented, skills approach in order to: 1) deal with the fear, 2) control attentional focus, and 3) enhance cycling performance. Dominant themes were:

    a.   Move toward ideal form and performance mind, rather than away from fear

    b.   Take advantage of biomechanical and strategic foci to direct attention.

    c.   Adopt proactive goals for performance, rather than focusing on reactive responses to the problem.

We met regularly from pre-season through the Olympics: once a week for 10 weeks in preseason, then about twice a month from May through September. We also communicated regularly on the phone, especially when Yvette was away at races.

The specific techniques were:

1. Relaxation, Breathing (her major stress response), and Centering
2. Imagery of excellent riding performance: Power Image (Power, Form, Control).
3. Focus on best biomechanical state: relaxed shoulders and chest, flowing pedal spin, sense of being "one with the bike".
4. Increased awareness on the bike.
5. Planning and imagery rehearsal of strategies for dangerous situations. Philosophical acceptance of the possibility of a fall.
6. Use of fear/arousal as CUE for relaxed breathing, focus on form, thoughts/feelings of best riding state.
7. Practice, practice, practice in imagery, during training and at races.

Outcome:

Subjectively, Yvette has given overwhelming endorsement for the procedures. She not only reported a tremendous feeling of accomplishment in beating the presenting problem, but also in her approach to g and development as a competitor. Yvette still reports some fear of pack riding and will avoid especially tight situations where possible, but she has skills to effectively deal with the situation when it arises and to be competitive in the process.

Objectively, she won several major U.S. criteriums last year and was competitive in all those where she was healthy. She felt well prepared for her Olympic ride and had a very strong race only to find herself trapped at the final sprint. She is one of the top riders in U.S. criteriums this season.

#13: Pre-Season Heisman Candidate

Introduction:

Jonas was a member of my general education class. Midway through the semester, the football team began to receive national publicity because of its aerial circus displays led by QB Jonas. This version of the Run and Shoot was amassing tremendous amounts of yardage with 40-50 passes a game the norm. Special media reports uncovered aspects of Jonas's personal life that were privately embarrassing to him. For example, during Jonas's high school days, he was virtually homeless living from house to house or car, wherever his friends would be his host.

As does occur, when one becomes a media "sport star," one's life is in a fish bowl. Because Jonas and I did not have a personal relationship beyond that of professor and student, I did not know how he was handling the attention and scrutiny, although he continued to play well.

During a course topic of media and stardom, he willingly allowed us to present a class scenario "This is Your Life, Jonas." He earned a C in the class. Events in Jonas's life began to change as the spring practice came to a close and the Intercollegiate Department decided to promote Jonas as a Heisman Trophy candidate.

The team suffered an opening loss to a Division II school, 42-41 and then suffered a humiliating defeat at a Div I power, 82-21. Personally, Jonas was not doing well. Fall camp performance had been mediocre. By missing some summer "voluntary" workouts, and being a bit rebellious, he had fallen in disfavor with the Head Coach (also the QB coach and offensive coordinator). The team failures were being attributed to Jonas's lack luster performance. He was a far cry from the Heisman Trophy and quickly dropped out of the race. This is when our close relationship began!

Intervention:

At our first meeting, Jonas opened up quickly and "spilled his guts" as to the tremendous responsibility he felt. Expectations had gone way out of his control. He felt the coach was mistreating him, and he was angry that the second QB was going to split time with him in the next game. He was experiencing the swift decline of a fallen star.

We identified the "problem" during the first meeting. Jonas decided that he was putting far too much energy and time into things he could not control.

1. The way the coach treated him
2. Media reports
3. Expectations of others
4. Whether the second QB played or not
5. Other players on the team
6. Opponents - the schedule

Jonas' first task was to take responsibility for his relationship with the Head Coach. Jonas began to ask for specific treatment and to reinforce the coach's appropriate behavior. For example: During games, when Jonas would throw an interception and come to the sideline, the Head Coach would "rip" him for the failure. After the one-sided interchange Jonas would get as far away from the coach as possible. As you can guess, the problem was not being addressed. Jonas was having a tough time reading defenses and needed help. I asked Jonas who would help him and he said the coach was one of the best in the country. I continued, "have you considered asking him to help?"

At the next game, I was on the sidelines and sure enough during the second series Jonas threw into double coverage and was intercepted. He came to the sidelines and the typical scenario took place. But this time, there was a different ending. Jonas received the tongue lashing, then asked for help. To his delight, the coach responded very positively.

Through our sessions, Jonas developed ways to improve his relationship with the coach. Because I also was spending time each week with the coaching staff, I specifically asked the coach what he could do to improve his relationship with his players. It helped.

The head coach basically used fear and punishment as motivation. Jonas had to learn to work through it and did. Also, he began to ask for different treatment and to reinforce the coach when he received it.

The main thrust of our sessions was taking responsibility for what Jonas could control. He quickly bought the whole package and placed his energy into development of his attitude, took charge of his motivation, used the coach as a resource, stepped up his pre game preparation, decided to be confident, and began to have fun again. He gave one media interview per week. He informed his live-in girlfriend that he was playing for himself.

The intervention strategies that gave Jonas a big assist to take charge was the development of a QB routine. Once he had established a set routine, he was sure to practice the exact routine often. The coach cooperated beautifully. Here is his routine:

After the play ended.
1. Check down and yardage
2. Look to the sideline for play call
3. Get over the center and call the play (run and shoot-no huddle)
4. While calling the play, survey the defense especially the safeties and possible blitzes
5. Audible: false or true; say the name of a car (Ford, Corvette)
6. Imagine the play unfolding (see and feel)
7. Trust; Just do it

Regardless of the situation of the previous play, Jonas would be confident (voice and posture), relaxed and alert.

Outcome:

Jonas worked with the No.2 QB and offered more leadership and support to other team members. The season went well. In the middle of the season, he came back very confidently from a poor game against a strong opponent. The key elements of the intervention were improving his relationship with the coach and developing, practicing his pre-play routine and taking full responsibility for who he was and what he did.

#14: College Quarterback

Introduction:

Dave is a college quarterback who earned the starting position during his sophomore year. His performance was below what was anticipated, and below what he demonstrated in practice situations. This pattern was repeated his junior year. Entering his senior year, Dave has once again earned the starting position by showing superior play during spring practices.

What can be done between now (May) and throughout the season to help this young man perform at the superior level he has demonstrated in practice situations yet never quite matched in games. If the team is to have a chance at a conference title and possible national bowl exposure, his play must not only be above average but extraordinary. If his performance is below average, most likely the team will lose faith in him and games will be lost that should be won. There is an equally talented yet untested backup sophomore-to-be quarterback.

The football program is entering its fourth year under a new head coach. The QB in question has led the team to a 3-8 record his sophomore year, and a 5-5-1 record last season. There is tremendous excitement about the upcoming season. Most of the starters are returning and the team is projected by sport writers to be among the best in the conference. The coaches and players feel the pressure.

Dave led his high school team to a state championship, yet he was not as highly recruited as could be because his performance was often ordinary. He was recruited based on his "flashes of brilliance" he showed at times. He is a superior natural athlete. He is 6'2", 200 lbs., runs a consistent 4.5 forty, has a 38" no step vertical jump, and is a very accurate short and long passer.

Dave appears to be insecure at times although there is a quiet underlying confidence. He seems to be satisfied with being good enough to start and does not push himself beyond that point. Higher personal goals have been set by him but the coaches question his dedication to them. He is very sensitive to feedback and is hurt by negative performance comments.

Dave has tested to be very intelligent, yet often appears tentative and insecure with change and sudden adjustments. He is not a natural "rah-rah" leader, but is highly respected by his teammates as a leader by example. His parents are very supportive, but this may be conditional. Dave's mother is very worried about injury, and his performance appears to decline when his parents are present. They attend every game, and his father is at practices more often than any other player's parents.

Although no specific sport psychology intervention techniques have been attempted, the Dave is very responsive to all types of coaching and is a very willing learner. Yet in actual games, these "learned" patterns disappear. He has never "put it all together" in high school or college beyond the occasional "flashes of brilliance" which are truly extraordinary to witness.

In games, Dave does not exactly "choke", but he fails to make the play although he appears to be trying hard. He seldom gets flustered, yet you are never sure "where his head is at". He appears to want to win badly, yet it appears at times that he is satisfied in the locker room at making it through the game without injury.

All of the above has been discussed with Dave with no effect on improving his performance consistency during his two years as starting quarterback. What should be attempted to assist Dave?

Discussion Questions

1. What are the most common theoretical explanations of the relationship among arousal, anxiety and performance?
2. What are three ways to recognize anxiety in athletes?
3. What are three relaxation strategies employed in applied sport psychology?
4. How might one decide on the appropriate cognitive-behavioral interventions for performance anxiety?
5. Were the techniques utilized in the case studies effective in assisting the athletes with arousal-reduction?, anxiety-reduction? How do strategies differ based on whether the issue is anxiety or arousal?
6. What were the unique pressures in each situation? Were they addressed appropriately?

7. Relative to each situation described in the case studies, what is the difference between perception of the situation and the reality of the situation? What factors determine whether there are differences?

References

Benson, H. (1975). The relaxation response. New York: Avon Books.

Hardy, L. (1990). A catastrophe model of performance in sport. In J.G. Jones & L. Hardy (Eds.). Stress and performance in sport (pp. 81-106). Chichester, England: Wiley.

Hanin, Y.L. (1980). A study of anxiety in sports. In W.F. Straub (Ed.). Sport psychology: An analysis of athlete behavior (pp. 236-249). Ithaca, NY: Mouvement Publications.

Hanin, Y. L. (1986). State trait anxiety research on sports in the USSR. In C.D. Spielberger & R. Diaz-Guerreo (Eds.). Cross-cultural anxiety (Vol. 3 pp. 45-64). Washington, DC: Hemisphere.

Hanin, Y. L. (1989). Interpersonal and intragroup anxiety in sports. In D. Hackfort & C. D. Spielberger (Eds.). Anxiety in sports: An international perspective (pp. 19-28). New York: Hemisphere.

Mahoney, M. J. & Meyers, A.W. (1989). Anxiety and athletic performance: Traditional and cognitive-developmental perspectives. In D. Hackfort & C. D. Spielberger (Eds.). Anxiety in sports: An international perspective (pp. 77-94). New York: Hemisphere.

Jacobson, E. (1938). Progressive relaxation. Chicago: University of Chicago Press.

Jencks, B. & Krenz, E. (1984). Clinical application of hypnosis in sports. In W.C. Wester II & A.H. Smith ,Jr. (Eds.). Clinical hypnosis: A multidisciplinary approach (pp. 574-590). Philadelphia: J.B. Lippincott.

Martens, R. (1977). Sport competition anxiety test. Champaign, IL: Human Kinetics

Martens, R. , Vealey, R.,& Burton, D. (1990). Competitive anxiety in sport. Champaign, IL: Human Kinetics.

Kerr, J.H. (1985). The experience of arousal: A new basis for studying arousal effects in sport. Journal of Sport Sciences, 3, 169-179.

Ogilvie, B. C. , Greene, D., & Baillie, P. (1997). The interpretive and statistical manual for the competitive styles profile and the learning styles profile. Los Gatos, CA: ProMind Institute.

Spence, J.T. & Spence, K.W. (1966). The motivational components of manifest anxiety: Drive and drive stimuli. In C.D. Spielberger (Ed.). Anxiety and behavior (pp.3-22). New York: Academic.

Spielberger, C. D. (1983). Manual for the state-trait anxiety inventory. Palo Alto, CA: Consulting Psychologists Press.

Weinberg, R.S. & Gould, D. (1995). Foundations of sport and exercise psychology. Champaign, IL: Human Kinetics.

Williams, J.M. & Harris, D.V. (1998). Relaxation and energizing techniques for regulation of arousal. In J.M. Williams (Ed.). Applied sport psychology: Personal growth to peak performance (3rd Ed). Mountain View , CA: Mayfield Publishing Company.

Wolpe, J. (1969). The practice of behavior therapy. New York: Pergamon.

CHAPTER 6

~ Confidence ~

William Moore, East Carolina University

If you could sprinkle magic dust on an athlete to produce one skill that would make the greatest positive contribution to his or her performance, what would it be? As a sport psychology professional and coach I would choose confidence; more specifically, a feeling of certainty about one's capacity to perform great. I believe that most coaches, given a choice between a talented player who lacked confidence and a less talented player with confidence, would pick the confident player. Confident athletes not only believe in themselves but also believe in their ability to acquire the necessary skills to succeed. Athletes lacking in confidence often focus on their shortcoming's rather than their strengths creating self-doubts and indecisiveness that undermine performance. For these reasons, a confident athlete with less talent will perform with more consistency and demonstrate greater persistence through difficult developmental challenges than a less confident athlete.

Coaches and sport psychologists often talk to athletes about *winning the inner battle* during performances. This is most often used as a way to help athletes recognize and accept that if they control their thoughts, emotions and attitudes during performance, they increase the likelihood of playing their best. The battle, more often than not, is to control the quality of the "inner experience". For many athletes, creating and maintaining that feeling of certainty which allows them to trust their skills during performance, is the ultimate inner battle.

This chapter presents an overview of confidence and trust as well as the habits needed to develop and maintain these skills. A three-phase trust training program is also presented as a means of structuring the development of trust.

Understanding Confidence

Sport psychologists consider confidence to be a "belief that you will successfully perform a skill at a desired level". In other words, confident athletes expect that they will "get the job done" and look forward to such an opportunity. This not only means they believe they will play great, but that they will also adapt successfully to unexpected demands or challenges. It is important for athletes and coaches to understand that thinking and acting confidently during competition is not dependent upon successful outcomes. We are all endowed with the ability to control our thoughts, emotions, and images. Therefore, athletes should not let their level of play dictate their confidence during performance. One of the easiest things for an athlete to do during competition is to "go with the flow". Simply stated this means, "I will be positive and confident when I am playing well and negative and frustrated when I am playing poorly." Once athletes begin to view confidence as a choice and take responsibility for it, their confidence begins to influence their level of play instead of their level of play influencing their confidence.

Confidence and Performance

The role of confidence in athletic performance has been studied from many different perspectives. However, two things are clear: 1) confidence is what separates good performers from great performers, and 2) confidence is a skill that athletes can learn and control. When athletes feel confident, they are able to focus more completely on the 'task at hand'. They are not as preoccupied with distracting thoughts and are better able to refocus following mistakes or unexpected situations. Confident athletes also manage their negative emotions more effectively and are more adept at expressing positive emotion following good plays. When athletes play with confidence, they are able to gain an advantage by being more aggressive or assertive during competition while keeping calm and relaxed during the heat of the battle. Additionally, coaches and teammates find it easier to believe in players who believe in themselves. This has a positive effect on the athlete's ability to maintain a relatively stable level of confidence over time.

Confident athletes have the ability to create and maintain a feeling of certainty during competition that allows them to trust their skills. A confident mindset is a positive emotional state in which the athletes free themselves of expectations, fears, and other conscious activity. In essence, the confident performer moves from the conscious control exhibited during skill acquisition to trust in the automatic selection and execution of movement sequences during performance. Therefore, when great athletes stop trusting, they stop becoming great athletes. Effective utilization of the tools necessary to stay confident and trusting during performance is what separates good athletes from great athletes.

Confidence as a Choice

Confident athletes perform better for a variety of reasons and there is no doubt that success breeds confidence in athletes. However, great performers don't depend on success alone for their confidence. Becoming competent in sport is an accomplishment, but becoming confident is more often a choice. Although developing confidence may require a greater commitment from some athletes than others, choosing to think and act confidently is still a matter of one's *will* to do so. Many athletes are convinced that their confidence should be based on external factors (most recent performance, on site warm-up, comments from coaches and teammates, etc.). They don't believe that confidence is something they can control and some perceive confident thinking as a form of self-deception. However, when the athlete's confidence is based on internal factors (thoughts, feelings, images), it is possible for them to feel confident despite unfavorable external factors, thus giving them a greater sense of control over their confidence during competition.

Every athlete has the tools necessary to become confident. It is a matter of whether or not they choose to use them correctly. These tools are:

- ◆ Free Will
- ◆ Self-awareness
- ◆ Imagination.

Free will is our ability to think or act independently of all other influences. We all have the ability to think and act independently, in spite of our circumstances. Consequently, confidence begins with us. For many athletes, this is a shift in perspective that is fundamental to becoming a confident player. Athletes can work diligently on the various aspects of their performance (technical, strategic, and physical) but until they deeply and honestly believe they can control the quality of their thoughts, they will never truly control their confidence. It is not what happens during competition, but the response to what happens that dictates confidence. Since we have the ability to choose our responses, confidence then is a choice. Confidence results from players proactively choosing correct responses during competition. Athletes who struggle with confidence tend to react to their situation. When they are playing well they feel positive and when they are playing badly their attitude is negative.

Becoming aware of our habits of thinking and responding is an important tool we can use to develop and maintain confidence. Habits of thinking and responding are powerful factors in the development and maintenance of confidence. Like physical habits, these habits often unfold automatically and without conscious awareness during performances. Self-awareness provides athletes the ability to stand apart and examine their habits, while free will provides the ability to change them.

Our imagination enables us to create feelings, pictures and thoughts beyond our present reality. Athletes use this tool everyday. For example, whenever they recall or review a performance or simply think about an upcoming event. The willingness to use imagination in ways that enhance confidence is an important tool in creating the necessary mindset for performance. Images are more powerful than words. Being able to utilize imagination to program effective responses is very helpful in creating a confident mindset.

Playing with Confidence

When you ask an athlete to describe what it is like to play with confidence, they often talk about what it *feels* like to be confident. "When I walk on the court I feel like I am going to win". "I feel like I can do no wrong". "I feel in control of my swing". For most athletes, this translates into a *feeling of certainty* that they will perform at their best. This feeling of certainty can be future-oriented. ("I feel ready to do battle!") or related to the present ("This ball is going in the hole!"). Confidence, like other feelings, arises from our interpretation of events in our lives. Therefore, how we think and what we recall from situations are powerful references used to draw conclusions about our capabilities. Confident athletes choose to think in ways that create a feeling of certainty prior to performances. For example, athletes are able to create images of themselves winning, executing flawlessly, or enjoying the unexpected challenges that may arise during performance. In essence, they expect to play great and look forward to the challenge of playing under pressure.

The opposite of confidence is a sense of doubt or uncertainty about meeting a challenge or executing a skill. When you ask an athlete to describe what it is like to play without confidence, they often talk about their *thoughts*. "Standing over the ball, I kept telling myself 'don't choke'." "I was thinking about not letting my team down." "Once I got behind, I was thinking, 'Oh no! Here I go again'." When athletes play with confidence, their mind is calm and they are *trusting what has been trained*. Trust is essentially the absence of thought. It is the absorption in or connection to the task at hand. A trust mindset frees the athlete from self-doubt or expectations and allows performance to unfold "automatically". The trust mindset is a confident state of mind where the athlete is free of conscious control and trusts the automatic selection and execution of skills during performance. This is often described by athletes as "playing by instinct", "trusting my eyes and reacting to what I see", or "putting it on automatic pilot". A lack of trust often results in the athlete thinking too much, over-controlling the correctness of the movement or trying too hard, all of which result in a breakdown of the movement's timing or sequencing.

Developing Confidence

There are not short cuts for instilling a feeling of certainty about one's performance. Obviously, some athletes are able to prepare, train and think less effectively than others and still feel certain about their performance; just as there are gifted athletes who need not train as much, physically, in order to win. However, managing one's confidence and performing consistently across competitions, are a result of effective habits of thinking and training. The effective habits necessary for instilling a feeling of certainty involve a true commitment to being prepared and choosing to be positive.

Commit to Being Prepared

The first choice an athlete must make is to accept responsibility for their physical and mental preparation. Athletes often think that this is the coach's job. A commitment to being prepared results in a feeling that you have done everything possible to play great. It is difficult to create a feeling of certainty about your performance if you don't believe you are prepared. Good preparation includes hard physical training, putting yourself under pressure in practice and developing a solid a pre-competition routine.

Train hard physically - Hard physical training is essential for excellence in athletics. Knowing that you have done everything possible to physically prepare yourself for competition is the first step in creating a feeling of certainty about your performance. For most athletes, there is a direct relationship between hard physical training and confidence. A rigorous and consistent physical training program increases confidence during pressure situations, delays fatigue that enables the athlete to compete at higher intensity for longer periods of time, and promotes faster recovery after or between performances. Feeling rested and ready to "fully extend" yourself prior to a competition is fundamental to believing you can get the job done. When trying to discern why a particular athlete is lacking in confidence, a good place to start is evaluating their physical training program.

Practice under pressure - Fully extending yourself in training also involves the frequency with which you put yourself under pressure during practices. ***Pressure builds diamonds.*** Athletes who seek challenges and repeatedly find ways to put themselves under pressure get the quality repetitions necessary to become a confident performer. When you look at consistently great performers you will see very competitive individuals. What we often don't see is the "single mindedness of purpose" with which they approach their practice sessions. Finding creative ways to instill 'pressure' into practice drills and activities is another aspect of preparation. This is especially true in individual sports were practices can become repetitious and boring, resulting in sloppy mental habits.

Execute pre-event routines - Good preparation also includes a set pre-event routine that consists of appropriate psychological warm-up combined with physical warm-up. The goal of a preparation routine is to achieve a desirable pre-event feeling and focus that sets the stage for a great performance. Each athlete should develop their own "personal formula" of activities that lead to confidence and a feeling of preparedness. This may involve combining positive thoughts focused on the process (i.e. enjoyment of the battle), imagining the 'feeling' of a great start to the performance with stretching and listening to music. Pre-event routines should be refined through practice but also need to be flexible. For example, an athlete may have one routine that is executed when the conditions are acceptable and time is not a factor and another that is executed when time is limited or the conditions are difficult.

Planning ahead and knowing when you will arrive at the site, eat, practice, and warm-up helps instill a sense of control over the competitive environment. Encouraging coaches to 'walk-through' the performance with athletes the day prior to competition is helpful for a variety of reasons. Walk-throughs give the athlete a cognitive understanding of what to expect and also provide a 'feel' for the competition environment.

Choose to be Positive

Making the commitment to stay positive while monitoring and eliminating negative thoughts is fundamental to maintaining confidence. Being positive is a choice that requires commitment and self-control on the part of the athlete. There are many forces that act upon athletes prior to and during performances that can pull them into a negative state of mind if the athlete allows. Thoughts play a critical role in shaping our emotional responses to events. It is important for the athlete to understand that it is not the events or situations in and of themselves that cause negative feelings, bur rather it is their thoughts relative to those events that determine the responses. Choosing to be positive is making a commitment to controlling one's inner dialogue and images.

Be a good self-coach - Being a good self-coach means making the commitment to give yourself what you need emotionally in order to stay competitive from the beginning of the competition to the end. This involves recognizing what you need emotionally and then having the presence of mind to give it to yourself. Therefore, if you need to be 'pumped-up' then you talk to yourself in ways that create positive emotion and if you are bored and need to be 'kicked in the butt' you do that as well. All consistent performers are good self-coaches. It is difficult if not impossible to consistently perform at a high level throughout an entire season without the ability to coach oneself emotionally.

The first step in becoming a good self-coach is to listen to what you say to yourself. This can be done by asking the athlete during practice to 'step outside of yourself' and just listen to what you say, not making any judgment or stopping any thoughts. Upon completion of a performance, ask an athlete, "If you could read a transcript of your inner dialogue during that performance, how would it read?", "Would it inspire you?", "Would you talk to your best friend that way?". This can also be used to increase awareness of the athlete's self-coaching skill.

Affirmations can be developed in advance of a performance to enhance positive self-coaching. Affirmations are strong, positive statements about something that is believable and has a realistic potential for becoming true. They should also be in a present, positive tense and not too wordy. For example, an athlete who tends to become over-anxious prior to a competition might repeat "I love the battle, I am a calm, peaceful warrior.". Such statements that are conscious, pre-planned and positive can effect one's mood and other subjective states that can transform the quality of a competitive experience. They may not immediately impact performance, but the quality and the enjoyment of the competition will be heightened. In developing affirmations, it may prove helpful for athletes to imagine the behaviors of certain animals and take on the qualities of that animal. For example, to act like a "caged dog" brings about images of reckless aggression and high energy.

Act like a confident athlete - It is obvious to most athletes that their thoughts and feelings during performance influence their body language. However, many athletes do not fully appreciate how their body language during performance influences their thoughts and feelings. Acting confidently can lead to feeling and thinking confidently. For example, acting "As If" you love the battle by walking with shoulders back, chin up, and facial muscles loose with a bounce in your step, will positively affects your thoughts and emotions.

Acting "As If" is a behavioral affirmation. Once you identity a desired feeling (i.e., confident, assertive, fearless), develop actions that display that feeling. It is not unusual for a recreational tennis player to play better after watching professional players on television. They see the relaxed tempo, focused energy and confident ease with which the pros play the game and act 'as if' they are great players as well.

Expressing positive emotion during performances can also help feelings of confidence. This may be difficult for athletes who play sports where the outward display of emotion is considered taboo. Helping them to role-play or "fake" an outward display of positive emotion can be helpful in getting them to release excessive control over their performances.

Create positive images - The pictures we create in our mind's eye not only affect our attitudes but also our motor responses. Images can be used to create feelings of certainty about outcomes relative to an athletic contest or a particular skill. For example, an athlete can visualize performing successfully prior to a competition, visualize a desirable "feel" prior to performing a particular skill or create a potential scenario. In each case, positive visualizations can create a feeling of certainty rather than doubt or fear.

Visualization is an active form of meditation in which you relax and view "images" or recall "how it felt" (kinesthetics) of great performances. Negative images often create self-doubt and tension that hinder performances while positive images relax the mind and body that allow for a clearer mind during performance. For many athletes, learning to control negative images that 'pop' into their minds or systematically create positive images requires practice.

Starting to train visualization is analogous to starting a fitness program if you are out of shape. The first two weeks are full of effort and somewhat uncomfortable. Most people have difficulty quieting their minds long enough to get images that are clear and controllable. Much like jogging, once you get into a daily habit the exercise becomes more enjoyable and effortless. Getting through the first couple of weeks seems to be the difficulty.

Understanding Trust

Great performances and our most meaningful experiences in life occur when we are totally absorbed in and connected to the task at hand. When we are in the process of doing, in a sense we become what we are doing, and suspend all judgments about our performances and ourselves. During skill development and refinement, conscious control over correctness of skill execution is beneficial to skill mastery. However, once the skill becomes well learned and the program automatic, this tendency to control interferes with performance. An illustration of releasing conscious control over performances is found in the following quote regarding a musician's task:

> "Ultimately, the musician must relinquish the illusion of moment-by-moment control, trusting the program to remember exactly how each finger must move. The musician becomes aware of only the feeling, the emotion in the music."

Similarly, an athlete, through structured practices and excessive instruction, often perceives the need for conscious control in order to produce the correct movement. Subsequently, they must release this "illusion" of moment-by-moment control and trust the motor program in order to attend to higher order aspects of the sport, such as strategy and cue utilization associated with their best performances. The trust mindset is a state that is free of expectations, doubts or other conscious activity, thus allowing the athlete to maintain a clear and present focus.

Trust as a Specific Performance Skill

The Ideal Performance State is viewed as a positive emotional state in which the athlete frees themselves of expectation, fears, and other conscious activity. In essence, the athlete has moved from conscious control exhibited during skill acquisition to trusting the automatic selection and execution of movement sequences exhibited during peak performance.

Motor learning theory recognizes the developmental process in skill acquisition as a shift from feedback-controlled (conscious), unrefined movements to smoother, completely open loop movements. Advanced skill performance requires an automatic mode to the accuracy, complexity, and speed of sport skills. In this context, it is important that athletes distinguish cognitive learning skills (self-monitoring, verbal cueing, etc.) necessary for acquiring fundamentals during practice from the performance skill, trust, which enhances the selection and execution of movement sequences during performance.

Breakdowns in Trust

The execution of sport skills involves three distinct processes: analysis of information, selection of the most appropriate motor program based on that information, and execution of the selected motor program(s). The challenge for the athlete during performance is to react to what is present. This means the processing of information and the sequencing of movements proceed effortlessly and naturally without any conscious interference. Breakdowns in trust occur at two levels:

      1. during the selection of movement sequences (processing breakdowns)
      2. during motor program execution (sequencing breakdowns).

Processing breakdowns - Processing breakdowns result from failure to attend to accurate information as a result of excessive thinking. In other words, the athlete doesn't trust what she sees and either second guesses herself or continues to think about what to do. *Jamming* is a breakdown that refers to excessive cognitive activity during the selection process. Much like static on the radio, excessive cognitive activity jams reception, preventing clear information processing. Examples would be a golfer standing over a putt too long, analyzing break and distance or a tennis player thinking about the position of their back swing instead of the on-coming ball. Jamming, or excessive thinking, can impair cue attention and ultimately execution. The golfer, for example, must learn to trust the automatic processing of information, often illustrated by lining up the putt, addressing the ball, and stroking the ball within a characteristic time period.

Sequencing breakdowns - Unlike processing breakdowns, sequencing breakdowns occur not as a result of inaccurate information but as a result of incorrect movement execution due to conscious control. These breakdowns can be identified as *aiming*, *pressing*, and *controlling*. *Aiming* is defined as excessive concern with the target, such as a quarterback aiming his passes resulting in over-or-under-throwing his target. Once the athlete becomes too concerned with accuracy, the tendency to consciously control execution heightens, resulting in alterations in the movement sequencing. *Pressing* occurs when the athlete tries too hard, such as a pitcher applying more speed to his fastball, thus changing his mechanics. This results in excessive tension from a perceived need to generate more force. Finally, *controlling* occurs when one attempts to exert excessive control over the movement sequencing results in ineffective movements, such as a figure skater who feels the need to control the performance of a triple axle due to the fear of falling. In order for the athlete to avoid these breakdowns it is important that he or she recognize under what conditions they occur and be able to distinguish between physical breakdowns (technique) and breakdowns in trust. Any of these breakdowns can result in an alteration in execution that negatively affects performance.

Training Trust

Trust is viewed as a separate psychological skill that is characteristic of automatic execution of well-learned movements. Therefore, the task for the learner is to develop not only the monitoring processes necessary for skill development, but also the ability to let go and trust during performance what has been trained in practice. Thus, trust is viewed as a distinct performance skill that can be trained.

The activities presented are crucial for preventing breakdowns in trust since these breakdowns result from a shift in attentional focus at the moment of skill execution. The central purpose of these activities is to keep the athlete in present focus, aware of only those things that are crucial to execution, nothing else. The goals are: 1) to develop a reference point so that the athlete knows when he or she is connected to, and trusting in, skill execution; and, 2) to identity when and how trust breaks down in terms of the specific skill and situation.

Make a Commitment to Trust

Competence comes from commitment to training while confidence comes from an honest commitment to trusting. For most athletes, trust does not come easily. Although they may have had moments of completely trusting their skills throughout a performance, generally athletes find it difficult to trust on a consistent basis. Recognizing trust as a performance skill that requires commitment to practice is essential to its development.

Given that trust is a difficult skill to acquire, the coaches needs to emphasize the importance of a disciplined approach to training, an approach that requires concentrated effort on the part of the athlete. This type of effort may be somewhat different than that required for physical training (fitness & technique) already practiced by athletes. The coach needs to acquire credibility with the athlete in terms of acceptance of trust as a volitional skill. This is difficult to accomplish since the concept of trust is counter to the way most athletes have been trained to approach their performance.

Practice Quieting Your Mind

The first step in learning to trust is being able to distinguish between the feeling of trust and the absence of trust. Quieting the mind is necessary for providing a reference point for feeling trust. Our capacity to trust our bodies to perform at their highest potential is in direct proportion to the stillness of our minds. When our mind is noisy, anxious or distracted, it interferes with the processing of information necessary for skilled performance. Certainly the most common means of gaining control over our thoughts and quieting our minds is through practicing meditation. This is done outside of team practice sessions and can provide the athlete with a clear reference point as to what it is like to have a quite mind.

Activities and drills that can be incorporated into practice sessions involve having the athlete become mindful of different 'feels', 'thoughts' and 'sensations'. The benefits of these drill are two-fold: first, they provide the athlete a clearer understanding of what a quiet mind and relaxed body feels like; and second, they provide the realization that the mental state acquired from these drills is the platform leading to trust. For example:

♦ *Feel* drills involve having athletes attend to the kinesthetic feel of specific movements in their sport. This can be done while the athlete is actually performing the skill movement as well as through concurrent visualization.

♦ *Quiet* drills involve the athlete monitoring thoughts related to judgments, technique accuracy, outcome, and process during skill execution. During these drills the athlete needs to learn how to identity such distractions and refocus. For example, a tennis player's focus only on the ball using the 'bounce-hit' method (Gallwey, 1976). This enables the player to monitor thoughts during the act of rallying with the goal of quieting the mind by focusing only on the 'bounce-hit.'

♦ *Connect* drills involve the athlete attending to present moment sensations during skill performance. These drills emphasize guiding the athlete through a series of sensory awareness exercises (i.e., "What do you hear when you swing the racquet?"). Again, using tennis as an example, the players now attend to the rhythm, the sounds, created by the rally.

Play in the Present

Coaches often emphasize to their players to "play one pitch, snap, or point at a time". Phil Jackson, coach of the Chicago Bulls developed the team motto, "Play hard, play fair, play now". Playing in the present involves attending to what is happening **here and now**. The *here* is the object of our attention (target, ball, etc.) and the *now* refers to what is happening in the present. Lapses occur when we project what is about to happen or dwell on what has already happened. Staying in the present throughout an entire performance requires a level of focused concentration that is very difficult if not impossible. The mind will wonder into the future, trying to anticipate what might happen and it often wants to replay mistakes.

Most sports can be divided into "on" periods where the athlete is in play and "off" periods that occur between plays. It is during these "off" periods that the mind can wander as long as it is brought back to the present just prior to the beginning of the next play, pitch, point, etc.. In many sports it is helpful to use verbal cues or to structure this "off" time into a set routine. Verbal cues such as "Breathe and focus" can be used to bring the athlete into the task at hand. Execution routines can be used for self-paced skills (e.g., penalty shots in soccer and ice/field hockey; tennis serve, baseball pitch, diving, golf swing, free throw shooting) as a means of preparing the mind for the present task. The purpose of the execution routine is to consistently put the athlete in a state that is most conducive to trusting their performance at that moment.

An example of an execution routine for a tennis serve is a three-step routine that moves the athlete from analysis to feel to trust. This structure is provided by three sequential steps: 1) "Check it out"; 2) "Click it in"; and 3) "Let it go". The server, at the end of the previous point, *checks it out*, by recognizing the score and the conditions, then develops a plan for the next point. The player then *clicks it in* by accessing the correct feel by clicking in the kinesthetic cues (exploding upward, the snap at the top) as means of selecting the correct motor program for the serve. Once the moment begins, the player *lets it go* as he or she begins the performance and clears (or quiets) the mind by releasing conscious effort, fears, or expectations and trusting the selection and execution of the motor skill. As previously mentioned, this step is the most difficult to take because it requires athletes to step into the unknown and accept that by releasing conscious control, they will, in fact, gain motor control. As with all effective routines, diligent practice and use of this routine puts the athlete in better position to capitalize on his or her mechanical aspects of performance. The execution routine has the ultimate purposes of consistently putting the athlete in a state that is most conducive to trusting performance at that moment.

Let Go of Conscious Control

One of the biggest obstacles athletes face in their development of trust is the tendency to judge aspects of their performances as good or bad and to classify their movement technique as right or wrong. This leads to an overly conscious concern for correctness during skill execution. This type of conscious control over motor skill execution is often reinforced during the early stages of the learning process. For sports that are highly technical and involve professional coaches it is not uncommon for athletes to be well trained in over-analysis. During the learning process they become hypercritical and judgmental which often lead to athletes who are great in practice but terrible performers. It is important for an athlete to distinguish between the cognitive learning skills necessary for skill acquisition and the performance skill, trust, which involves letting go of conscious control.

Helping athletes let go of conscious control begins with the practice of non-judgmental thinking. Obviously, there are times when athletes must make judgments regarding the correctness of their skills. However, many athletes don't understand the relationship between their overly judgmental mind and their inability to release control. It is similar to having a very judgmental parent standing over you while you are washing the dishes after dinner. Knowing that you are being judged on every move, you become conscious of not making a mistake and therefore try to control every move. Not only does this lead to more mistakes but it also take away from the enjoyment.

Recognize Breakdowns in Trust

When developing any skill, it often becomes necessary to recognize breakdowns in execution and the conditions under which they occur. In order to identify breakdowns in trust, it is helpful for the athlete to monitor trust and breakdowns that occur during practice situations. This can begin with an understanding of cause and effect relationships in skill execution. Often physical mistakes are a result of breakdowns in trust. For example, a golfer may decelerate the club head on a putt (effect), this is seen to be caused by the head lifting prematurely. However, 'over-controlling' the putting motion, may have caused the head to lift. For athletes whose skills are well learned, it may be more effective to address breakdowns in trust first and physical mistakes second.

A Trust Training Program

Athletes can acquire trust in a couple of different ways; trial and error experience, or a planned program. One way is to access the skill of trust through long-term trial & error experience as a competitive athlete. This process is similar to the development of many other psychological skills that athletes acquire over time, such as concentration and mental toughness. A major advantage to providing a structured skill-training program is to increase the likelihood that psychological skills will endure during competition. This is accomplished through the establishment of a firm foundation of references which the athlete, coach, and sport psychologist can access during difficult times. The trust-training program contains three phases: 1) Education, 2) Skills Training, and 3) Competition Simulation.

Education Phase

The purpose of the education phase is to provide the rationale for trust as a specific performance skill and to gain a commitment from the athlete to train for trust. This is an important phase from the standpoint of keeping the athlete in the program during the difficult times that often occur during training.

Provide a Rationale for trust - The rationale for trust can be understood using a motor programming model describing the selection and execution of motor programs. This process is analogous to a computer routine: information is stored from previous movement experiences (schema), a motor program is then selected based on desired movement specifications determined from processing stored and current information, then the program is executed. The execution process and outcome are then stored for future reference.

During skill instruction, the athlete is trained to consciously attend to proprioceptive feedback in order to develop and refine correct technique. However, this conscious monitoring of technique is a hindrance to the natural (automatic) execution process associated with skilled performance. Therefore, during the education phase the instructor needs to convince the athlete that the mentality that is necessary for skill development (self-monitoring, verbal cueing, etc.) is counterproductive for skill execution. This practice mentality can be referred to as the *training mindset* and is often associated with a "good attitude" necessary to overlearn skills.

The development of the *trusting mindset* begins with the athlete's understanding of the motor program schema as it relates to conscious and automatic processes. It is important for the instructor to provide examples of everyday, somewhat complex motor tasks that are performed in an automatic fashion, such as opening and walking through a door, using a keyboard for typing/word processing, and brushing teeth. The neurological and attentional processes involved in performing these tasks are often ignored or taken for granted. For example, getting out of one's own car requires sequencing of movements, timing, feedback, and precise execution. These tasks are accomplished without much conscious control or attentional focus and as conscious control increases, the result is noticeable and sometimes frustrating!

Gaining a commitment to trust - The success of gaining a commitment form the athlete to train for trust is impacted most by the education phase in terms of its thoroughness and persuasion. The instructor needs to "sell" the concepts of trust in order to gain the athlete's commitment to work through this seemingly simple skill. Thus, the education phase of trust training has to be solid success if the athlete is to then progress to specific training activities that will build trust during sport performance.

Skills Training Phase

The purpose of the skills training phase is to assist athletes in acquiring trust under a variety of supervised conditions. The athlete must establish sufficient levels of concentration, confidence, and composure during his or her sport skill performance. Thus, the initial component of this training phase consists of appropriate activities designed to build and enhance these three fundamental skills.

Self-Coaching - These activities are important to increase the stability of trust by improving the athlete's self-coaching abilities and accessing the feelings and focus associated with trust through visualization. Self-coaching involves both self-talk and energy management. This involves being a good emotional coach to oneself, not a technical coach. Consequently, the athlete gives him or herself what is needed emotionally in order to stay competitive (focused and intense) throughout the duration of an event. Self-coaching is important for the stability of trust because as performance decreases, the challenge to trust increases. Thus, good self-coaching provides a stabilizing effect on trust even with swings in performance.

Developing self-coaching involves three steps: 1) recognizing self-coaching as a performance tool that requires practice; 2) practicing a self-coaching sequence that involves recognition of self-coaching statements (positive or negative), stopping ineffective self-coaching statements, and replacing such with an effective one; and 3) developing and making use of affirmation statements. Again, it is important for the instructor to assist athletes in monitoring self-coaching practices. This can be done in two ways. One way is using a monitoring sheet during practice where players evaluate their degree of self-coaching skills using a 10-point scale. The second method is to have them keep journals describing situations throughout the day and in practice during which they had opportunities to use self-coaching.

Mastery Imagery - The second confidence training activity makes use of mastery imagery to recreate the mental and physical conditions that are associated with the feelings and focus of trust. First, drawing upon past performances and using his or her imagination, the athlete writes a script describing what his or her perfect performance would be like. Next, the athlete uses this script to practice imaging (including visualization) the feelings of enjoyment and freedom associated with trust. Use of these two training activities provides a foundation that the athlete can draw upon during the course of a competitive season.

Concentration routines - For self-paced skills, execution routines that are completed immediately prior to the skill are trained during this third phase. As mentioned previously, the purpose of such a routine is to consistently put the athlete in a state that is most conducive to trusting performance at that moment. An example of a three-step service routine was presented earlier under *Play in the Present*, consisting of "Checking it out", "Clicking it in", and "Letting it go". Developing and refining the execution of the routine can involve both the steps in the proper sequence as well as the amount of time in which the routine was completed. Consistency in both cases is desired.

Competition Simulation Phase

The third phase of the training program involves evaluation of these psychological skills by monitoring performance during structured competitive simulations. For example, a tennis player plays points against an opponent while self-monitoring psychological skills between points or after a predetermined number of points (3,5,7,etc.). This method employs the use of monitoring sheets that the athlete completes immediately following points played. Video recording can also be used as a method for the athlete to recall and describe his or her use of these skills after a series of points. Both of these monitoring activities have the advantage of allowing a structured interaction between the athlete and the sport psychologist regarding psychological skill performance under competitive situations.

Summary

Confidence and trust were discussed as skill that can be developed and maintained through the use of specific training activities. Both are interrelated skills that have profound influence over the quality of athletic performance. Confidence was seen as a feeling of certainty about one's performance that comes from a commitment to being prepared and choosing to be positive. Trust, the ability to free oneself from fear of mistakes in execution or outcome and release control during motor skill execution, is an on-going performance goal for athletes. During skill development and refinement, conscious control over the correctness of skill execution is beneficial to skill mastery. However, once the skill becomes well learned and the program becomes automatic, this tendency to control interferes with performance. Motor control theory provided that rationale for letting go of conscious control, thus allowing the automaticity of movement sequence selection and execution to occur. As with all performance skills, trust can be trained by following an appropriate training program.

Case Studies of Confidence

#1: Female Collegiate Basketball Player

Introduction:

Jessica is a 19 year old sophomore basketball player. She had an outstanding high school career, a great shooter, did not play very much her freshman year. The presenting problem is that she is tentative, not very confident, and often wonders if she fits in at this level (i.e., nationally ranked women's program). Jessica suffers from "stinkin' thinkin'" and has difficulty letting go of a mistake or missed shot. Her coach suggested that she come in to work on developing that confident look about her.

In the initial interview, Jessica talked about differences between high school and college (i.e., attitude, expectations, coaching styles, social support systems, freshman adjustment issues, etc.), perceived sources of current stress, role expectations, and what she feels she needs to do to pick it up a notch.

Intervention:

Much of the intervention centered around goal setting (for practice and competition), relaxation and visualization, affirmations, and the concept of "ACT AS IF"!. Personally, I find this to be a very powerful concept, an extension of visualization, goal-oriented affirmations, and "scripts of excellence" we have discussed when making individualized audio visualization tapes for athletes. The aspect I like is that it seems to be more feeling-oriented and focuses more on positive beliefs rather than positive task-oriented thoughts.

Together, Jessica and I developed an audiovisualization tape centered around being ready, being prepared, TRUSTING herself as well as her preparation, and ACTING AS IF she is going to be successful. We worked on visualizing herself being aggressive and confident, coming off the bench energized, adrenaline pumping, ready to have an impact both offensively and defensively, executing the things she has to do to be effective in her role (i.e., movement without the ball, coming off the pick decisive and ready to shoot, acting as if she is going to make it, getting back on transition, defensive intensity, boxing out on the boards, etc.) . In addition, we worked on rekindling the old "shooters mentality" (i.e., don't think - see it, feel it, trust it - feeling herself shooting with good form, soft touch, smooth to the finger tips, swish!) and some coping imagery skills so if she made a mistake, she could let go quickly instead of catastrophizing or musterbating.

Outcome:

Jessica reports that "Acting As If" really hit home. After the first couple of games, she worked her way into the #3 guard position, made some valuable contributions in key situations. Her stats picked up, so did her intensity, enthusiasm, and focus. More importantly, she felt a lot more confident, ready, and in control.

#2: Elite Pole Vaulter

Introduction:

Joe was a former All-American pole vaulter. After graduation he set out to fulfill his goal of jumping in the Olympics. While in college, Joe had jumped 18'6" and had cleared 18 ft. in competition numerous times. Eight months out of school, Joe was mired in a slump and was seriously contemplating quitting the sport and getting on with his life. In the eight months following graduation, his highest vault was 17 ft. Joe came to discuss his decision to quit.

Joe's coach also called to tell me that Joe was stronger, faster, and had tested out in the five primary vaulting drills better than in any previous season. He was convinced the problem was not one of technique or training. He wanted Joe to talk to someone else before he made the decision to quit.

Joe said that he was only working part time so that he could train. He also said that he was still training with his college coach. On both counts he felt guilty. First, he felt that he should pull more financial weight at home since his wife was working full time. Making extra money by jumping in big meets was his original intent. Secondly, he felt that by training with his collegiate coach, valuable time was being taken from the younger vaulters.

He acknowledged that a jumper must clear 18 ft. after college to be invited to the money making meets or to secure financial support from a sponsor. His highest jump in 8 months had been 17 ft.. Because of the pressure to jump high and the failure to do so for 8 months, Joe had lost faith in his talent and he had lost sight of his goal. He was convinced that he was "washed up."

Intervention:

I felt that three people needed to be communicated with by Joe; his wife, his coach, and himself. Guilt will destroy a person's focus and motivation if it is not addressed quickly. As was the case with this athlete, many times there is no external foundation for this emotion. By sharing these burdensome feelings with his wife and coach I knew he would find support rather than anger and disappointment. I encouraged Joe to have heartfelt conversations about the issues we had discussed with his wife and with his coach, individually.

Next, I asked Joe to write a letter to his best friend. He thought this was a peculiar request, so I started the letter for him, "Dear Joe,". He immediately recognized that he was to write a self-addressed letter to himself. I told him that I wanted him to tell "his best friend" several things. First, tell the friend why he (Joe) had the audacity to think he could be an Olympic champion. Did he have the talent, and if so, what are his greatest assets as a vaulter. Joe was to discuss his greatest achievements as a vaulter.

Joe was also to identify what it took to jump high in the past and identify what it felt like. He was to discuss the investment he had made in training and the payoff to be expected from staying with it through the years. I also asked Joe to recall his greatest jumps and discuss the mental routine that he used to ready himself. He was to recall the specific mental preparation strategies that we had worked on through the years. I finished by saying not to end the letter until the addressee was convinced to pursue his goal with a new vengeance, or conclude that it is over.

Outcome:

Joe talked with his wife and coach. He received total support and encouragement to pursue his training in the current manner. He learned that his guilt was self-generated. Joe also brought in the letter that he had written to himself; it was seven pages in length. The letter was positive and uplifting. He was able to see that his talent hadn't left him, rather he had locked it inside. He re-established his mental strategies for the vault and made a commitment to his pre-jump mental routine.

We chose sections of the letter to be read onto an audio-cassette tape. This tape became his mastery tape for competition. He listened to it several times a day, especially on meet days.

By severing the baggage of guilt and pressure, Joe was able to focus on what matters most in the vault on meet day, positive mental preparation. He was able to focus on the process rather than the outcome. By doing this, 18 ft. was not seen as a barrier, but as a challenge that could easily be overcome, to which his performance history attested.

Joe's next meet came two days later. He jumped 18'1" which qualified him for his first money meet, the Melrose Games in New York. He jumped 18'4" there, followed by 18'8" (a new PR) in Los Angeles the next week. His next meets followed in this order: 17'11", 18'4", 19'0" (PR), 19'2" (PR).

Currently, Joe is ranked #1 in the U.S. and #5 in the world. To think that he was ready to hang it up. This case demonstrates the fact that when the mind isn't functioning properly, talent becomes dormant.

#3: Female Baton Twirler

Introduction:

Sheri is a nationally competitive baton twirler whose primary concern was that she was not performing as well in competition as she did in practice. Sheri is a very perfectionistic, goal-oriented individual. She has difficulty enjoying competition and experiences fears of dropping the baton. Sheri expressed that she gets frustrated when the routine isn't perfect. ("If I miss one trick during practice, I must catch it ten times before I leave.") Her primary desire is the development of greater confidence so that she can perform up to her practice standards and beyond in performance.

Intervention:

Together, we developed a three phase "trust training program" to enhance her self-confidence. The first phase was an "education phase" that would provide a rationale for the trust, explain the characteristics of trust, and identify breakdowns in trust. We began by discussing the model of motor programming and the dynamics of practice vs. performance.

In addressing the characteristics of trust, we talked about the issues of specifying what trust entails: the degrees of magnitude associated with trust and the issues surrounding stability of trust. The goal of this discussion was to establish the perspective that trust is a "volitional" skill; one that an individual has the choice of making.

The final component of the educational phase involved identifying the breakdowns in trust. I pointed out the potential for jamming, pressing, aiming, and controlling. I explained that jamming is akin to "paralysis by overanalysis"; an inability to perform due to too much being processed, not just the essential focal points. Sheri could readily identify how, in her performance routines, she was allowing external stimuli and factors creep into her attentional focus; thus, hurting her performance. Pressing was outlined as the mistake of trying too hard instead of trusting oneself and one's ability. Sheri believed this too be the crux of the problem, relating this to her earlier comment of having to make 10 good catches to rectify for one bad.

I explained to Sheri that aiming concerns the development of too fine a target area; one that is unreasonable to expect consistently, and potentially detrimental to performance. Finally, controlling was identified as the process of trying too hard to maneuver the baton and its movements; not releasing oneself from allowing the movements to take their course. This error of trust results in a "mechanical" approach to performance. Sheri could see how this "mechanical" approach could be limiting to performance.

The second phase instituted was a Skills Training phase that emphasized concentration, confidence, and composure training. The concentration training centered on the development of a "trust reference point" and monitoring the breakdowns in trust. The development of a trust reference point involved identifying a focal point that would free conscious control. Three types of drills Sheri was encouraged to utilize were "feel" drills, "quiet" drills, and "connect" drills. All three drills were explained in relation to the building of trust.

To monitor breakdowns in trust, Sheri utilized a monitor sheet. Sheri, during her practice would indicate whether she trusted her performance (yes/no) and recorded a connect percentage. This allowed Sheri to quantify her performance to provide evidence of her progress in concentration.

Confidence training activities focused on improving self-coaching skills and incorporating mastery imagery in Sheri's preparation for performance. To enhance her self-coping, Sheri maintained a performance journal that monitored the self-coaching goals she set in practice. The mastery imagery was incorporated as a means of developing the feel of trust in a mastery performance.

Composure training activities involved mistake management and the development of a preparation routine, both with the goal of aiding Sheri in the ability to cope with non-mastery performances. The mistake management hinged on the ability to refocus after drops. The preparation routine was created with an emphasis on adaptability and relaxation. In other words, the routine must be adaptable to a variety of circumstances, and the intent of the routine was to develop a sense of relaxation.

The third, and final phase, was a simulation phase that involved a dress rehearsal and post-rehearsal monitoring. The dress rehearsal was conducted with the full routine in the presence of distracters. Post-rehearsal monitoring asked Sheri to rate her ability to refocus after mistakes on a scale from 1 to 5, identify a percentage of her tricks that she trusted, and rate her mental preparation on a 1 to 10 scale.

Outcome:

Sheri worked very hard and attempted to incorporate each element of the phases. She really connected to the monitoring of mistakes as a means of developing an understanding of the quality of her performance. This understanding translated into enhanced confidence which aided her ability to trust her skills. She also commented that the dress rehearsal was very helpful due to its "real" feel.

Sheri followed the mental training with wins at State and Regional competitions. Her coach reported improvement in skill as well as mental approach to competition and practice. Sheri also expressed an increase in her enjoyment during competitions and felt that she was performing much closer to her potential.

#4: Elite Female Diver

Introduction:

Heather is a 27-year old member of the US National Team in Diving. Heather has been a member of the national team for 4 years. She has been diving since the age of 7 and competing at the national level beginning with the age group Nationals since the age of 10. As a collegiate diver she was a 4 time all American and placed in the top five at the NCAA's on a number of different occasions. She has had mixed success on the national and international level. She has generally placed in the top ten on the 3-meter springboard and has usually placed in the top six in the 10-meter platform. Perhaps the highlight of her career was winning outdoor nationals on the 10-meter platform. She has also represented the United States in a number of different international competitions.

Heather's national outdoor 10-meter platform championship was very much out of character with her placing at other national meets in the past five years. It also perhaps provides a glimpse of her potential. Heather has a reputation as a very hard trainer, but someone who never quite has been able to break through in terms of top placing at the national level. Heather and I began working together last November. Since that time we have met on a weekly basis through April. Initially, she was administered a battery of tests in order to assess her psychological state with regard to athletic competition prior to any intervention. Since that time we have focused on a number of different areas, but most specifically anxiety control and management, cognitive restructuring, and visualization.

In the past Heather has had more confidence in her physical ability and physical training than she has in her psychological ability and training. In fact, in retrospect she has often overtrained physically in order to try to compensate for a lack of confidence. Early in our work it was emphasized to her that while she is at the upper end of the continuum in terms of physical conditioning that the potential for improvement from a psychological point of view is tremendous given her pretest results.

Intervention:

Because of the nature of the program in which Heather participates it is very easy to get lost in the shuffle. Heather dives for a prominent program which is coached by a former United States Olympic coaches. Three of the seven divers on the United States Olympic team in 1988 were from the same program.

Because it is highly competitive, in the past Heather has had a great deal of difficulty in being more assertive and in letting her coach know what she needs as an athlete. Part of her lack of assertiveness stemmed from a lack of confidence and the feeling that perhaps she did not deserve equal attention. Early in the intervention she was encouraged to be more assertive and vocal in terms of expressing her needs. Also some changes in communication between her and her coach were facilitated which have since proved to be helpful to both of them.

An examination of the pretest scores reveals that there are a number of different areas that are major concerns. Given the talent and ability that Heather possesses it is obvious that her self-concept scores reflect a very poor internal picture of her capability. Therefore, some of the early sessions revolved around bolstering general is obviously impaired by anxiety, and Heather exhibits extremely high levels of both cognitive and somatic anxiety. Her cognitive anxiety, (negative self-talk"), however, is much more problematic with respect to her athletic performance. Therefore, a great deal of attention early on was also given to helping her to learn cognitive restructuring techniques and encourage her to apply them both in practice and in her life generally. Heather was highly motivated and was readily able to learn and apply cognitive restructuring skills. Goal setting also was one of the earlier focuses of treatment. While Heather had some goals they were not clearly stated nor were they as progressive as they should have been. She was encouraged to set specific goals both short term and longer term. She was also asked to develop strategies to address these goals. Her Achievement Motivation Scale test scores indicated that a stronger or primary motivation for her initially was to avoid failure. This attitude in and of itself is indicative of significant anxiety and lack of confidence. A major task in the intervention was to help her to set aside her fear of failure and to focus on the process of performing effectively and successfully.

Outcome:

An examination of the pre- and post-test results indicates apparent dramatic changes in Heather's perception of herself and also in terms of her information processing and interpersonal style. While these results may seem quite dramatic, it is my belief that the capability has been there, simply her lack of belief in that capability has prevented her from realizing a good deal of her potential. Certainly, because of her physical capability, her intellectual capability, her motivation, and her work ethic, Heather could definitely be one of the top divers in the United States if not in the world. Therefore, the dramatic changes in her self-concept in her levels of confidence, motivation, in her ability to focus and in her overall level of psychological skills appeared to be more commensurate now with her achievement levels than they were previously.

Heather did not have any major competitions during the time from January to April. She placed well (top 6) in an international meet in March and was pointed to the U. S. Indoor Nationals in mid-April. After visiting a competing program in late March, she began to think about switching coaches and programs. This decision began to "cloud" her mental focus and the sports psychology work. Although her (then) current coach reported excellent practices, Heather "bombed" at Nationals. She failed for the first time in several years to make finals (top 12) in either 3 Meter Springboard or 10 Meter Platform.

I believe that Heather's psychological testing represented somewhat of a "flight into health" phenomenon. I also think that her failure at Nationals resolved any remaining dissonance about the coaching/program change.

I spoke with Heather after the U.S. Outdoor Nationals where she performed very well - 5th on Platform, 3rd on 3 Meter Springboard (her highest finish ever - only 2 points out of 2nd place). She stated that she felt the psychological skills were essential to her performance. She has continued to work on mental skills daily (visualization, self-talk monitoring, etc.), and it appears that the skill levels manifested on testing in March were behaviorally apparent and internalized by August. She is also now very happy diving for the new program.

This case study is a combination failure/success example and points out the complexity of the dynamics which affect performance and also the seeds of mental skill training sometimes take time before they begin to blossom.

#5: Professional Male Golfer

Introduction:

Peter was a talented young professional golfer who had played on a "mini" tour for three previous years. Though he was talented, he had failed to qualify for the PGA Tour for five straight years; once by only one shot. He had dedicated this particular year to gaining muscular strength and working on his mental game. He was referred to me by another sport psychologist due to my knowledge and experience with golf with the specific purpose of developing an on-the-course pre-shot mental routine.

Peter was an extremely talented player. He had all the tools necessary to qualify for and succeed on the PGA Tour, with the exception of a consistent mental game plan. He had a tendency to focus on mechanics. This led to his focus being behind the ball. To be successful at this game, one's focus must be on the target (in front of the ball) in an effort to develop a picture and feel for the shape of the shot.

Intervention:

Golf is one sport where it helps if the consultant has played the game. Together, we developed a mental routine which could be used over every shot Peter would face. This routine incorporated the four phases of concentration: broad-external, broad-internal, narrow-internal, and narrow-external (assessing, analyzing, rehearsing, and performing). For a golfer to say that he/she has concentrated over a shot, each phase must be used. To develop a mental routine the golfer must choose cue words for each phase of concentration. These words were used to trigger the mind to attend to the appropriate information necessary to pull off the shot. They also act as a block to negative input.

The pre-shot mental routine that Peter and I developed was: a) "Observe" - take in all the important external information (i.e. the wind, lie of the ball, elevation change, hazards, layout of the hole, etc.). [Broad-external], b) "Strategy" - develop a plan from the information received from the first cue word (i.e. choose a target, club, and type of shot to be hit). [Broad-internal], c) "See it" - visualize the shot. Paint a picture on the canvass of the mind. [Narrow-internal], d) "Feel it" - allow the shot to be felt by the muscles. Pre-feel the stroke that is about to be made. This is a kinesthetic feel that is being attached to the picture which was visualized. [Narrow-internal], e) "Trust it" - this cue allows the mind to turn over the reigns to the muscles to execute the swing that has been pictured and felt. The focus is entirely on the target as the swing is "trusted" because trust is "earned" by the previous cue words. [Narrow-external]

This mental routine incorporates all the relevant information necessary for hitting a golf shot while at the same time sequencing the information in the most efficient manner possible. This routine resembles a funnel as it starts from a broad view and is narrowed to a single thought and corresponding singular action (the swing). To play golf, one must be aware of an enormous array of information, yet process it down to a single thought that corresponds with the initiation of the swing.

Outcome:

Peter began practicing the routine with putts, chip shots, and then moving to full shots on the driving range. Once the routine become comfortable on the range, we moved to the course and hit various shots using the routine, but not playing for score. Finally, Peter played nine holes attempting to incorporate the routine on each shot. After two days of intense practice, Peter was ready to use it in a tournament setting. He made a commitment to go through the routine over each shot and kept a concentration score for each round.

Three weeks later, he won the State Open tournament by shooting 17 under par. The following week he entered an official PGA Tour event on a sponsor's exemption. He shot 17 under par again and won the tournament. This gave him a two-year exemption on the PGA tour and an answer to his childhood dream.

#6: Female College Volleyball Setter

Introduction:

Candace, a three-year starting setter on the volleyball team and a psychology major with a coaching specialization, was enrolled in an Independent Study course with me, Applied Sport Psychology. We had progressed through a number of topics through the first six weeks of the semester. Candace's last two assignments were essays related to: 1) Personal Responsibility and 2) Developing a Great Attitude.

During one of our weekly meetings, we discussed psychological routines applicable to self-paced sports skills specific to golf, tennis, baseball, etc. We identified volleyball skills that were self-paced such as serving and service receptions. I asked Candace what her routine was for those two skills. After discussing her two routines, we began investigation of her routine as a setter.

For my own information, I was interested in the similarities between Candace's psychological routine as a setter compared to golfers and quarterbacks. I explained to Candace the psychological routine patterns of golfers; and then proceeded to ask her what her routine was.

I did not initiate this discussion because of any identified problems, just as a means of facilitating the discussion.

Intervention:

Over 3 years of competition, Candace had established herself as one of college volleyball's premier setters. As she began to explain her routine as a setter for her team's offense service returns, a definite pattern unfolded. I asked her to explain each of the steps to me.

I asked her to tell me what she did when she is setting great. At first, Candace said she currently was not setting great. I asked her when she last set great. She remembered it was against UCSB. I asked, "What did you do?" She explained her routine during that match. As we listed the steps, Candace stopped and said, "I am not doing that now.", referring to #5 - deception.

Routine
♦ Get signal from coaches
♦ Awareness of hitters
♦ Position of blockers and strategy
♦ Select best option and alternatives
♦ Deception
♦ Second awareness of blockers
♦ Trust (term selected from golfer's and QB's routines)

I asked her what she could do to include deception. Candace said that she could and should always practice with a purpose in mind. I asked her how often she practiced deception. She said that, at present, she did not practice deception very often.

We talked about how often she practiced her entire routine exactly as she did it during matches. It was becoming apparent that she was getting away from her routine in practice and this was transferring to her performance. Consequently, we attempted to determine how Candace could include her routine in practice; including her coach in the process.

Outcome:

With the approval and assistance of a very cooperative coach, Candace practiced her routine more often and followed the coaches' lead in the refinement of deception.
Her routine changed and matured throughout the season. For a majority of the season, her routine was similar to that previously listed.

Candace worked on this routine and with a lot of practice it became fairly automatic. Once she was able to run through her routine smoothly, she simplified her cognitive routine and then anything else became habit. Candace's adapted/cognitive routine was:
♦ signal
♦ position of blockers and hitters strategy
♦ best option
♦ deception
♦ trust

This routine included everything that she actually thought about before the opponent served the ball. Candace only used the fourth step about 50% of the time. This is due to the fact that by the end of the season most of her deception became habit. However, she did use it at specific times when she knew she could deceive a specific blocker. For example, if Candace knew that a blocker liked to cheat, she would use her deception to show one set and then would set somewhere else.

The steps that disappeared from her adapted routine became habit by the end of the season. Through the season Candace was able to practice her original routine in games as well as in practice. By repeating the routine again and again these steps became automatic. Without realizing it they had vanished from her cognitive routine and therefore, the routine became simplified.

#7: College Softball Player

Introduction:

Mary is a college softball player with great ability. She has played softball for many years and was a high school all-star. Her primary position has been catcher. Mary is viewed as an integral player since she has power with the bat and a strong arm. The team relies heavily on her, but out of nowhere she has developed a very bad habit of routinely missing the pitcher on her throw-backs in practice and in games. Seemingly at random, according to Mary, she returns pitches by throwing the ball to the ground or far over the pitcher's head. Some return throws are perfect; then, like a curse, a wild throw may happen.

Mary is seeking help for this because nothing like this has ever happened to her before. The coach is extremely upset with her and has threatened benching her in humiliation for not "concentrating". She has become very frustrated with the situation; becoming emotional and breaking into tears when discussing the problem. According the Mary, the more she tries, the more difficult the situation becomes. She is evidencing a strong sense of disbelief and fear of not being in control "of this simple thing." Mary wants to regain self-control and not worry about this erratic behavior.

Intervention:

Rather than viewing this situation as a "concentration" issue, I decided to address it as a confidence issue. Mary was definitely influenced by her coach's actions in the situation, so I established an understanding of her perception of her coach (respect, ability, etc....). I sensed there was sound respect for her coach. We discussed elements that were essential and nonessential for her position as catcher. I had her expand on her abilities as an athlete; an exceptional one to this point in her life. She shared her past accomplishments, showing pride in the recollection. For an assignment, I had her write a letter to herself as if she were her own best friend. The best friend should tell Mary about the best friend's perspective of her abilities and accomplishments.

There were no apparent deficiencies in her performance other than the actual release of the ball that was either too early or too late, at times; thus accounting for the erratic throws. I did not use any technical skill analysis pertaining to her performance style, because I did not want to foster or suggest a "paralysis by analysis" effect.

Once we identified and focused on Mary's concerns, we discussed images of self-control in several situation on the field from warm-ups to on-base pressure situations. With various situations, I directed her through several guided imagery sessions imparting full control and involving a "breathe → set → throw" performance routine.

In working with guided imagery and game situations, I asked Mary if she would consider a motivational cue word, **BEST**. The cue, meant to represent *B*reathe *E*asy, *S*et, and *T*hrow (trust). For her routine, Mary would pound her glove, execute a breath (deep), set, and throw back to the pitcher (or to a base in a game situation). We aimed for simplicity, repetition, and automation of her routine to minimize the throwing errors.

We discussed that the pitcher should not be viewed as a threat, rather a warm and willing friend. This was to make a motivational target. Finally, and importantly, Mary decided that she would treat all errors as one *less* mistake learned.

Outcome:

With each subsequent practice, mistakes became fewer and fewer. Mary struggled to overcome this behavior but the routine did have a positive impact on her performance. She finished the year at catcher, contributing to a respectable team record.

Discussion Questions

1. Why is it important to "be your own best friend"?

2. How does an athlete know when it is time to quit? What signs do you look for? What are the differences between signs that suggest an athlete is in a slump, or at the end of his/her career?

3. Discuss the idea of "dormant talent" vs. "lost talent".

4. How does a mental routine help one's confidence?

5. Why is it necessary to be sequential in a performance routine? What are the guidelines one should follow in developing and refining a routine?

6. What is meant by the phrase, "trust is earned"?

7. How can one objectively measure an athlete's use of a routine during competition?

8. When should a referral be made to another applied sport psychology practitioner?

References and Resources

Gallwey, T. (1976). The inner game of tennis. New York: Random House.

Gauron, E.F. (1984). Mental training for peak performance. Sport science associates.

Huang, A.C. & Lynch, J. (1992). Thinking body, dancing mind. Bantam Books.

Jackson, P. & Delehanty, H. (1995). Sacred hoops. New York: Hyperion.

Moore, W.E. (1987). Covert-overt service routines: The effect of a service routine training program on elite tennis players. Dissertation Abstracts International, 48, 85-A.

Moore, W.E. & Stevenson, J.R. (1991). Understanding trust in the performance of complex automated sport skills. The Sport Psychologist, 5, 281-289.

Moore, W.E. & Stevenson, J.R. (1994). Training for trust in sport skills. The Sport Psychologist, 8, 1-12.

Orlick, T. (1986). Psyching for sport: Mental training for athletes. Champaign, IL: Leisure Press.

CHAPTER 7

~ Concentration ~

Jeff Simons, Victoria University, Melbourne, Australia

Concentration problems are among the most common performance issues presented to sport psychology consultants by athletes and coaches. Obviously, concentration is a psychological concern and integrally linked to sport performance. Yet, it is not easy to define and understand concentration, much less determine how it might be improved in athletes. Most everyone would claim that it is important to 'pay attention' and 'concentrate', but what are the necessary, sufficient, or optimal dimensions of performance concentration? Distractions and lapses in attention are often easy to identify, but how clearly do we understand, plan, and execute superior concentration skills? Most evaluations of concentration are inferred after the fact from the quality of performance. If one performs well, he or she must have been concentrating well—if performance is substandard, concentration must have been poor. However, simple claims and "post-hoc" explanations when speaking of concentration are not particularly useful. Given the advances in practical sport psychology, there is little excuse for leaving such an important mental skill to chance and trivial evaluations. With proper information and training, athletes can develop superior concentration skills for competitive performance.

The terms 'attention' and 'concentration' are often used interchangeably. This is not much of a concern in everyday conversation. Yet, to discuss the concepts more clearly, a couple of working definitions may be helpful. Attempts at precise scientific definitions have failed to come to a conclusive description of attention. In general though, *Attention* is the process of applying mental resources, giving consideration or thought. It is essentially the state of mental information processing. Although we all think we know what it is, attention is difficult to fully comprehend because it is the medium of our known experience, both conscious and subconscious. (It is somewhat like a fish comprehending the meaning of 'water'.)

The word 'concentrate' means to collect, focus, or intensify something. Accordingly, *Concentration* may be defined as the control or focus of attention. It is the mechanism by which attention is directed. In Moran's (1996) terms, concentration can be viewed as the "mental effort aspect of attention." (p. 41) Clearly, the two words are not mutually exclusive of one another, as there is always some concentration aspect of attention, and attention is what concentration is directing or focusing. In this chapter, I will use 'attention' to denote the awareness itself, and 'concentration' to refer to the process of directing or controlling attention. Because concentration is the control function of attention, it is a more accessible concept for understanding the relationship to performance.

The existing scientific evidence supports the view of concentration as a skill. It is not simply some innate mental resource that we differentially allocate to various tasks. We learn to concentrate, and we can train to concentrate better. Furthermore, the specific concentration abilities to deal with distractions or to counter the effects of anxiety are also skills that can be improved through practice. This assumption of concentration as a skill is key to most psychological interventions.

Basics of Concentration

Concentration is complex. Consultants need at least a basic understanding of the processes involved so they can provide practical and effective help to athletes and coaches. It does little good to simply attribute performance problems to poor concentration or to exhort athletes to concentrate! Some technical knowledge is required in order to actually do something about it. Detailed discussions of attention and concentration can be found in many sport psychology texts (e.g., Abernathy,1993; Boutcher, 1992; Hardy, Jones, & Gould, 1996; Nideffer, 1993; Summers & Ford 1995; Weinberg & Gould 1995). For the most extensive treatment currently available, a book on concentration in sport performers by Moran (1996) is highly recommended. For the purpose of this chapter, I will present some basic concepts that are central to effective sport psychology practice. Although there is much yet to be learned through scientific research, these concepts have served well in practical applications.

Attentional Capacity

There is a limited capacity to attention. We can draw on only a finite amount of attentional resources at any given time. Consequently, if most of attentional resources are dedicated to processing one particular set of information then there are few resources available to process other data. To illustrate how this can become a difficulty in sport, consider the common problem of distractions. A distraction attracts attention to something irrelevant to performance, thus occupying some portion of one's capacity to pay attention. That portion of attention, then, is not available for concentration on relevant performance cues. The common result is a reaction or response to the distraction and an inability to handle performance demands. Both effects are detrimental to performance. Thus, given capacity limitations, the athlete may be doubly impaired by a single distraction.

It is probable that our total capacity is not a singular quantity, but rather a collection of attentional pools. For instance, there may be separate attentional resources for different senses, such as sight, hearing, and touch (cognitive scientists currently do not know exactly what is shared and what is unique). Therefore, the amount of capacity available may be increased by using multiple attentional pools. Increases in general information processing capacity may be possible, but it appears that most concentration improvements involve either decreasing demands on capacity or accessing more pools, or both.

Control vs. Automatic Processing

A common distinction is made between Control Processing and Automatic Processing. Control Processing involves deliberate, conscious attention to sort out perceptual data, make decisions, and execute actions. It is exemplified by the significant effort needed to pay attention to a new complex task. Think, for instance, of a beginner's first attempts to dribble a basketball.

Early in learning, a large amount of conscious thought must be applied in order to process information and control responses. The beginner must watch the ball and try to anticipate the unfamiliar bounce, as well as attempt to coordinate body movements to provide the right amount of force and control in maintaining the dribble. Each bit of input and output information requires attentional space, and therefore, the demands of a new task typically exceed the learner's capacity. In our example, the overload becomes apparent as the learner fails to keep up with the perceptual-motor demands and dribbling deteriorates. Even later in learning, new complexity or new skills will require Control Processing, as when dribbling must be transferred to movement on the court against a defensive opponent.

Once skills are well-learned, information processing can become seemingly reflexive, requiring very little conscious thought. Input and output information is quickly and easily handled according to experienced knowledge and response habits. This Automatic Processing is evident in the easy attentional flow of the expert. To the professional basketball player, for example, dribbling is second nature—just another aspect of walking or running on the court. Although the expert may experience a keen sense of awareness, she or he exhibits little effort to concentrate as complex decisions and actions are executed.

The amount of attentional capacity that is required for any particular task essentially depends upon the degree to which the performer must use Control Processing versus Automatic Processing. The more Control Processing, the more mental effort and greater dedication of attentional resources. The more Automatic Processing, the less mental effort and more attention available for additional information processing. Therefore, training an athlete toward Automatic Processing through overlearning provides a distinct advantage. However, it should be recognized that there is a loss in performance flexibility once perceptions, decisions, or skills become totally automatic. Stereotypical habits may create some limitations to performance when task demands are variable. For example, a tennis player may need to adjust an automatic timing response to the bounce of the ball when moving from hard court to grass court surfaces. At the highest levels of expertise, successful performers operate under a high degree of Automatic Processing, yet appear to readily access Control Processing for dealing with changes in strategy and unexpected circumstances.

Analytic vs. Integrative Processing

The brain has different ways of dealing with information. As a useful heuristic, a distinction can be made between processing in the left- and the right-hemispheres of the brain (this is not a precise scientific distinction, but it is an effective practical concept). Roughly, the left-brain is involved with verbal, logical, and analytical reasoning. This 'analytic' hemisphere processes data in serial fashion, appropriate for language, computation, and logic. It is the seat of conscious decision-making and the self-talk of our 'thinking mind'. Analytic information processing is essential to strategic aspects of sport, such as a football quarterback 'reading' a defense or a pitcher choosing a pitch for a certain game situation. Given that it can consciously guide a series of decisions and actions, the left-brain is typically most active when Control Processing is required. But, because analytic processing deals with information in serial or sequential fashion, time can become an issue in executing any set of thoughts or actions. For example, a batter does not have sufficient time during a pitch to analyze all perceptual data and consciously initiate each motor aspect of a swing. Left-brain processing simply cannot keep up with the rapid demands of complex physical performance.

The right-brain, on the other hand, is active in visual-spatial awareness, imagery, creative thought, and execution of motor skills. It can engage in parallel processing across multiple sensory channels, appropriate for holistic understanding of patterns in simultaneous information. If the left-brain is the 'thousand words', the right-brain is the 'picture'. Just some of the richness of this processing may be experienced, for example, when one becomes absorbed in the multitude sights and sounds of a film or music video. The right-brain is the center of 'knowing', feeling and doing. There is reason to believe that much of intuition, far from being a metaphysical or chance occurrence, is an expression of knowledge formulated in this non-verbal hemisphere. The right-brain appears to be most involved during Automatic Processing, especially with physical skills. Parallel processing means that far fewer attentional resources need be expended per unit of information relative to serial processing. For that reason, right-brain thinking is often perceived as rich in content, quick in processing, and a lower drain on attention.

Both analytic and integrative processing are essential to sport performance. Intelligent analysis, decision-making, and strategy require the logical left-brain. Analytic processing is also central to learning and adapting new skills. The right-brain becomes increasingly important to performance as expertise allows athletes to react intuitively to situations and execute motor skills without conscious thought. Once skills are well-learned, the two hemispheres can share the work, with each performing at its specialty—the left-brain objectively analyzing the situation and guiding strategy, while the right-brain takes control of executing the skills under the circumstances encountered. During optimal conditions, the timing and degree of contributions by each is determined by the moment-to-moment processing required. Accordingly, descriptions of flow experiences by athletes highlight a seamless coordination of the two hemispheres.

Even though there may be a rough correspondence between Control Processing and analytic processing, and between Automatic Processing and integrative processing, these concepts are not equivalent to one another. Control Processing can be required by the right-brain, such as when one is learning to discriminate complex patterns of information. To illustrate, it may take a great deal of conscious effort for a gymnast or diver to learn the kinesthetic feel of a half-twist executed correctly. Likewise, Automatic Processing of left-brain decision-making is common in experienced performers, as when strategic decisions in ball games become essentially unconscious. Perceiving the goalie shifting weight toward one side, for example, a soccer player may instantaneously change a goal kick into a pass to a teammate on the opposite side. The distinction between Control and Automatic Processing is primarily in the degree of conscious attentional effort required, whereas the difference between analytic and integrative processing is in the sequential versus simultaneous nature of dealing with information and controlling responses.

Direction of Attention

Perhaps the most obvious aspects of concentration involve the directing of attention and the relative division of attention. In any performance situation, there is a question of what a person is paying attention *to*. It is useful to conceptualize three types of attentional direction. First, attention may be directed mentally, including cognitions (thoughts, self-statements, decisions, worries) and emotions. Second, it may be directed within the body (somatically), reading body states and kinesthetic orientation. Third, attention may be directed externally to the information in the environment as received by our senses. The effectiveness of information processing in performance will depend to a great degree on the direction of attention and the ability to switch appropriately between mental, somatic, and external focus as the situation requires.

Direction of attention is determined by circumstances and the person. Extreme and novel information most naturally attracts attention, whereas habituation to persistent stimuli can essentially eliminate conscious awareness. These evolutionarily adaptive processes explain why many distractions involve new or unusual stimuli, and why concentration lapses are often a result of 'sameness' or repetitive stimuli. Other than extreme stimuli, the most dominant force to direct attention is volition—what we choose to concentrate on. Explained simply, our selection of attentional focus is based on knowledge (what we know how to do), intention (what we mean to do), and motivation (how interested we are in doing it).

Given the enormous potential of sensory and mental stimuli available to us at any moment, selective attention is an essential concentration tool. We direct attention like a beam of light in the darkness as we select the information we wish to process. It is important to realize, however, that a practically infinite amount of information simultaneously exists outside of this selective beam. For instance, notice what you are sitting on right now as you read this passage. Feel the pressure against your body. Take a moment and concentrate on the feelings. You may have noticed a striking degree of sensation when you switched your attention. The point here is that the sensory information already existed, but only became a significant part of your experience through your powers of selective attention. Whether or not the focus is helpful is dependent on the objectives in any given situation. In the case of sport, selective attention is effective when focus is directed to the relevant aspects of performance in the face of all other potential pieces of information that could be processed.

Selective attention is not the only concentration tool. We also have the ability to divide attention between two or more tasks. The classic example of divided attention is the number of actions accurately performed by an experienced driver navigating familiar streets. Not only may the driver execute multiple pedal and steering actions while visually scanning the road, but he or she may also be listening to the radio, talking to a passenger, or planning another part of the day. The ability to divide attention effectively can be most simply attributed to the use of Automatic Processing for most of the required demands. Laboratory studies consistently reveal performance decrements when even just two simultaneous tasks require significant Control Processing. It is easy to see how experienced, highly skilled athletes are so much better equipped than novices to monitor and act on multiple levels during performance.

Thoughts and actions tend to follow whatever is most dominant in consciousness. Most often the dominant cognitions and feelings are determined by our choice of focus and our decision about what action we wish to take. This means that our choice of focus, coupled with a definite intention, tends to lead performance. If we want to catch a ball, we turn our focus to track it and we activate our intention to intercept its flight with the hand we choose. The conceptualization of 'catching the ball' is set foremost in consciousness. To be successful, an athlete needs to choose thoughts and actions well, and then set an intention for action to dominate attention before and during performance. The athlete needs to be clear on what information is relevant and what actions are desired. Obviously, doing so at a high level requires coaching, skill, and experience. But the principle holds true even for the beginner. Whatever is foremost in attention serves as the primary guide for information processing and performance.

There are some features of consciousness that compete with intentional thought and make it difficult to hold the desired attentional focus. Most significantly, there appears to be a complimentary process that checks to see if one is attending to anything other than the desired thought. The rough explanation for this is that a comparison is necessary to evaluate whether or not we are doing what is intended. Unfortunately, this monitoring system can throw unwanted thoughts into the focus of attention. If these thoughts are extreme, or in any way interesting or threatening to the person, attention is naturally attracted to them. For instance, while one is trying to focus only on performance, the monitoring system may produce a random thought about being socially evaluated. Because social evaluation tends to be taken seriously and typically triggers self-observation and worry about personal success or failure, the athlete may suddenly feel self-conscious and/or anxious. Once such a focus is activated, it interferes with performance focus.

If there is primarily one single thing that a person does not want to attend to, the comparison system devotes most attention to checking for that one thing, which may compete directly with any chosen intention for attentional dominance. For this reason, instructions to 'just ignore' something often fail to help. In the case where there is no intention other than to not do something, the comparison system draws the focus of attention directly to it. To illustrate this effect, try not to think of a red hen right now. The result is as common as swinging at a bad pitch, moving directly to the wrong position, or hitting the ball right into the net.

The key for dealing with the unintentional effects of the monitoring system is to make certain that the intended direction of attention is very clear and dominant, while reducing concern about conflicting notions that spontaneously arise. Intentions should be formulated in the positive, to direct what is desired, rather than avoid what is not desired. For example, any important 'nots' (e.g., 'do not hit the ball long') should be replaced with 'dos' (e.g., 'do hit the ball short of the line'). Any information irrelevant to performance needs to be considered unimportant.

Intensity and Duration of Attention

Attention can be focused narrowly on a single thing, or it can be spread broadly across a wide array of potential sources of stimuli. In this respect, attention can be likened to an adjustable beam of light. When tightly focused, it illuminates thorough detail of the single object of attention. As the beam is broadened, it takes in a greater scope, but with less discrimination of any particular piece of information. Narrow attention is often referred to as 'hard focus,' while broad attention is commonly called 'soft focus.' For each aspect of a given activity, there will be an appropriate width of attention to match the relevant cues and necessary actions.

The ability to sustain any particular breadth of focus over extended periods of time is another performance skill. Maintaining concentration for long periods is fatiguing. Furthermore, tasks requiring vigilance can be especially difficult due to the boredom factor of habituation. Opposite of the involuntary attraction to extreme or novel stimuli, the attentional system naturally tends to disregard information that remains constant or uneventful (are you still aware of the feelings in your seat?). For this reason, some sports, such as archery and shooting, provide a challenge in the very uniformity of the task over long series of performance trials. During prolonged performance, it is necessary to keep attention from wandering off toward internal or external diversions, or to shut down waking consciousness entirely and go to sleep. The key to concentration for long duration performance is maintaining one's interest in the stimuli. This can be accomplished by constant scanning of individual features, by fascination in the details of performance, or by enjoying the meditation-like state of alert soft focus.

Attentional Switching

There is virtually no sport that demands only one type of attention. Instead, sports present a variety of demands for direction, breadth, intensity, and duration of focus. Consider a batter in baseball who mentally goes over the game situation walking to the batter's box, scans the positions of defensive players, focuses in on the third-base coach for the offensive signal, reads kinesthetic cues while setting up a good batting stance, studies the pitcher, chooses an intention for what type of pitch to go after, checks to make sure the body is ready and relaxed, watches the pitcher wind up, focuses in on the release point of the pitch to pick up the ball as quickly as possible, watches the ball, makes the decision to swing, and makes minute swing adjustments to get the bat to successfully connect with the ball. In less than ten seconds, the batter's concentration must shift attention in several different directions, with varying breadth and intensity of focus. And this is not at all unusual in sport situations. Consequently, the ability to switch attention as necessary is a central concentration skill.

Successful attentional switching goes beyond simply having discrete abilities to develop specific types of focus. Just being able to hold a broad external or narrow somatic focus, for example, is not enough. Effective concentration involves the smooth coordination of transitions from each appropriate focus to the next. The athlete needs to be able to switch attention easily and at will from reading the environment to checking body position, and so on. The implication is that concentration training should include the transitions between each required performance focus along with development of any specific focus.

Arousal-Attention Relationship

Arousal is an innate concentration mechanism, integrally linked with attention. It is difficult to separate variations in arousal from the dynamics of attention. For example, arousing from sleep is accompanied by the activation of conscious attention to the environment, and panic is marked by both high arousal and intense focus. One simple relationship between psychophysiological arousal and attention is fairly well established. As arousal increases, attentional focus narrows. Under conditions of very low arousal, attention is diffuse, without much detail perceived in any one of a wide array of stimuli. To illustrate, think of a player sitting on the sidelines after practice, lazily watching the next squad going through training, not paying attention to any one thing, but generally taking in the overall environment. As arousal increases, so too does the detail on sources of information. Perhaps our player notices some movement and noise to one side of the field which peaks his interest, increasing arousal and attracting attention in that direction and onto a single group of athletes. At extreme arousal, only one or two cues are intensely processed. Now the player suddenly realizes that a ball is rapidly coming at him, arousal jumps and attention becomes intently focused on the flight of the ball and a quick head movement to avoid being struck. Based on this effect, raising and lowering arousal is a common method for naturally adjusting the breadth and intensity of attentional focus.

For any given task, errors of overinclusion (attending to too many irrelevant cues) may occur when arousal is too low, and errors of underinclusion (failing to attend to relevant cues) occur when arousal is too high. Put another way, low arousal problems relate to an inability to adequately concentrate in on only relevant task cues, and high arousal difficulties relate to the inability to process sufficient task cues or control the intense, reactive focus. The notion that there might be some optimal level of arousal for processing only the cues relevant to the task is one explanation for the popular inverted-U hypothesis for the arousal-performance relationship.

Beyond attentional narrowing, arousal can have other concentration effects, particularly when anxiety is the arousal source. For example, some experts claim that people will tend to switch to their preferred direction and breadth of attention when arousal becomes high. In effect, heightened arousal is thought to activate whatever attentional processing is most habitual for the performer. For example, someone who is typically introspective and analytical might be expected to focus attention in a broad mental direction under conditions of high arousal. Whether this arousal induced concentration is helpful or harmful will depend on the appropriateness of the preferred attentional style to meet the task demands.

High arousal can also stimulate rapid switching between various sources of information. Given the narrowed focus under high arousal, the effect is rather like trying to scan every aspect of a large dark warehouse with an intense pinpoint beam of light. Attention jumps from one thing to the next, trying to take in sufficient information. Another effect of heightened arousal is the tendency for attention to become focused mentally on thoughts and emotions. This is particularly the case when rising arousal levels are due to anxiety. The worry and self consciousness effects of anxiety tend to direct attention mentally.

Individual Differences

All psychological evaluations and interventions must be flexible to differences in performers. A few obvious, but important points should be stated to reinforce the need for individualized concentration skills training. Each person has different experiences and varying levels of concentration abilities. Degree of expertise will determine the athlete's ability to engage in Automatic Processing versus the need for Control Processing. Furthermore, some people will find certain types of concentration easier than others. There is some support to the idea that people have preferred concentration styles, relating to direction, breadth, intensity, and duration of attention. For instance, one person might find it natural to focus externally on a wide variety of cues for a long period, whereas another person might find it easy to hold a single thought to control a precise closed skill movement. In addition, athletes' motivations to attend, their chosen directions of focus, and their intentions for performance will each alter attention in any given situation. All of these points suggest that a single, 'cook book' approach to concentration training is not very feasible.

Most Common Concentration Issues in Sport

Despite the complexity of concentration, the most common difficulties encountered in sport can be placed under three basic categories. Because they are all concerned with attention, the problems and interventions will regularly cross categories. However, it is helpful to the practitioner to separate concentration issues into problems of appropriate focus, distractions, and anxiety.

Appropriate Focus

Many concentration problems relate to the failure to pay attention to the right things, at the right time, for the right duration. The judgment of relevant versus irrelevant cues for any performance suggests an appropriate focus of attention. The first attentional concern is understanding the correct focus, the second is having the ability to concentrate accordingly. First, the athlete must know which cues are essential to performance. For example, a backcourt volleyball player receiving serve needs to know what information to gather from the flight of the ball to intercept it and effectively bump it to a teammate. Next, the athlete must have the ability to concentrate on those cues to the exclusion of irrelevant ones. So, our volleyball player needs to be able to concentrate with an external and fairly narrow focus of attention to process those relevant cues from the ball's flight, while disregarding irrelevant information, such as movement on the opponent's side of the court. In many cases, attention needs to be divided between several aspects of performance, and switched as action progresses. This would be true for the volleyball player. Besides the ball, the receiver needs to be aware of the movement of teammates, particularly the setter, who should receive the bump from the backcourt. Then, once the ball was delivered to the setter, attention would need to shift to process the information necessary to move back into the proper defensive position for the ball's return.

Appropriate focus will, of course, also involve aspects other than direction and breadth. Intensity needs to match the degree of detail required and effort may be needed to maintain focus for long duration. Furthermore, the performer needs to be able to recognize when appropriate focus is lost and then have the ability to re-establish correct concentration. Problems of appropriate focus are clearly connected to sport knowledge and experience, coaching, and training. Dealing with such problems is fairly straightforward, accomplished through teaching strategies of the sport and training desired concentration patterns. Athletes need to understand what to observe and do, and practice the process of observing and doing.

Distractions

The second category of concentration issues is the direct compliment of the first and includes all forms of distractions. The basic problem of distractions is that they attract attention away from appropriate focus and onto task-irrelevant cues. Distractions consume attentional capacity, while providing no resource for effective performance. If a player is paying attention to something happening off the field, there is no benefit to on-field processing of information. In some cases, distractions capture virtually all of the performer's attention, thus eliminating any possibility of attending to sport demands. Moreover, distractions often evoke reactions, both psychological and physical. A player may get angry or respond to a spectator, for example. At best, these responses are a waste of effort. More often, they ruin performance and/or place the athlete in a more difficult situation (e.g., penalties). External distractions include irrelevant aspects of the action in progress, as well as people or things in the surrounding environment. Internal distractions include self-talk, indecision, other personal interests, worry, and emotions. The first steps in dealing with distractions are to specifically identify them and to then determine why they are able to attract attention away from the performance focus. Training should then center on decreasing the distractibility of the athlete and increasing the ability to maintain appropriate focus.

Anxiety

The third category of common concentration issues involves anxiety and its effects. Because anxiety is arousing, it narrows attention. For this reason, anxiety sometimes actually aids performance when a more intense focus on relevant cues is needed (e.g., when we decide we had better 'get serious' about performance). In many cases, however, anxiety pushes arousal beyond optimal levels, and performance suffers. It is common to see anxious athletes exhibiting levels of activation too high for their best performances, especially in important competitions.

Anxiety produces more than just arousal effects on attention. Anxiety activates protective mechanisms and the attention drain of worry. The major protective device is to rely on the most basic or habitual ways of processing information and responding. Thus, anxious performers tend to use their preferred attentional style (whether it is helpful or not) and exhibit 'fight-or-flight' decisions and reactions. Avoidance behavior is another of the natural reactions to anxiety, so anxious athletes can be expected to make attempts to withdraw from competitive situations, physically or psychologically. There is also a tendency for anxious people to revert to their most well-learned motor patterns, overriding intentions for some or most specialized performance skills.

Anxiety stimulates cognitive focus on past events and future possibilities as worries about success and failure dominate attention. Worry is a common internal distraction which robs attentional resources from the performance at hand. At high levels of anxiety, attention tends to become compulsively fixed on a limited number of cues or to switch among a multitude of cues uncontrollably as the person attempts in vain to find the information with which to resolve the discomfort in the situation.

Dealing with anxiety effects on attention takes a two-pronged attack. The first approach is to manage the anxiety itself. As anxiety is controlled, the concentration problems ease in direct proportion. The second approach is to establish effective focus and skilled actions as habitual, and convince the athlete that such concentration provides the best response possible to the anxiety provoking situation. In other words, we want to maximize Automatic Processing of skilled performance and develop the trust necessary to allow performance to flow without mental interruptions. Naturally, both approaches require considerable time, effort, and training, but they can be accomplished.

Diagnostic Process

Nearly any performance issue presented by an athlete will include concentration concerns. The consultant will want to listen carefully to the descriptions of the perceived problem to determine whether or not concentration is indeed the central issue. For instance, an athlete may ask for help with concentration when the major problem is actually competitive anxiety (concentration problems are more socially acceptable than admitting to anxiety). Dealing with difficulties such as anxiety will likely involve concentration training, but in such cases it may be secondary to other mental skills. Once the decision is made to address concentration, the following questions can be used for diagnosis and intervention.

♦ *What are the concentration demands of the performance?* Establish at least a general understanding of the sport (e.g., open versus closed skill, fine motor versus strength or power task) and any particular concentration demands of the performance situation (e.g., positional responsibilities, opponents, environmental or personal distractions). Attentional demands should be analyzed for direction (mental, somatic, external), breadth, intensity, duration, and switching required. Gather information from the athlete, coaches, and other resources.

♦ *Does the athlete have sufficient knowledge of correct focus?* Can the athlete adequately describe optimal focus for performance? Does he or she know which cues are relevant and which are irrelevant? Can the athlete plan and react strategically, make effective decisions, and develop a clear intention for action?

♦ *What distractions are present and how does the athlete react to these?* List prominent internal and external distractions. Discuss the degree to which these may interfere with performance. Explore how these distractions affect the athlete and how they are currently handled.

♦ *Does anxiety play a significant role in concentration problems?* Determine the degree of anxiety encountered during performance, especially when concentration is known to suffer. Explore the source(s) of this anxiety and the nature of the athlete's anxiety reactions, particularly how they relate to concentration.

♦ *Is motivation an issue in the inability to maintain focus?* Lapses in concentration may be due to a lack of interest, particularly if the athlete cannot understand the reasons for paying attention to certain aspects of performance. Investigate whether the athlete finds meaning in the task, and whether competing interests may be attracting attention. Is there a boredom factor due to restricted stimuli or a repetitive task?

♦ *Does the athlete have appropriate concentration skills for the performance demands?* Examine typical patterns of concentration. The athlete may simply have insufficient experience in focusing, maintaining, or switching attention. The preferred attentional style of the athlete may not match the demands of performance. For example, he or she may do well with singular focus, but be relatively unskilled at maintaining a relaxed broad, external focus for vigilance across a wide spectrum of information. Conversely, the athlete may be most adept at scanning the environment, but have difficulty staying focused on a few specific cues.

Intervention Approaches

There is little empirical or practical evidence to conclude that general exercises have much effect on concentration skills for competitive performance. The popular 'concentration grid' and multi-channel distraction tapes, for example, are useful tools for demonstrations, but their efficacy in training applicable skills is questionable. Part of the problem may well be the difficulty in getting athletes to dedicate adequate practice time to exercises so far removed from their sport. That is, general training may work, but only if athletes can be convinced to train sufficiently. Practical experience indicates that this is unlikely. In any case, specificity of training is highly recommended, both for the motivation of the athlete and for the likelihood of transfer of concentration skills to sport performance. Toward that end, simulation training through mock competitions and/or imagery rehearsal provides the most effective tool outside of competitive experience for developing effective concentration skills.

Some suggestions for dealing with concentration problems have been offered throughout this chapter. The following brief descriptions outline the most common intervention approaches (note: although anxiety management is relevant and important to concentration, it is covered in another chapter). Practical applications will need to be dynamic, with due consideration given for the principles of concentration, the demands of the sport performance, and the uniqueness of each athlete.

Train Appropriate Focus

The most obvious intervention for concentration problems is also the central objective of all other interventions. Effective concentration means directing attention to relevant information and appropriate actions. All concentration training should help athletes to discriminate between relevant and irrelevant cues and to link specific circumstances with potentially successful actions. Although any aspect of attention might be addressed, the primary emphases may need only be on direction and breadth of attention. That is, training may chiefly stress the manner in which attention should be focused alternately between mental, somatic, and external directions, and how wide a number of cues need to be processed. At this most basic level, actions may be planned to work from a simple contingency plan (i.e., 'If X situation, then Y action').

Training in appropriate focus will initially involve a significant amount of Control Processing. This will be demanding on conscious effort and attentional capacity. Furthermore, development of factual or strategic knowledge will require analytic left-brain thinking, however, a high degree of analytic processing may well interfere with the integrative processing required for complex sport performance. For these reasons, performance enhancements may not be observed immediately. The gains from improved concentration will appear as appropriate focus becomes automatic and integrated into the flow of performance.

The bottom line of appropriate focus is for the performer to be clear on what she or he needs to pay attention to and what actions are desired (e.g., 'see the ball, hit the ball'). Processing may be conscious and analytic where complex decisions must be made (e.g., deciding on a golf approach shot to a difficult green) or where performance requires flexibility from habitual responses (e.g., slight adjustments in form to handle environmental changes). Otherwise, the majority of decisions and actions best flow from Automatic Processing guided by simple thoughts or images. These guides need to be most dominant in the mind and comprised of intentions for perception and performance. They should indicate what TO DO.

Simplify Concentration Focus

With the complexity of sport performance, it is possible for appropriate focus to be described in intricate detail. Highly analytical athletes and coaches, especially, may find themselves overcomplicating concentration demands. This may not only be confusing, but be a distraction to performance as well. Many concentration difficulties arise from athletes trying to focus in too many directions and on too many cues. Even if these are all potentially relevant to performance, it may be far beyond attentional capacity to keep up with every one of them. In such cases, application of the K.I.S.S. (Keep It Simple & Smart) principle is an effective intervention. Most competitive demands can be faced with (1) a clear objective (what you want to achieve), and (2) a collection of one to four intentions for thinking and action (what you want to consider and do). If this simple set proves insufficient, it is a sign that further training is needed to make more aspects of performance automatic. In that case, simplify the performance demands for the athlete in the short term, and plan long-term training for mastering additional skills.

Whether or not a focus is simple will depend on the individual athlete. Some athletes will readily deal with facts and analytic information, whereas others will find this difficult, exhausting, and even de-motivating. Some athletes will easily handle holistic awareness of rich somatic data and a wide array external cues, whereas others will find such information confusing, beyond interpretation, or overwhelming. A skill that is well learned can be executed with a simple thought, but complex novel skills will require much more attention. The goal in interventions is to capitalize on what the individual performer can do easily, and work to make less familiar demands easier to handle through knowledge, experience, and training.

Deal with Distractions

The simplest way to deal with distractions is to remove them altogether. There is no sense in going to elaborate lengths to handle distractions if they can simply be avoided. If, for example, an athlete gets distracted warming up with competitors and it is possible to arrange a secluded space, do so. However, most distractions—both internal and external—are a natural part of competitive performance. Each distraction may have its own specific characteristics and unique effects on a particular athlete. Therefore, detailed exploration of the distraction and its effects on the performer is almost always beneficial. The consultant will then need to address the specific issues that arise. There is no easy way to describe all the possible interventions that a sport psychology consultant might employ to aid a particular athlete with specific distractions. Each case will require a collection of professional skills.

Beyond the complexities of dealing with specific distractions for unique individuals, there are a couple of general suggestions for interventions. Many distractions are distracting because they are novel or extreme—they activate our natural orienting response. Loud noises, bright lights, quick movements, and any other strange or sudden sensory input naturally draw attention. Preparing for such distractions through simulation training can make them seem less novel or extreme to the athlete. Potential distractions that have become normal and expected occurrences lose much of their power to distract. Think, for example, of the professional basketball player who can shoot free-throws under conditions of extreme crowd noise and visual distractions behind the basket. Simulation training can involve mock competitive situations, as well as imaginary rehearsal of performing in the face of distractions. Actual and imaginable overexposure can serve to desensitize the athlete.

The other general approach to dealing with distractions is to train the athlete to view anything other than task focus as irrelevant. When the desired focus is considered of paramount importance, people tend to disregard anything other than this dominant intention. Development of such concentration requires both a clear, motivated intentional focus and a firm belief in the irrelevance of other stimuli. This does not mean that extraneous stimuli must be totally blocked, however, only that they are given little attention and allowed to pass easily out of consciousness if irrelevant to performance. One world class cyclist referred to this type of concentration when he commented in a session that "if a train were to crash next to the road during the final sprint to the finish, I would know that it happened, but I wouldn't waste any energy in reacting to it—all my attention would be on my body, my bike, the pack and the finish." When performance focus is clear and of dominant importance, attention will generally stay on it.

Develop Plans and Routines

Competition plans and pre-performance routines can be excellent concentration guides. They serve to organize knowledge of relevant and irrelevant cues, and provide a blueprint for intentional focus and action. Plans can be drawn up for any aspect of training, traveling, or competing. In as much as they give the athlete a sense of security and effective strategies for preparation and performance they are invaluable. Routines are typically designed to focus mind and body control down to the absolute essential elements of performance. The objective is to have the body in the appropriate physiological state, the mind confident, positive and aware, and the perceptual-motor system operating from a clear intention for action. As usual, the simpler the plans and routines, the easier they will be to execute in and around competition.

Refine Specific Expertise and Trust

Attentional capacity can be better managed by shifting from Control Processing to Automatic Processing and accessing more attentional pools for information processing. Automatic Processing is largely dependent on training and experience, so there is little substitute for the normal emphasis in sport on physical practice and performance opportunities. However, coaches and athletes can be more efficient in developing automaticity of desired skills (1) by implementing consistent high quality practice (i.e., train the precision desired in competition to 'groove in' correct performance), (2) by stressing right-brain processing (e.g., training performance by 'sense' and 'feel'), and (3) by using imagery rehearsal (e.g., increasing quantity and variety of the athlete's competitive experiences through imagined performance).

Just as attentional demands can be reduced through automaticity, relative attention capacity may be enhanced by accessing a wider range of processing pools. Although we don't know the actual limitations, there is sufficient evidence to suggest that emphasizing different sensory modes for information processing can effectively increase the field of concentration. For example, once dribbling a basketball can be done by proprioceptive and kinesthetic feel, vision is free to process other information. Similarly, using auditory cues may eliminate the need to look at a teammate for strategic information. The overriding tendency of most athletes is for visual processing to dominate attention. In a great number of cases, auditory, proprioceptive, and kinesthetic processing are just as valuable for performance, if not more so. Expertise in the use of these sensory systems will not only enhance most physical skills, it will open up greater attentional capacity during competitive performance.

The development of greater Automatic Processing and broader use of multiple sensory modes requires that much of performance control be turned over to right-brain, integrative functioning. Unfortunately, we tend to think that the 'intelligent' left-brain needs to be in control as much as possible (this appears true at least in Western cultures). 'Thinking' oneself right out of the game is a particularly left-brain fault, as are trying too hard and the ineffective 'guiding' of complex motor skills. The ability to actually use the more effective right-brain processing in physical performance is dependent on the ability to trust control to that hemisphere. A whole chapter could be written to address the issue of trust. At it's essence, trust in sport performance is based on the faith to allow information to be processed and actions executed in the integrative fashion too quick for full analytical review. Performance needs to be trusted to flow without the interfering need to consciously control or analyze it.

Trust is trained by experience in the integrative processing mode. It also relies on the development of a core belief that best performances flow from sensing and doing, rather than complicated analytical thought and trying. As an athlete becomes familiar with integrative functioning and can realize the intelligence in trusting, then concentration can be freely directed as needed to meet the performance demands.

Conclusions

Concentration is integral to sport performance. It is the mechanism by which we control attention to receive information, to process thoughts, and to direct actions. Concentration is complex, and effectively helping athletes and coaches with concentration issues requires a certain level of expertise. This chapter has introduced a basic working knowledge of concentration for sport psychology consultants. Like physical skills, concentration skills can be enhanced through intelligent planning and diligent training. Throughout a quality training program, specific consideration need be given to concentration principles, to sport demands, and to each athlete's abilities. Importantly, it should also be emphasized that intervention methods go beyond simple corrections for concentration problems. They provide the basis for development of optimal concentration skills and therefore optimal performance. Virtually every performer can gain from improved concentration.

Case Studies of Concentration

#1: High School Baseball Pitcher

Introduction:

Charles is a varsity high school pitcher. Historically, Charles has been a promising pitcher with "control" being a primary strength. However, he has recently experienced uncharacteristic lapses of control. In discussions with Charles, no other factors appeared to be intervening variables, so we went to work on developing stronger concentration skills.

Intervention:

I initially asked Charles to recall a time when everything felt great and automatic. In his response he used the expression of "being in the groove". I then asked him if a suitable goal would be to always feel that way on the mound. He responded that such a goal would be great. I suggested that he could learn to put himself into the "groove" when he wanted or needed to rather than just hoping it would happen.

Together, we devised a plan to develop this ability to put Charles in the groove. It began with the building of a "memory bank" of how the groove feels so that it can be recalled whenever desired. This feeling needs to be actively stored by taking the time to savor it and not let it be taken for granted. The second phase of the plan was for Charles to make a commitment to take control over the mental side of his pitching by learning to use a "reset" routine any time he felt out of synch.

The reset routine consisted of:
- ◆ Observe what is going on, what is wrong, what needs to change?

- Make a <u>strategy</u> for correcting the problem. Do you need to make a technical change or just regain your rhythm?
- Recall your desired feel from memory and <u>feel yourself</u> making the desired change or in the desired rhythm.
- Say a <u>trigger</u> phrase or word to yourself to establish the change you desire. Rhythm, relax, drive, snap, pull down, flow,...

Charles was to practice this every so often in practice (every 15 pitches) so that it became comfortable. It can't just be pulled out during the next game without it having been practiced. Therefore we developed a game strategy:

- When you are in the groove just let it happen and let it be natural; you don't need to always be thinking about it.
- When you are not in the groove, then use the reset routine to work back into the groove. Some games you may not even use the routine and some you may use it three or four times but you will have it when you need it.

Outcome:

Charles' coach commented that he was pitching great and seemed to be in "control of himself". During his last outing he was called into a tough situation in relief and struck out 4 of 5 batters faced and walked none.

#2: Male College Basketball Player

Introduction:

Felipe is a varsity NCAA Div-1 basketball player. Five games into the season, Felipe is shooting 30% from the charity stripe. Concentrating mostly on mechanics the previous year, his shooting percentage was approximately 40%. Citing the lack of success the previous year and the extremely poor shooting the current year, the coaches are now ready to have him work on mental aspects.

Intervention:

During the first session we discussed mental principles of free throws. This necessitated addressing how the free throw, a relatively simple skill, can become extremely difficult. The intervening factors include:

- Situational Pressure (game is on the line; crowd is harassing the shooter, etc.)
- Poor Past Performance (missed a few in a row; missed during crucial part of game; % going down, etc.)
- Media Perception (poor shooter from the line; free throws cost team game)
- Fan's Expectations ("Oh no, not him on the line!")
- Over Analyzing Mechanics (blowing every miss on a mechanical flaw)
- Forcing, Pressing, Guiding (I have to make this; I can't miss another, etc.)

We discussed that in order to make a free throw into a simple shot again, one has to block out all the factors listed above.

Felipe wanted to know how? How could he block these factors? We discussed two key points:

1. Replace the wrong thoughts with positive thoughts.
2. Know ahead of time what you are going to think at the line. Then there is no room for the negative to enter.

We talked about how all performance is controlled by thoughts; it is no different with free throws. Therefore choosing the right thoughts is the key to becoming a great player.

An effective means of establishing consistency is to develop a mental routine by picking three cue words, which trigger the mind to mind to think of the most important thoughts possible. These three cues are: 1) VISUALIZE, 2) FEEL, and 3) TRUST.

SEE IT: Visualize the shot. This focuses the mind on the target and sends positive information to the muscles for "feel."

FEEL IT: Feel the rhythm and the smooth motion of the shot just visualized. This sets the muscles up to shoot the shot with a smooth, relaxed, rhythm.

TRUST IT: As the shot is initiated one thought should fill the mind. Trust is one of the most powerful trigger words in performance.

We then went to the gym where Felipe completed the following:

a) 25 shots against the wall, concentrating on going through the routine out loud.
b) 10 shots from 10 ft., concentrating on routine out loud.
c) 10 shots from top of key, concentrating on routine out loud.
d) 20 shots from free throw line concentrating on routine out loud.

To conclude, we simply reviewed what we had done.

During our second meeting, I asked how the adjustment to using the routine went during practice. He shared that he thought it went well; he felt comfortable with the routine. We then went to the gym and repeated the same drills completed during the first meeting.

For the third meeting, I had Felipe make an audio tape using a script I wrote based on what he said during our first session. He was free to change any word or phrase to fit his needs. He was told to listen often (5-10 times per day) as we would not get together for one month due to the Winter Break.

Initial Audio Tape Script

With each game my confidence is growing. I see improvement... I believe that I will continue to improve... I trust my routine and am committed to it for the season... It is working just like Dr. _____ said... In the beginning it was new and a little distracting, just as he said... I know that when I come to a change I may go backwards one step before I go forward two... I have been patient as I have gone through the one step backwards... I am now GOING FORWARD... My shots are starting to fall... I will continue to be patient... I will continue to improve as the tournament nears... I know that change takes time and my patience is beginning to pay off... I will continue to improve at the line... I will surprise the crowd in each game to come... I believe in my routine...I can see myself at the line... I look forward to shooting free throws now because I am improving ...The Ref hands me the ball. I take a deep breath and as I do my shoulders,

arms and hands become relaxed. It is a good feeling. I then take 3 dribbles, loosening my hands
and fingers I then look at my spot on the front of the rim... I am totally focused on this point.
As I say "SEE IT.", I can see the shot traveling through the air, into the basket.
I then say "FEEL IT.", and I feel the rhythm of the shot. It feels smooth and confident... I then
say "TRUST." as I focus on the front of the rim and release the ball. My eyes never leave this
point on the rim... swish. It feels so good when I follow my routine; I know that I will continue to
improve. I can.

After returning from Winter Break, we met again and discussed his progress and commitment to routine and tape. In terms of focusing, Felipe's eyes were leaving the rim and moving to the ball during release. He then was missing long by focusing on the space above the middle of the basket. We attempted to remedy this by having him change his focus to a point on the front of the rim and not allowing his focus to move to the ball during the shot. Felipe then made a new tape, incorporating these ideas with his routine.

We continued to meet and make new audio-tapes to reflect changes in thought, focus, or routine and to keep the script fresh. The following is the final script in preparation for the NCAA Tournament:

The NCAA TOURNAMENT IS HERE... I have looked forward to these games... As I look
back over the past few weeks I am pleased with my progress... With each game my confidence
has grown... I see continued improvement in my shot... My free throws have been great. I will
continue to shoot well from the line... I know that all I have to do is trust my routine. I will
continue my commitment to it.. I have shown everyone that I am a good free throw shooter... My
confidence is back... I have been patient, it has paid off... The plan that I have followed has been
successful... I will continue to go through my routine... I look forward to stepping up to the line...
I look forward to getting fouled... I look forward to having other teams foul me... The free throw
line is a great place to be... I look forward to stepping up to the line with the game on the line... I
look forward to shooting free throws when the pressure is on... I will simply go through my
routine... Deep Breath 3 dribbles... See it... Feel it... Trust it... Swish... Deep Breath... 3 dribbles
See it.. Feel it... Trust it.. Swish... My routine gives me confidence... It makes my shot feel
automatic and smooth... When I go to the line I am totally focused... My concentration is
powerful... My thoughts are positive...The ref hands me the ball I take a deep breath As I do my
shoulders, arms, and hands become relaxed...It is a good feeling... I then take 3 dribbles
loosening my hands and fingers. I then look at my spot on the front of the rim... I am totally
focused on this point....My concentration is powerful...I can see the shot traveling through the
air, into the basket...I feel the rhythm of the shot... It feels smooth and confident...I focus on the
front of the rim and release the ball... My eyes never leave this point on the rim... Swish. It feels
so good when I follow my routine; I know that I will continue to improve I can shoot free throws
well I have proven this over the past few games... I will continue in the games to come See it ..
Feel it Trust... Swish... Deep breath 3 dribbles... See it ..Feel it Trust .. Swish. I am right on
schedule...My work is paying off .. My shots will continue to fall...I am committed...See it...
Feel it...Trust... Swish.

The following shows Felipe's performance at the free throw line, relative to the intervention being conducted.

Stages	Games	FT's Made-attempted (%)
Pre-Intervention	5	6-20 (30%)
Initial Contact-First Tape	13	16-45 (36%)
Second Tape	4	3-13 (23%)
Third Tape	8	19-38 (50%)
Fourth Tape	2	4-7 (57%)
Conf./NCAA Tournament	5	16-26 (62%)

Outcome:

Reviewing the season, certain obstacles were noteworthy. The first was media pressure; articles written in local newspapers and repeated questions about "Why can't you shoot free throws?". A second obstacle was staying committed during continued poor shooting. A final obstacle was that Felipe was a "reaction" ball player who was being asked to think sequentially. In the beginning the routine was a distraction itself.

Implications of this case are:

♦ During learning phase the routine may be a distraction and cause player to stay the same or even go backwards before progress is made. Patience and commitment are a must. There is No Quick Fix!

♦ We focused on shooting well during the tournament from day 1. We made a long term goal and commitment to be patient; the work will pay off at tournament time.

♦ Patience and long tern commitment paid off as Felipe shot 62% during tournaments (conference and NCAA).

♦ The tapes reinforced the use of the routine which kept the goal alive across the season.

The routine is important for several reasons:

1. One knows what one is going to think on the line. The thought process at the line becomes focused and consistent.

2. Thoughts have been chosen ahead of time, so there is no need to worry about what to think. There is no need to block out thoughts.

3. There is no room for outside factors which complicate the simplicity of the free throw because of the focus.

4. It frees the athlete up to shoot the ball with a fluid motion and rhythm rather than tension.

5. It gives the athlete a goal to work towards besides making the shot. Making the shot becomes the consequence of going through the mental routine.

Felipe encountered several things that others are likely to experience with the institution of routines:

1. The mental routine will be distracting in the beginning. After 20-50 shots the hand will be "triggered" by the words. The shot will then begin to feel automatic and fluid.

2. One must be patient at the line. The routine ups the odds of success. However, a miss will sometimes happen. Learn how to respond effectively. Respond by saying "I'm Due Next Time."

3. One must make a 100% commitment to the routine. It is fact (not some theory) that thinking this way increases an athlete's chances for success.

4. One should have a "Passion" to go to the line. Look forward and dream about going to the line with the game on the line.

#3: Female Junior National Distance Runner

Introduction:

Janice is a very talented 17 year old high school senior middle distance runner. She was a member of the USA World Track and Field Championships Team. Janice asked to see me regarding her ability to concentrate during races. She was specifically having a difficult time coping with the pain and discomfort she was experiencing during the course of her races.

She felt she could have performed better in her recent races but the "period of fatigue" she anticipated and experienced before and during her races (1) created self-doubt regarding the race outcome; and (2) affected her ability to maintain her racing pace and "stay in the race." She was attempting to qualify the next day for the world championships in the 3000 meters, a distance which she had not run competitively for the last four years (her previous best was 10:04). She had already qualified for the team in the 1500 meters and therefore felt the upcoming race was a "no pressure" situation.

Intervention:

The evening before her qualifying race we spoke at length about her perceptions and feelings regarding her racing ability and effectiveness. She needed to recognize the fact that fatigue is an integral part of her sport and that she must understand the "ebb and flow" of athletic competition. She would need to accept the fact that she must endure the difficult and challenging aspects of athletic performance in order to achieve effective and consistent performances. I reassured her that this process was under her control and challenged her with the following statement: "Do you train to train or do you train to race?"

I encouraged her to trust in her preparation and had her talk about her accomplishments and athletic talents in an effort to reinforce her feelings of competency. It was important to help her identify her skills as a middle distance runner (i.e., is she a power or a flow/temp runner?; her sense, control and ability to run an appropriate pace; her finishing ability and talent, etc.) in order to help her positively reaffirm her athletic talents as well as to have her reflect on her past successful racing experiences.

I suggested that Janice establish, in writing, a flexible race plan which incorporated:

♦   The lap or pace times she needed to reach her overall qualifying time of 9:35;
♦   Physical skills she could incorporate into her race plan to help her effectively deal with the discomfort/fatigue she would experience during the race (i.e., pumping her arms vigorously in order to regain her desired tempo, controlling her breathing rhythm, etc.);
♦   Cue words which triggered the use of specific racing strategies and physical skills (i.e., "tempo," relax and flow," "lift and sprint," "control"). These cue words were to

be used during the actual race.

I asked Janice to review her race plan with her coach prior to the race.

Outcome:

Janice achieved her goal (9:30) by running 9:28 the following day. She was very excited and felt in control throughout the entire race. She continued to work closely with her coach to implement strategies to insure her performance effectiveness and went on to qualify for the-3000 meter final at the world championships, improving her personal best to 9:25.

#4: PGA Player

Introduction:

I was contacted by Chuck at the end of May, approximately halfway through the year. At that time he was about 90-100 on the money list and had made about $65,000. Chuck indicated that he had an inability to concentrate on the course. He was very indecisive about club selection. He was also very intrapunitive. Perhaps one of the most demanding, negative self-talking athletes I had spoken with in 10 years.

He indicated a desire for help. Chuck had a previous encounter with a sports psychologist 3-4 years ago that was not positive. This sport psychologist had contacted him and wanted to caddie for him and become ego-involved with his career. He was willing to contact me because of a referral from his attorney/agent who was familiar with me. He wanted advice over the phone and I obliged to some degree. However, an initial meeting was arranged for his hometown during the week in May when he was not playing in Atlanta.

Intervention:

I traveled to Chuck's home and spent 2 days with him. I utilized a paper and pencil "Golfing Profile" form to gather some intake information. This inventory proved very useful. We talked for 2-3 hours, went to the course and hit balls, played 9 holes and met again the next day with his wife, also a very good golfer. I determined that his concentration problem was due to high internal overload; that is, he was thinking too much on the course.

I watched Chuck hit shot after shot where he wanted the ball to go. Yet, he was always overly critical of the result. I utilized Nideffer's Model of Attentional Control to explain to him where his attentional difficulties occurred. I did a lot of listening and guiding his own discoveries and insights into his problems. I utilized SCORE as a way to go over his pre-shot routine, S (Scan), C (Contemplate), 0 (Overall feeling), R (Ritual), and E (Execute). We decided to cut down the amount of time in the scan and contemplate areas and to concentrate on the feel, ritual and execute stages. Our plan to eliminate or cut down the time for second guessing club selection, negative self-talk time and accentuate the good feelings associated with past performance. We needed to get him to literally learn to play out of his head.

Outcome:

I made four personalized audio-cassettes over the following 3 months and have communicated over the phone several times; usually after competitive rounds from the tournament site. Chuck had 3 top 10 finishes in those months including ties for 2nd, 5th, and 7th. He has also had several top 20 finishes, including a major, and has not missed a cut. His income increased to where he had broken into the top 50 on the money list. He has become less intrapunitive and more trusting of his decisions on the course.

#5: Male College Discus Thrower

Introduction:

Roland is a sophomore discuss thrower who has both Olympic aspirations and capabilities. He has had to overcome tremendous adversity in his life (Hodgkin's Disease is in remission, appendectomy a few months before the Olympic trials his freshmen year). Roland is extremely dedicated and committed to excellence. He understands principles of mental training very well and we have worked extensively in the areas of goal setting, visualization, and mental readiness states to perform. He has developed a motto he lives his life by: "Inch by Inch is a cinch, yard by yard is hard".

Roland has a tendency to go to his own beat. Although he is very loyal and dedicated to those people he considers close, he is somewhat of a social isolate among his teammates. He does not tolerate other people's little idiosyncrasies very well (which includes what most people consider typical college student behaviors). He has his own set of values he lives his life by, and his way of dealing with people he cannot tolerate is to avoid them altogether (as he puts it, "get rid of the distraction"). In addition, he does not handle criticism well and I have had to intervene in coach-athlete and athlete-athlete relationships involving Roland.

Unbeknown to me (and others), he broke up with his long time girlfriend prior to the conference meet (one of his only true sources of support at the university) and consequently, did not perform well at all. The incident came to my attention when talking indirectly with another track athlete about the event itself. Knowing something about Roland's values and sense of loyalty to those he considers close, I sought him out immediately.

Intervention:

We talked about the break up, its sources and consequences, and his poor performance at conference. Since NCAA's were coming up soon (a very important goal for him) and he had been training well prior to conference, intervention focused on letting go of the conference meet, the face of adversity, distraction control, and seizing the opportunity at hand.

One of the ironies of the situation was he had to compete in New Orleans, site of a poor performance in Olympic trials qualifying meet the year before (coming back from chronic shin splints and bout with appendicitis). Therefore, I did some coping rehearsal techniques to help him reaffirm his goals and stay focused on the task at hand. Other distraction control techniques addressed the break-up with his girlfriend, dealing with the weather, and people's perception of him choking at conference. In addition, we talked about his tendency to rush himself when he becomes over aroused after fouling and the need to take it one throw at a time.

Outcome:

Roland won the NCAA crown by 5' on his last throw. He and his coach called from New Orleans in celebration of the victory. He said our work on dealing with distractions, trusting himself and keeping "his" focus in the heat of the battle was a big part of his success at the meet.

#6: Elite Female Pistol Shooter

Introduction:

Tyra is a national level female pistol shooter. She sought sport psychology assistance to help her break through a performance barrier that she felt prevented her from competing successfully against the best women in the country and gaining a place on international teams. An experienced competitor in her early thirties, Tyra was conscientious in her training and dedicated to improving in a sport she loves. She reported frustration in losing concentration in competition, particularly after one or two poor shots in a row. Tyra felt that eliminating bouts of inconsistency in the midst of competition would likely produce scores that would allow her to step to the next level of ranking in her sport. After considerable exploration of the issues, we decided that we would work on her concentration skills through development of a dependable pre-shot routine for the precision segment of Women's Sport Pistol competition.

Intervention:

The first step of the intervention was to have Tyra thoroughly review her thoughts and actions in competitive performance. She already was in the habit of keeping extensive notes on her shooting, so it was fairly easy for her to review past performances, as well as record observations of current training sessions to ascertain her pre-shot patterns. Although she had some general habits for preparing herself and performing, Tyra did not have a consistent routine. Therefore, I asked her to create a sequence of thoughts and actions that would describe how she might want to approach each shot. On one side of a blank page she wrote down the Mental Aspects, and on the other she listed the Physical Aspects of her proposed sequence. She consulted with her coach for advice and to make certain that all important elements were included.

Working from her draft, we then approached development of the routine from the basis of concentration principles. The objective was to create a simple series of steps that would allow Tyra to focus in on the relevant information, while disregarding irrelevant cues. Physically, we wanted her to feel stable, relaxed, and kinesthetically aware of her motor actions. Psychologically, we wanted her to be present-minded, calm, confident, and clear on her intention for performance.

We created a six-step performance routine. Labels attached to each step were, 'Ready,' 'Observe,' 'Intention,' 'Perform,' 'Analysis,' and 'Reset.' At the "load" command from the range official (beginning of each set of five shots), Tyra would deliberately count out the rounds and load her pistol. She would indicate 'Ready' to herself as she felt the gun in her grip and brought her focus to the task. She then moved on to 'Observe' as she set herself into her stance and looked to the 10-ring of the target, connecting to it mentally by thinking "you're mine." Maintaining her stance and a lowered gun, Tyra would then set her 'Intention' with a mental image of the shot, emphasizing the feel of the trigger pressure, the movement of sights into line, and the straight shot of the bullet through the center of the target. Once she had 'seen it and felt it', she was ready to trust her performance and do it, so advanced to 'Perform.' Coordinating her breath with her movements, Tyra would raise the gun, then lower the gun while feeling the trigger and watching the sights, staying focused through the break of the shot through the target. The resulting shot then received a quick review during the 'Analysis' step, only to draw objective information (e.g., shot on or off). Finally, Tyra went to 'Reset' to conclude that shot and be clear to move on to the next. If the shot went well, she would say "keep it," and if it was not what she wanted, she would say "let it go," and imagine a shot through the ten-ring. When she felt comfortable with 'Reset,' Tyra would begin the next shot by focusing back to her grip and 'Ready.'

Tyra devoted time at each training session to specifically work on the routine. At first, she would sometimes get confused, distracted, or forget parts of the routine. She also found times when concentration on the routine disrupted her ability to shoot well. Tyra kept notes and steadily became familiar and comfortable with the routine, both in concept and in practice. Once established, Tyra found it easy to perform the routine on each shot and remain well inside the six minute time limit for each series of five shots. Refinements in the routine will likely continue over her career.

Outcome:

The initial work that Tyra put into developing her routine paid off within several weeks of training. At the national championships she performed with better consistency than ever before and won the open Women's Sport Pistol event. Tyra reported that she executed her routine over 85% of the time during precision shooting, and that it seemed to give her better control. She noted that she had been able to recover immediately from several poor shots during the competition. Beyond being an effective technical procedure, Tyra indicated that the routine gave her confidence in a definite mental focus that she could rely on during the entire performance.

Tyra has since further refined her pre-shot routine. She has changed a few of the mental and physical cues in the sequence. As her routine has become automatic, her coach has encouraged her to become less conscious (analytical) of the process and more intuitive (integrative) in her performance. We are using imagery rehearsal to reinforce this trend. She now only needs to think through the steps at times when she is distracted or has lost the 'feeling' for her shots. But, when she feels the need, her routine is always there for her to direct her performance. Based on her improvements and perceived potential, Tyra has been selected for an elite athlete program to train for international events and the next Olympic Games. She continues to develop mastery in her chosen sport.

Discussion Questions

1. Describe the meaning of the words 'attention' and 'concentration'. Discuss the different ways that athletes and coaches use these terms, and suggest how a sport psychology consultant might explain them to clients.

2. Consider golf putting, a floor routine in gymnastics, and a team ball sport, such as soccer, basketball, or volleyball. How might the three levels of attentional direction be differentially required in these sport activities and at different moments within competitive performance?

3. Describe the arousal-attention relationship. Provide examples of sports which might be best performed under low, moderate, and high arousal, and explain the reasoning behind your choices.

4. Relate a situation where you have witnessed a distraction that disrupted concentration and hindered competitive performance. Describe the situation in terms of attentional principles.

5. Describe a situation where you have had difficulties with concentration. Using the diagnostic questions in the chapter, determine the major problem(s) for you. Suggest an intervention approach to work on the difficulty you experienced.

6. For each case study, identify into which of the three categories of common concentration issues that the case would be placed. Explain each case study in terms of the general concentration issue involved.

7. For each case study, identify the intervention employed. How does the intervention address the concentration problem?

References

Abernathy, B. (1993). Attention. In R.N. Singer, M. Murphey, & L.K. Tennant (Eds.), Handbook of research in sport psychology (pp. 127-170). New York: Macmillan.

Boutcher, S.H. (1992). Attention and athletic performance: An integrated approach. In T. Horn (Ed.), Advances in sport psychology (pp. 251-265). Champaign, IL: Human Kinetics.

Hardy, L., Jones, J.G. & Gould, D. (1996). Understanding psychological preparation for sport: Theory and practice of elite performers. West Sussex: John Wiley & Sons.

Moran, A.P. (1996). The psychology of concentration in sport performers: A cognitive analysis. East Sussex: Psychology Press.

Nideffer, R.M. (1993). Concentration and attention control training. In J.M. Williams (Ed.), Applied sport psychology: From personal growth to peak performance (2nd ed.) (pp. 243-261). Mountain View, CA: Mayfield.

Summers, J.J. & Ford, S. (1995). Attention in sport. In T. Morris & J. Summers (Eds.), Sport psychology: Theory, applications and issues (pp. 63-89). Chichester: John Wiley.

Weinberg, R.S. & Gould, D. (1995). Foundations of sport and exercise psychology. Champaign, IL: Human Kinetics.

CHAPTER 8

~ Coach-Athlete Issues ~

Jodi Yambor, Thomas College

In the world of sports, the word "coach" has taken on a variety of connotations. They include leader, teacher, role model, disciplinarian, friend, counselor, parent-substitute, trainer, psychologist, strategist, and recruiter. For many, the term "coach" personifies outstanding individuals who are dedicated to the pursuit of excellence through their teaching, service, and personal example. However, for others, the word "coach" may bring back negative memories of conflict, frustration, resentment, anger, and unfulfilled dreams. The reality of sport is that the quality of the sport experience for all athletes will likely be no better then the personal, moral, and leadership qualities of the coach who is providing that experience. (Vernacchia, McGuire, & Cook, 1992)

Coaches who positively affect the lives of their athletes cultivate relationships with them based on two-way communication, mutual trust, and respect. If this type of relationship fails to develop, numerous problems may arise, including those pertaining to playing time and personality differences. What follows is an elaboration of the coach-athlete dynamics. Recommendations for the applied sport psychology professional are given both for working with the athletes to address these issues, and working with the coaches. Much of the information is approached from a "working with the coach" perspective. This is intentional, because the sport psychology professional, many times, must work "through" the coach to address coach-athlete issues. The coach is viewed as essential to the success of applied sport psychology interventions whether or not the coach is "part of the problem."

Playing Time Dynamics

Almost every athlete is extremely concerned with the quantity and quality of playing time they will receive. One main reason athletes participate is to showcase their skills and abilities in competition. Everyone knows that starters, and, to a lesser degree, substitutes receive more attention, benefits, recognition, and tangible rewards than do bench warmers.

Conflicts relative to playing time actually begin during the recruiting process. Frequently, coaches only tell athletes what they want to hear when they are trying to get them to join their team. By the same token, athletes frequently only hear what they want to hear when coaches speak to them. This is supported by the findings of Henschen and Miner (1989) who report that in the process of interpreting verbal and non-verbal messages, information may be lost or distorted. Consequently, the athletes' role expectations are often way out of line with reality well before they ever set foot on the court, field, or deck.

After tryouts and initial practices are held, the coach names the team and starters. In many cases this is a very subjective process, which can be affected by a variety of things. Coaches are frequently accused of "playing favorites" and often place athletes in roles with which they are not accustomed to playing. Subsequently, these athletes tend to question the integrity of the coach; frequently, badmouthing the coach to teammates, other coaches, teachers, parents, or anyone who will listen.

Throughout the season, the playing status of some athletes changes due to team rules violations, academic problems, missed or poor practice sessions or "bad attitudes", whereas other athletes status remains unchanged. If team members are treated inconsistently by coaches it serves to fuel both coach-athlete and intra-team conflict.

Personality-Related Conflicts

There are countless "personality conflicts" that could arise between coach and athlete. In this chapter, the discussion will be limited to those conflicts related to leadership style, communication style, and coach-athlete relationships.

Leadership Style

Often personality conflicts can be attributed to the leadership style of the coach. LeUnes and Nation (1989) report that the majority of coaches tend to adopt a task oriented leadership style which is very directive and purposeful. However, Carron (1988) found that more experienced athletes preferred democratic coaching behaviors which involved independent action and stressed personal authority and independent decision making. Carron also determined that male athletes tended to prefer a more autocratic style, whereas female athletes had a preference for more democratic behavior from their coaches.

Communication Style

Highly interrelated with leadership style is communication style. Some coaches do not like to communicate, nor do they feel the need to regularly communicate with their athletes. Often, coaches who believe they are "all-knowing", don't feel the need to interact with their athletes. If any communication does take place, it is one-way from coach to athlete. Coaches who use this style frequently perceive athletes' questions as a lack of respect or personal affronts. Consequently, their lack of communication, poor communication and frequent miscommunication causes conflict.

Other coaches cause conflicts with their athletes by choosing to communicate in a negative manner. They yell and scream at their athletes, and generally tell them what they are doing wrong. Often, they even direct derogatory comments toward their athletes in an attempt to motivate them. Carron (1988) found that athletes desire socially supportive coaching behaviors, which express a concern on the coach's part for the well being of each athlete by emphasizing a positive team climate and warm inner personal relationships. Interestingly, Tuffy (1995) found that coaches reported differences between male and female athletes, not so much in what they communicated to them, but in how they communicated. The coaches tended to be blunt and confrontational with male athletes. However, because of the perceived tendency of females to internalize poor performances, internalize criticism, and to react emotionally in these situations, coaches tempered their critique of the female athlete's performance.

Coach-Athlete Relationships

Additionally, coaches who are cold or indifferent may develop problems with their athletes. Many athletes have a strong need to be liked by their coach and to develop a relationship with them that extends beyond the boundaries of the sport. Consequently, they will not be happy if the coach is only concerned with them as an athlete as opposed to a total person. Tuffy (1995) found that female athletes want and need more from their coach then just basic coaching. Female athletes want a relationship and frequent individual communication with their coach. Tuffy suggests that because the coach-athlete relationship is of value to the female athlete, she wants the coach to demonstrate that he or she also values the relationship.

Performance Implications of Coach-Athlete Conflict

Coach - The performance implications of coach-athlete conflict for the coach depend on a number of things, including: the coach's personality, leadership, and communication styles; the talent and ability level of the athlete; the degree of influence the athlete has on fellow teammates; the intensity level of the conflict; how well the coach handles conflict; how directly the coach works with the athlete; and the degree of pressure on the coach to win. Ultimately, the coach is in a power position and can choose to deal with the athlete in a variety of ways:
- They could try to work things out with the athlete.
- They could maintain the status quo.
- They could ignore the situation.
- They could be harder on the athlete.
- They could dismiss the athlete from the team.

Potentially, conflict with an athlete could cause the coach to become angry, anxious, defensive, depressed, irritable, and fatigued. It could decrease their efficiency, effectiveness, and self-esteem, which could lead to lower levels of motivation and make their job less enjoyable. Conflict with an athlete could also negatively effect a coach's personal life, social life, health, and well being. It could push the coach into a state of burnout.

Athlete - The performance implications of coach-athlete conflict for the athlete also depends on a variety of factors. Some of these factors are: the personality type and communication style of the athlete; the support system available to the athlete; the importance of sport participation and performance to the athlete; how important it is for the coach to like them; how well they get along with their teammates, and; the degree of influence they have on their teammates.
Conflict can occasionally have a positive effect on athletes; causing them to work harder to prove the coach wrong. Probably more often, however, conflict causes the athlete to become

depressed, resentful, and angry. Their practice performance may decrease even more due to their inability to concentrate, lack of motivation, their decreased sense of self worth, and the feeling that playing the game just isn't fun anymore. It often makes them wish they had joined another team. It can also have an adverse effect on their academics, personal, social life, and overall health. Athletes are also likely candidates for burnout.

Interventions for Coaches

Communication Keys and Recommendations

There are a number of options coaches can choose from to help prevent problems with their athletes. First, the coach must communicate in order to establish credibility and to begin developing a trusting, caring relationship with their athletes. Coaches must remember that actions speak louder than words, so they should be encouraged to demonstrate honesty and caring, and serve as a good role model. Coaches should also become familiar with non-sport related things about your athletes, sharing "non-coach" things, spending time with the athletes outside of practice, letting the athletes get to know the coach's family, participating as a team in various activities unrelated to sport, and having an open-door policy to be available to the athletes.

It is also extremely important that the coach communicate to each athlete what his or her role is on the team. This communication should take place as early in the season as possible. Every athlete has a role expectation, which may or may not be accurate. Therefore, it is the coach's job to provide role clarity for the athlete and if necessary assist them with role acceptance and role performance. It is advisable for coaches to reduce uncertainties for their athletes as soon as possible.

In order to further improve communication early in the season, the sport psychologist could have the coaching staff brainstorm to come up with a list of characteristics that describe their ideal athlete. At the same time, the athletes can brainstorm and come up with a list of attributes for their ideal coach. The coaches and athletes then share their lists with each other and discuss them. Later in the season, the coach and athlete can each be given 3" x 5" cards and asked to write five things they like about each other on the cards. Possibly, depending on the team and their situation, they could also be asked to write three things they would like to see each other improve. This information could then be shared and discussed.

Communication skills development can also help the coach. Some suggestions are that the coach should communicate in a direct manner rather then hinting or implying. Send messages that are clear, consistent, and complete. Repeat important information and then ask for feedback to determine if the message was accurately received. Coaches must also make sure that their verbal and non-verbal messages match, because they do not want to send mixed messages. It is important to remember, however, that coaches must communicate in a style that is consistent with their personality and coaching style (Wooten, 1992). Additionally coaches should strive to create an environment which encourages athletes to freely initiate communication.

Coaches can also practice being effective listeners. They need to give their undivided attention to the athlete, squarely face them, utilize an open posture, lean toward them, use frequent direct eye contact, relax, attempt to empathize with the athlete, and restate in their own words the message they heard from the athlete.

Coaches need to remember that information is power. Consequently, they need to develop systems to uniformly and consistently disperse information to their team. Perhaps it will be delivered by the team captain, or on larger teams, through a team council. Regularly scheduled team meetings provide a sense of stability and organization as well as improving communication.

Coaches can also learn how to deal with conflict situations. Ravizza and Sime (1991) suggest using "5 on 5" for mediation and conflict resolution. The first step is to inform both coach and athlete that they each have 5 minutes to express their respective concerns. While one party is speaking, the other person listens, then they switch. The mediator would then initiate discussion between the two sides and close the session.

I use a technique that is similar to "5 on 5", but expands on it. I ask the athlete to express their point of view while the coach listens. Then the coach presents their perspective while the athlete listens. Then the athlete must try to place himself or herself in the position of the coach and present the coach's outlook. The coach must then attempt to put him or herself in the athlete's position and argue from the athlete's point of view. Finally, they discuss the situation. This exercise helps develop empathy and gives each party an opportunity to better understand and become more sensitive to the other person's point of view.

Using the Myers Briggs Type Indicator can also improve communication between coach and athlete (also between athletes). The Myers Briggs Type Indicator measures psychological types by reporting an individual's preferences on four scales. Each scale represents two opposite preferences. The four bi-polar scales indicate; direction of interest (extroversion-introversion); perception (sensing-intuition); judgment (thinking-feeling); and lifestyle (judging-perceiving). Individuals who have the same strengths in a dimension will usually seem to "click." They will really hit it off with each other, whereas people who have different strengths in a dimension will most likely not see eye-to-eye on many things and will have difficulty accepting some views, opinions, and actions of the other person. The higher the number of dimensions on which two people differ, the greater the likelihood of conflict and/or misunderstanding. Conflict may also occur when people must utilize dimensions in which they are weak, or when others point out deficiencies in these areas.

When extreme opposite types must work together, an understanding of types does much to lessen the friction. Disagreement is much less annoying when the coach recognizes it would hardly be normal for the athlete to agree. The athlete is not purposely trying to be difficult; he is simply being an opposite type. Types are not good or bad, right or wrong, they are simply categories which are related to behavioral expectations. Rather then be overly concerned about differences we need to understand and accept each type and value the perspective people of that type can provide. Taking time for a team and it's staff to learn and understand not only their own types but those of their teammates and coaches, will help make interacting with each other a much more enjoyable and fruitful experience. (Yambor, 1995).

The Competitive Learning Styles Inventory developed by Ogilvie and Green (1992) is another test which could be used to help understand and improve communication between the coach and athlete (B. Ogilvie, personal communication, December 12, 1996). It may be impossible to stress enough the value of effective communication between coach and athlete to minimize conflicts and enhance performance.

Goal Setting

Coaches can also utilize a goal setting program to help eliminate conflicts. Goal setting clarifies expectations, directs attention to the task, mobilizes effort, facilitates motivation, enhances task persistence, encourages the development of new skills and strategies, and improves performance. According to Botterill (1983) a goal setting program has three phases:

- ◆ **Planning** - involves learning the basic guidelines for goal setting and developing a system for recording athlete's goals.
- ◆ **The Meeting** - is where the athletes will be educated about their role in the goal setting process. First, the athletes must be introduced to the principles of goal setting either as a team or individually. Then they should be encouraged to develop and record their goals. It is strongly suggested that the coach meet individually with the athlete to discuss his or her goals. Coaches should act as facilitators rather then dictators in the goal setting process (Botterill, 1983).
- ◆ **Evaluation** - emphasizes the fact that timely evaluation is important to a successful goal setting program. Coaches are often hesitant to initiate a goal setting program because they fear the evaluation process will take up to much time. Actually, goal setting in some cases can even save time for the coach.

Gunesch (1992) has stated that goal setting can help make athletes less dependent on coaches. With goal setting, athletes are more likely to know what areas they need to work on in each practice and are more focused over the course of the season.

Reinforcement Principles

Sport psychology professionals should also work with coaches to develop appropriate reinforcement strategies. The following are reinforcement principles that can be employed to modify athletic behavior:

1. **Target behavioral objectives** - identify and establish performance goals and the specific behavioral skills used to obtain the goals.
2. **Stress positive reinforcement** - recognize and reward athletes for correct performance in practice and/or competition. Allow athletes the opportunity to learn or improve skills in a comfortable and encouraging setting.
3. **Provide feedback when mistakes occur** - In the learning and performance phases of motor skill acquisition emphasize improvement. It is normal and natural for mistakes to occur during the learning process. In order to facilitate learning; provide the athlete with information regarding corrective feedback.

4. **Reward athletes immediately when skills are performed correctly**.
5. **Link rewards to correct behavior** - The athlete should know why they received a particular reward. The athlete must know exactly what they did correctly in order to repeat this behavior in the future performance situation.
6. **Reward athletes if they are approaching success** - Typically, athletic skills are very complex and will be learned gradually over a period of time. If athletes are "close" to the response you are seeking, it is helpful to reward this performance in order to encourage their persistence toward the task and to help to prevent frustration.
7. **Reward athletes occasionally once they have learned a specific sport skill or movement pattern** - This will help maintain the athlete's interest in correctly practicing and performing the athletic skill.
(Vernacchia, McGuire, & Cook, 1992, p. 111)

Interventions for Athletes

Acceptance of Responsibility

There are a number of things that can be done by the athlete to help prevent or minimize conflicts with the coach. First and foremost, the athlete must be willing to take personal responsibility. Responsibility means being accountable for your own behavior, actions, and performance. Many athletes don't act as if they are responsible for what they do or cause to happen. They attempt to give the responsibility away or share in only a part of it. The degree to which each player holds themselves accountable for their actions will be a major factor in determining the degree of their learning, improving, or succeeding (Dorfman & Kreehl, 1989).

Communication Skills

Athletes need to develop and practice good communication skills as discussed in the coach's section. It is extremely important for the athlete to be assertive and take the initiative to communicate with the coach. Greenberg (1990) suggests the DESC formula for being more assertive:
1. Describe the situation as you see it.
2. Express your feelings regarding the other person's behavior or the situation.
3. Specify the changes you would like to see take place.
4. Outline the consequences you would expect.

Another technique which may help athletes be more assertive with their coaches is to have the athlete practice role playing with the sport psychology consultant. The sport psychology consultant will act as the coach, and the athlete will discuss any issues they would like to talk about with their coach. This can help the athlete clarify their position, increase their confidence, and decrease their anxiety about discussing issues with their coach. Additionally, if there is a problem with the coach, the athlete should go directly to the coach instead of discussing it with their teammates. If speaking individually with the coach is too threatening, the athlete could ask the sport psychology consultant to talk to the coach for them. If a sport psychology consultant is not available, the team captain could serve as an intermediary.

It is important for athletes to become more aware of their non-verbal communication, particularly, their body language. I have often seen athletes yawning, joking, looking around, picking their fingers, messing with their shoes, talking, and rolling their eyes while their coach is speaking. These behaviors are often perceived by coaches as being extremely rude and indicating a lack of interest or commitment by the athlete. If athletes want to send positive messages to the coach, they could practice good listening skills as discussed in the coaches section.

Athletes can also communicate positive messages through their demonstrated effort. They could put out extra effort in practice and try even harder. They could spend additional time practicing, arriving early for and leaving late after workouts. They could even thank their coach for a particularly good training session.

Coping Skills

Athletes who must deal with negative coaching behaviors can be taught how to cope by using cognitive restructuring, visualization, and positive affirmations. Balague (1993) suggests that older athletes can "translate" coaches' criticism into instructions and that asking for technical clarification often helps. She also maintains that younger athletes may prefer to develop visual imagery that gives them a sense of control. Some examples are: a) visualizing the coach's behavior as a storm and b) "putting on" a rain coat or "opening an umbrella" until it passes.

Another way to combat negative feedback is to develop and use personal affirmations. Affirmations are positive self-statements that consciously affirm or confirm qualities, skills, and attributes that already exist in an individual. Top performers frequently use affirmations in many ways to remind them to reinforce their positive performance abilities. Although affirmations are usually used to deal with negative self-talk, they can also be used to combat negative talk from others.

Bridging the Gap

Frequently, a sport psychology consultant needs to help bridge the gap between the coach and the athlete. Often this can be accomplished by assisting them in reestablishing communication and improving their interacting skills. On some occasions however the sport psychology consultant might offer to speak to the coach for the athlete or speak to the athlete for the coach in order to help open the lines of communication. Often, sport psychology consultants are used to assist athletes in conforming to their assigned roles. The consultant can also help to provide crisis intervention services or serve as a facilitator during conflict resolution. Initiating and developing a goal setting program and providing information relative to reinforcement can also help the sport psychologist narrow the distance between the coach and athlete. Additionally the sport psychology consultant can individualize or personalize performance enhancement programs and just be there to listen and lend support in all areas of the athletes' and coaches' lives.

The sport psychology consultant should avoid the temptation to coach, especially if they are knowledgeable about that sport. Especially, when helping the athletes with visualization and self-talk, ask them what cues work for them. If they aren't sure, have them ask their coach. Don't volunteer technical or strategical cues for the athletes.

Coaches like to work with sport psychology consultants in a variety of ways. Most commonly the coach has the consultant work with the team as a group or individually. Some coaches like to meet with the sport psychology consultant and learn all about performance enhancement so the coach can apply what is learned with their own team. Other coaches want to work directly with the sport psychology consultant on their own performance issues. Finally, others want the consultant to work primarily as a counselor, dealing individually with athletes' personal concerns.

Before a sport psychology consultant should consider working with a coach or a team it is important to understand the sport, speak the sport's language, and, if possible, develop a relationship with the coach and athletes. After the relationship is established, find out what the coaches and athletes believe works for them and build on that information. I believe the coaches and athletes should be actively involved in developing their performance enhancement program. The sport psychology consultant should offer options and make suggestions, but the coach and athletes should make the final decisions. Through this process, the coach and athletes are given more control. Consequently, they are more committed and dedicated to their program.

Case Studies of Coach-Athlete Issues

#1: College Volleyball Freshman

Introduction:

Ingrid was a highly recruited volleyball player who came in and had an immediate impact on the team her freshmen year. As the season progressed, she began to suffer from motivation and concentration problems. Interpersonal jealousies began to develop within the team, she was experiencing typical freshmen adjustment stressors (academic, athletic, personal, and social), and to top it off the coach (who has a Master's degree in sport psychology) constantly insults her and the team with degrading, badgering comments.

These things went on throughout her first year, she was able to cope with the distractions and make a significant contribution to the team during the season. However, during the off-season, her visits to my office were more frequent, she was fed up with the coach's constant evaluation and degrading comments, hates playing for the man, basically feels she cannot be herself, really misses her high school coach who would do anything for her or the team. This has effected her motivation and self confidence, as well as her academic and social life as a freshmen student-athlete.

Intervention:

Interventions involved both Ingrid (i.e., assertiveness skills and communication training, distraction control) and the coach. The coach responds well to honest, direct, communication and most of the girls on the team know he has a heart of gold and would do anything for them in time of need. However, the coach is set in his ways and it is disheartening to see him be so demeaning and belittling (particularly with his background in sport psychology).

Overview:

This situation brings up a number of complicated issues; in particular, coach-sport psychologist interactions and dealing with a variety of different coaching philosophies. The coach's position is that the girls have to learn to be mentally tough, handle criticism without taking it personally, come together as a team, be ready to play without letting interpersonal jealousies get in the way. Although the team traditionally does very well year in and year out, and he expects a lot out of the ladies, the bottom line is he does create fear of failure tendencies & self-esteem problems (as evidenced by Ingrid). Furthermore, his methods of motivation translate into more work for me (the ladies are in my office a lot).

A secondary issue is coach-athlete compatibility. I come across many student-athletes who wish their college coach was more like their high school coach. But is this really possible? How do socialization factors influence the equation (i.e., high school buddies, social support networks, differences in both athletic and academic demands/ environments, other transition issues, etc.)?

#2: Male College Basketball Player

Introduction:

Paul was a highly successful black collegiate basketball player during his two year college career as a center and impact player. His basketball honors during this time included NAIA All-District Team, District Player of the Year, and NAIA honorable mention All-American.

Paul had failed to meet his academic responsibilities and was declared ineligible for the first half of his senior basketball season. Specifically he failed to attend class which resulted in a failing grade in the course. His coach was upset with Paul's academic performance and suspended him to two weeks, feeling that Paul had let the team down by not meeting his academic responsibilities. The coach asked Paul to meet with me to resolve this conflict in their relationship and to help Paul set appropriate academic and professional goals.

Intervention:

Paul was initially belligerent in our first meeting since he had been receiving a very aversive reaction from his teammates and coaches regarding his ineligibility due to his failure to meet academic standards. We had established a good relationship over the past two years and eventually Paul began to express his feelings regarding his situation.

During our conversations it was my goal to help Paul identify and clarify his understanding of the academic responsibilities he had as a student-athlete. We also identified the source of conflict between Paul and his coach as well as a need to resolve this conflict. I encouraged Paul to identify his future professional goals, in terms of his livelihood, once his basketball career was over. He was a very intelligent and aware individual who expressed himself well, and who, as in the case of many athletes, was unprepared to meet the academic demands required of student-athletes at our university.

During our sessions Paul expressed his desire to pursue a career in law enforcement. He was aware that he did not need a college education to do this and although he wanted to play basketball he was essentially unmotivated to pursue a degree.

As a result of our meetings, Paul and I decided to:

- Identify in writing his personal, academic, and professional goals as well as strategies he could employ to achieve these goals.
- Meet with the head coach to resolve their personal conflict.
- Implement time management strategies to help him achieve his academic and athletic goals.

With constant attention and support Paul was initially able to implement many of the strategies he had formulated. Paul, his coach and I met in my office to clarify and resolve their conflict and to specifically identify his academic responsibilities as a team member. We used a "5 on 5" format, that is, each person speaks uninterrupted for 5 minutes expressing their perspective regarding the conflict. The sport psychologist serves as a facilitator. Paul's coach expressed a sincere concern for Paul's personal welfare and future once his basketball career was over. During this meeting Paul clearly expressed his desire to pursue a career in law enforcement. As a result of this meeting Paul agreed to do all that he could to meet his academic responsibilities.

I worked with Paul to: (1) identify resources which were available to him (academic advising and tutorial services) which could help him achieve his academic goals and; (2) to learn the appropriate strategies (i.e. time management, etc.) he needed to integrate into his daily schedule if he were to be successful in meeting his academic responsibilities.

Outcome:

My gut level feeling was that Paul was very confused and uncertain about his future and essentially would go along with any suggestion I made in order to be able to have his suspension lifted. I personally felt it would probably be best for Paul to leave school once the season was over to pursue a career in law enforcement. I did not express this to either Paul or his coach.

I learned that Paul failed all his courses during the winter quarter. He was allowed to enroll during the spring quarter.

#3: Critical Gymnastics Coach

Introduction:

I was contacted by a former student of mine who asked me to call the coach of a gymnastics club in the area for a consultation. My student was an assistant coach working at a local gymnastics club.

During my interview with the coach she stated that the main problem was dealing with the hyper-emotional behavior and erratic performance of one of her "elite" gymnasts. The coach was considered one of the best coaches in the country. Her club was located in a wealthy suburb and encompassed a variety of programs, from initiation to rhythm for 2-4 year olds to elite level competition. I offered to explain some basic principles about sport psychology and brought her some outlines about psychological skills training and what sport psychology could and couldn't do. The coach was basically uninterested and never read the materials, stating instead, "The girl has the problem, give it to her."

Mallory is a 17 year old girl who moved from her hometown in the South to train. She had made the National team the year before but felt that to improve she had to train with this coach. Leaving her family and friends had proved difficult and she appeared depressed. She had no outside interests or friends other than sport, but she was doing well in school. Mallory appeared to be very perfectionistic, minimizing her accomplishments. When we spoke about gymnastics she identified inconsistency as her main problem.

In the State championships a few weeks prior to my meeting with her she had performed erratically. Her technical level was very good but she had difficulty modulating her emotions. When coach criticized her, she would become angry, argumentative and a yelling match often ensued. She felt she could win the National but doubted her ability to keep her focus of attention.

Intervention:

With the Nationals 5 weeks away we agreed to work on attention/concentration. She practiced some focusing and centering, specific to each routine which she practiced during training sessions. She also developed a specific pattern of behavior and activity prior to the beginning of each of her routines, including some specific positive thoughts and points to focus her attention. She responded very positively to the interventions and coach then felt that I had to accompany her to Nationals. After discussion with Mallory we agreed that she did not need me there and I did not go. Mallory won the National and coach was very happy, attributing great weight to sport psychology saying, "I don't think there is a need."

After nationals another athlete of the elite team requested to work with me and coach wanted a Junior (13 year old) to also work with me. I went twice a week to work with them in the gym and to observe practice. The coach's style was a very domineering, punitive one. She would often yell and insult athletes and someone would cry in practice almost daily. All three athletes included in their statement of goals for mental training to learn how to deal with coach.

I attempted once to talk to the coach about her negative approach and its effect on athlete's self-confidence. This backfired as the coach got very angry because athletes were talking to me about her rather than about "their problems." At that point I decided to focus on teaching the athletes how to cope with her. Different approaches worked with each of the athletes. The older ones could "translate" coach's criticism into instructions and learned that asking for technical clarification often worked. The younger athlete, shy and unable to speak up, developed some visual imagery that gave her a sense of control (she would see coach's behavior as a storm and she would "put on" a raincoat or open an umbrella until it passed).

All three girls did very well, made national team and performed in international competitions. Coach got very used to having me around and would complain if I was out of town for more than two weeks. The following Fall the parents of some of the other athletes requested that I work with their daughters. I realized then that a problem of "jealousy" was developing as the coach had asked me to work with the athletes she perceived as best. The mother of an 11 year old, a very motivated and gifted girl, requested that I work with her basically to equate her with the "elite team."

Outcome:

Several issues have emerged this year that I feel are not resolved: Eating disorders is a potential problem as the sport, judges and coaches insist on thinness. Small, skinny 11 and 12 year olds feel and fear being fat. My attempts at helping athletes change their eating habits from starvation diets to eating frequently small amounts of food have met with the response of coach yelling at an athlete eating an apple during a 5-hour practice, "You will get so fat...".

Recently I intervened, helping Mallory decide not to go to nationals after being diagnosed with two stress fractures a week prior. She risked a more serious injury that would prevent her from competing at Olympic Trials. The coach was furious at Mallory's decision stating that she "would have to have been broken in two before refusing to compete at nationals."

Parents have great conflict among themselves with major rivalry and jealousy that spills onto the gym and the girl's behavior. The coach does not seem to listen to me very much, but wants me around all the time and would want me to attend all major competitions.

My plan for next year is to have a few sessions with parents, to give a workshop on psychological skills training to all gymnasts in the competitive program, and an educational session on eating disorders to be given by a nutrition specialist.

#4: Male Junior National High Jumper

Introduction:

Mel was an 18-year-old male high jumper and member of the USA Junior National Track and Field Team which was preparing to compete in the World Championships. He had just completed his senior year in high school and was the USA junior national champion in the high jump. Mel had performed poorly in two meets prior to the world championships which were held in the USA. He was viewed by the coaching staff as disruptive and I was asked by the coaching staff to speak with him during the team's training camp since they were thinking about "sending him home." Mel agreed to meet with me even though he was reluctant to do so. He was belligerent at the beginning of our meeting. Mel's mother was going to accompany the team to the world championship meet. She was the only parent to do so. She stayed in the same hotel with her son and ate meals regularly with him.

Intervention:

Mel appeared very apprehensive about his upcoming performance at the world championships. He seemed to lack confidence in his abilities and skills, especially since he had performed poorly in the regional and international competitions which were held prior to the training camp and world championships. His inappropriate reactions (i.e., temper tantrums, swearing, sulking, etc.) to this newly experienced lack of success caused him to distance himself from his coaches and teammates as a result of such self-pitying and brooding behaviors.

I expressed concern for his situation and made him aware of the coaches' intentions to "send him home" if his disruptive behavior continued. We then discussed the inappropriateness of his behaviors (i.e., missing or being late for team meetings, poor practice attitudes, etc.) and he expressed his desire to discontinue these behaviors in the future and to focus on his upcoming performance in the world championships.

He really needed feedback from his coaches to help him make the technical corrections necessary to succeed at the world championships but he had alienated both his teammates and coaches so they were avoiding him. We discussed this problem and identified behaviors for Mel which would help him interact more cooperatively with his teammates and coaches. He agreed to behave appropriately and cooperatively with his teammates and coaches.

I also suggested that he focus on the specific aspects of his high jump technique (performance goals/strategies vs. outcome goals) which would, if corrected, improve his performance effectiveness. I suggested that he re-establish a working and social relationship with his coach in order to facilitate this process during practice sessions.

Outcome:

Mel made an effort to implement the strategies we had talked about but didn't seem successful in getting the coaching help he needed. I observed Mel's performance during the trials of the high jump at the world championships. He was not jumping well and when he was about to take his final attempt at the qualifying height I observed his mother moving to the wall at the edge of the track near the high jumping area.

As Mel was preparing to jump I heard her yell, "You better make this, I didn't come all this way for nothing. Needless to say, Mel missed his final attempt and was eliminated from the competition. He was not happy with his performance and was unapproachable immediately after the competition. In our subsequent conversations he did express appreciation for the support and suggestions I had provided for him throughout the trip. It should be noted that Mel qualified for the USA team the following year and won the high jump event at the world championship.

#5: College Football Player

Introduction:

Mark was a 20-year-old black, male athlete who had been a High School All-American, recruited to play football at a Division I NCAA University. He was academically well-qualified, but performing marginally in academics Mark was seen as a classic example of the entitlement problems in sport, (i.e. athletes who are pampered, coddled, favored, given extra benefits, undue attention, and unrealistic expectations). He was immature emotionally, lacking a sense of responsibility. He was also overly-sensitive to criticism of his performance, not accustomed to realistic evaluation.

Mark was thrown into the spotlight unexpectedly. He loved it. The opportunity and the attention fed his ego further. However, he was placed in circumstances beyond his knowledge, skills, and training. Because of his innate ability (size, speed, etc.) his mistakes were overlooked by his position coach. At the end of the season, he performed poorly in a Bowl Game and hurt the team performance a great deal.

During his second year, a new coach was assigned to the position Mark played. His coaching style was diametrically opposed to that of the previous coach. Mark experienced a rude awakening. He went from the favored, over-privileged status to a situation where his performance was scrutinized intensely; and even minor errors in judgment were criticized candidly and openly in front of his peers, resulting in great embarrassment.

In his first year, Mark had a coach who tolerated mistakes on the assumption that his innate talent would offset the errors and eventually work out to where the performance would achieve the consistency that was needed to excel. In the second year, however, the new coach was a perfectionist who demanded consistent technique and minimal mistakes regardless of innate talent or ability. Ironically, in this sport environment, feedback is delayed for 24 hours. The intense practice periods are filmed for careful analysis. The following day, each player's performance is critiqued verbally and illustrated vividly on the screen in the team meetings. Mark's errors in performance were blatantly obvious, and the coaches' feedback was unmerciful.

Mark was not accustomed to criticism or to the experience of "falling from grace." He had never been faced with such adversity, though it was probably very appropriate in this situation. The over-privileged, macho character was suddenly transformed into a fragile, overly-sensitive, resentful, young man who felt he was being persecuted unfairly, perhaps, even subject to racial discrimination. His reaction seemed irrational to most observers, including other coaches. Unfortunately, a few of the other players and staff sided with the athlete, which fueled his resentment even more.

Most of the time he repressed his feelings and displayed the typical "macho" image. His typical response to a sincere inquiry, such as "How are you doing?" was to say, "I'm fine! Hey, it' s no problem." Some weeks later, however, Mark lost all the hair on the back of his head--a dramatic stress-related condition called "alopecia." He wore a cap to cover the area, but refused to talk about the condition or to address the relationship between alopecia and his conflict with the coach.

Later, the conflict heightened to a crisis level. The athlete was convinced that he was being unfairly persecuted and that the coach was prejudiced against him, in part, because of race but also because of his affluent lifestyle. His girlfriend was from a prominent, wealthy family. He drove her sports car, lived in her plush apartment, and ate at all the expensive restaurants. His coach was incensed by his arrogant, contentious attitude. As this conflict reached a peak, the athlete threatened to transfer to another university where he thought he would be appreciated for his natural ability.

Intervention:

Recognizing the possible loss to both the team and to the individual, the coach and Mark were receptive (independently) to the proposal for a conflict resolution session. At a predetermined time, the coach and the athlete were brought together in a "mediation-like" setting. Ironically, the coach and Mark were together (with other team members present) for one hour meeting time and two and one-half hours of practice daily throughout the season, yet neither had initiated any specific communication on the conflict issue. Mark and the coach were instructed in the intervention described figuratively as the "Five and Five," referring to two separate periods of five minutes of commentary by each party which was intended too clear the air.

When the session began, the tension in the air was so thick that you could cut it. Both the coach and the athlete were visibly distressed by the confrontation. The first step in the mediation was to inform both coach and athlete that they would each have five minutes (uninterrupted) to express their respective concerns. Mark was encouraged to go first and he did. He lambasted the coach, the program, touted his own credits and concluded with the threat that he was going to transfer.

When Mark finished his five-minute tirade, the coach followed with his response. He was much more open and conciliatory. His initial statement almost blew me over. He said, "Son, if you feel this way, I think you probably should transfer."

The coach continued, however, with a very sincere statement about his concern for the long-term success of the athlete and his program. He acknowledged how much natural ability and talent the player had, but stated candidly that if he didn't learn proper technique, he would never reach the height of his potential (to play pro ball). He concluded his dialogue with the glorious statement, "If you are not happy here, then maybe you had better transfer." The mediators closed the session with several platitudes highlighting the possibility for better understanding and communication, but no great optimism for either to occur.

When the session was ended there was no substantial resolution; however, apparently everyone left with a greater level of understanding. Mark went on to play two more seasons under the same coach. He never acknowledged any appreciation or acceptance of the coach's style or philosophy. Several months later I heard from the coach that Mark took the initiative to appeal his complaints to the head coach. His efforts apparently were misguided and were to no avail. However, when this second confrontation was terminated, Mark seemed to accept the situation and to benefit from the rigorous training with less complaint and somewhat more success. At first we were offended that the athlete did not seek our assistance in mediation during the second confrontation. However, upon reconsideration, we realized that he had apparently learned something from the "modeling" in mediation, that is, perhaps he discovered that he could initiate action or confrontation without hostility on his own.

Outcome:

Yes, his hair did grow back; and, yes, he did reach his ultimate goal of being a professional athlete. According to the athlete, he felt that he had achieved success in spite of the coach. According to the coach, the athlete still had not mastered the skills of his position satisfactorily.

Ironically, this personal conflict was an illustration of typical "real life" problems. It was complicated by a perceptual distortion (i.e. the athlete's unwillingness to acknowledge his performance flaws and his tendency to project blame upon the coach, claiming prejudice as well). Finally, the athlete repressed his feelings to such an extreme that his emotions erupted with a psychogenic physical/medical manifestation, i.e. Alopecia.

The symptoms of hair loss fluctuated in accordance with exposure to the stressor (i.e. the coach). During the off-season and after graduation, the athlete had all his hair grow back. Now, five years later, the athlete is still active in professional football and has no further symptoms.

The authors agree that the intervention was only partially successful. The conflict between the athlete and the coach was never completely resolved. However, the athlete seemed to learn how to deal with it sufficiently well so as not to result in transfer or dropout. The coach may have learned something about negotiation and about the special needs and sensitivity of some athletes. Under the circumstances, the intervention appeared to be the only reasonable approach. The conflict resolution strategy (Five and Five) has been used successfully in numerous other coach/athlete conflict situations, each with more or less success in resolving the problem. By contrast, the first author has encountered numerous other cases of alopecia (hair loss), partial or complete. In each case, there existed some unresolved personal problem or severe anxiety concern. In some cases the hair loss was completely abated with intervention, in other cases the alopecia fluctuated in accordance with the exposure to the stressor.

As a result of this dramatic illustration, we are considerably more sensitive and alert to the possibility that medical symptoms (i.e. hair loss, stomach ache, panic attack, and depression) may be due to some unresolved conflict between the athlete and one of many persons (e.g. parent, coach, significant other). Exploration of these issues and prompt resolution of the problem is very important both for performance and personal health and well-being.

#6: College Softball Team

Introduction:

The softball team was experiencing a disappointing year following a successful campaign the previous year. The team began the year with a West-coast tour against top competition and, though having played well, came back with a losing record. Through these first games, the players and coaches believed the tone of the year was being established as one in which the team appeared to play to the level of their competition and, inevitably, lose by one or two runs consistently. The team had not hit a stretch where everything appeared to be going well and improved prospects were believed to be ahead.

The coach contacted me to discuss the team's status and my perception of what I might offer. Her assessment was that the team had the talent to play much better, but had the tendency to get down and shoot themselves in the foot. The coach stated that she had attempted to build the team's confidence and focus them on positive thoughts. However, the team was unable to incorporate or practice what was being stressed.

Prior to my meeting with the team, a member of the team asked to talk to me. She shared with me that some knew I had met with the coach and wanted me to hear "the team's" perspective as well. The team's perspective was that the coach was inconsistent in her words and deeds. In other words, the coach was telling them to be positive, that she believed in them, and she wanted them to be a cohesive unit (not having cliques). However, according to the team member, the coach was not being positive, was overly critical of their skill and effort, and played favorites which resulted in cliques. Consequently, the coach was perceived to be a significant force in the team's lack of success.

Intervention:

I met with the team and proceeded to focus on five tasks: 1) Identification and riddance of negatives, 2) Development of personal affirmations, 3) Defining success, 4) Identification of situational triggers and cues, and 5) Reorientation.

The identification and riddance of negatives involved recognizing thoughts when oneself or a teammate makes a mistake. We then discussed the effect of such negatives on performance. The players wrote down the thoughts they developed when things went wrong, then tore them up (symbolic of getting rid of negatives).

To develop personal affirmations, I paired the players with the purpose of sharing positives that each perceived about themselves, the team, and playing collegiate softball. A group discussion followed to develop a collective understanding of the positives on the team.

As a group, we defined success. This involved identifying what constituted success as a fielder, hitter, pitcher, and teammate. Stress was placed on the responsibility that all teammates had in the success of each other.

The players were then asked to individually identify a cue based on their responsibilities (i.e. center fielder & leadoff hitter, first base & clean-up hitter, starting pitcher). They were instructed to write these cues on paper and keep the paper in their pockets while they were playing. If they needed a reminder or a focus cue, they could take out the paper, read the cue, and get back to business.

The final task was a reorientation. Collectively, the team outlined goals for the rest of the year - from that point forward. Each team member was asked to commit herself to these new goals.

Outcome:

The team did sweep their next double header, but that effort was followed by a quick return to the previous pattern of playing down or up to their competition, but rarely over. I believed, going into the situation, that the problems were much deeper than what I was addressing. If nothing else, I was attempting to establish a smokescreen through the end of the season. I was hoping that the team could focus on positives, overlook possible differences with the coach, experience some success, and have many of the problems fix themselves. However, the attempt was unsuccessful.

The solution to this situation lies in addressing the real roots of problematic circumstances. During the middle of a season, however, time may not be a luxury that would allow for an intervention that would have been more comprehensive and effective.

#7: College Coach's Stress Affecting The Team

Introduction:

This case involved work with a highly successful team sport coach. The coach is well-respected in her sport and has been successful at the national and collegiate levels. She has been supportive of the work of the sport psychology consultant over a period of years with her teams, promoting an on-going involvement for the athletes through team and individual athlete contacts. In addition, the sport psychology consultant is frequently used as a sounding board for the coaching staff on issues of player behavior, team concerns and coaches' issues. A good working relationship, as well as mutual liking and respect have developed between the coach and consultant.

The athletes who play for this coach typically respect and admire her. They all trust her coaching ability. They have voiced complaints in team meetings, however (without the coaching staff present) that they wish the head coach could control her stress level before and during competitions. They have stated that it is difficult for them to concentrate and prepare or perform well when she is stressed and takes it out on them. An assistant coach has confided that the head coach's stress level has a negative impact on pre-competition warm-ups and on athletes' attitudes and anxiety levels. The sport psychology consultant observed that the coach is not as effective as she might be, indeed as she usually is in other situations, when she becomes uptight around competitions.

The athletes did not wish their coach to be any less intense or competitive, but they did find her stress level contagious at best and upsetting at worst. They coped with the situation by sort of accepting that "Coach always gets this way before competition." Some tried to block out what she said and did, with the risk that they might miss some valuable information or coaching feedback. The coach was aware to some extent that her stress level was high, but did not seem to be aware of how bad it really was. She had discussed with the consultant the effects of stress on her health, and stress and athletes in general, but to this point the consultant had not actually addressed the issues in a way that resulted in any measurable differences in relation to her team's concerns.

Intervention:

The dilemma for the consultant centered around a reluctance to cross some imaginary line between giving advice as the sport psychology consultant and avoiding the perception of "telling the coach how to do her job." The consultant did not want to damage the working relationship or credibility that had been established, but at the same time felt that for the athletes' sake some intervention was called for. In addition, the consultant hesitated to present information to the coach which might be taken in the wrong way or misinterpreted.

This situation is not unlike others faced by consultants in which coaching actions, behaviors or words are perhaps having a less than positive effect on the athletes, and the sport psychology consultant needs to somehow discuss the notion of a coach changing his or her behaviors in order to improve interactions with athletes. These situations present some sensitive issues in dealing not only with coach-athlete relationships, but also with the coach-consultant relationship.

In this case it was necessary to first clarify and prioritize the issues at hand. In reviewing the issues it was noted that the coaching behaviors related to high stress were having a negative impact on athlete preparation and performance. The situation had been going on for some time. Therefore, intervention was warranted. At the same time, it would be necessary to discuss the issues in a way that was positive in tone and did not cause further stress for the coach.

In this case there was no fear that the coach might "take it out" on the athletes, rather the concern was that information pertaining to the notion that her team did not like the way she behaved around competition might be taken personally, thus producing disappointment or feelings of self-consciousness for the coach. The coach is someone who is deeply committed to her athletes and to her job, and it was reasoned that there should be a way to approach her which utilized these strengths in order to begin to remedy the situation.

Discussions with the coach therefore at first centered on what the athletes' needs are surrounding competitive situations, for example, in terms of support, feedback, information and coaching behaviors. It became obvious through discussions that the coach felt it was very hard for her to be all the things her athletes needed because she felt a lot of pressure placed on her from the coaching situation in terms of knowledge, decisions to be made, and consequences of performance. She expected her athletes to "take care of themselves" in terms of readiness to perform. Further discussions centered on coaching stress and how to alleviate or cope with the stressful lifestyle coaching entails. In addition, ways to pay closer attention to the impact her attitude and behaviors has on her athletes, as well as ways to refrain from communicating her stress were explored. This was a particularly sensitive area since it involved sharing with the coach that some of the things she said and did in interacting with the athletes prior to and during competition were at odds with her stated philosophical beliefs about helping athletes perform to their potential.

Outcome:

There were no simple solutions to the issues presented in this case and in fact it is an on-going process for this coach to gain control of her stress and tension levels as well as educate her athletes in mental training techniques to deal with stressful competition situations. Without undermining the coach, it has been necessary to help the athletes learn to deal with having a highly competitive, intense individual for their coach. They also have had to come to terms with being responsible for their own pre-competition preparations and mental readiness. The coach is working to monitor and control her own stress levels in order to cope more effectively with the pressures of her job.

Finally, it should be noted that several other tactics could perhaps help alleviate the situation described. Since the coach is receptive to Mental Training sessions for the team, one such session might center around each individual's needs in terms of feedback from coaches and teammates at competition. After a discussion about individual preparation for competition, athletes could disclose for example, whether they preferred to be encouraged and cheered on by others or left alone to get ready. The team could brainstorm ways to prepare as a team while respecting individual differences. Another topic might center around discussion of the coaching staffs expectations for athletes' preparation and performance in terms of attitude and readiness, and athletes' expectations/preferences for coaches' involvement in that process. A communication workshop which would include assertiveness skills and coach-athlete interaction enhancers might also be helpful for this team.

#8: College Volleyball Setter

Introduction:

Susan is a third-year sophomore collegiate volleyball player who had transferred to the school to follow her coach. Susan is a hard-working, potential-striving setter for the team. Setter is a new position for her as she red-shirted last year to work on the adjustment. Consequently, she is being asked to be the center of a team coming off a very successful year for a school with a history of outstanding setters.

My initial contact was from Susan's coach who wished to discuss the situation prior to me meeting with the athlete. Through this discussion, the coach shared her perspective that Susan's quality of play had dropped along with a decline in enthusiasm. The coach also believed Susan was expressing self-directed antagonism as well as antagonism toward the coach. Susan's coach was frustrated at being unable to understand the changes that had taken place which were impacting Susan's performance. The coach believed Susan was feeling pressure from an incoming player, was experiencing burnout, and might not understand some personal changes the coach was experiencing. Susan's coach wanted her to relax and regain her prior level of performance.

Intervention:

Susan, upon the urging of her coach, met with me to discuss the situation. Susan shared that she was not having fun and was experiencing difficulty identifying positive factors associated with playing volleyball. Susan also acknowledged that both she and the coach were undergoing personal changes resulting in greater separation. For her part, Susan perceived herself as maturing and focusing on other matters outside of volleyball. She also believed her coach was polarizing on her coaching responsibilities.

Susan was unclear how she fit into her team's future and perceived herself as a liability to the team due to a poor attitude and poor play. She was angry with herself and was "beating herself up", taking primary responsibility for the team's poor performance.

Through a series of meetings, specific issues were highlighted for special attention. An initial task was for Susan to identify the positives she historically received from volleyball that led to her committing so much of her time and effort to the sport To do this, Susan was to make a list of the positives she derived from her participation and to identify those that were still present.

I shared with Susan my perception that she was expressing no intention of quitting during the current season. Instead, she was contemplating what to do following the season. She expressed that she was unaware of this mindset until it was reflected to her, but agreed that was indeed the case. I then suggested, since she was not going to quit at the time, she make a commitment to evaluate the issue after the season was complete. This was strongly stressed as it was believed she truly needed to take stock of her emotions and thoughts during a time when she could be more objective and feel less pressure.

A third task was for Susan to recognize the extent of her control of her team's performance. She was to analyze this as well as the role of her teammates and coaches in the team's performance. This was suggested to allow Susan to gain a more accurate perspective of her role in the team's performance.

A final task was for Susan to have a non-volleyball discussion with her coach concerning a variety of issues she had identified. These included Susan's perception that she was maturing, looking at career issues, and allowing distance for the coach to fully address her own responsibilities. A final component of her conversation with her coach was to communicate her resolve to finish the season, making a full commitment to herself, her team, and her coach.

Outcome:

Susan was able, with time to reflect, to identify many factors that made volleyball enjoyable for her. She was able to tap into these factors by looking at the list she had developed at any time she was feeling a drop in enthusiasm. A pivotal point in Susan addressing her lack of enthusiasm and poor play was the self-realization that she did not have to make a decision at the present time. Susan was putting an extreme amount of pressure on herself to make a decision during the middle of the season that she had no intention of enacting until the end of the season. In delaying the decision and committing to address the issue at the end of the season, Susan felt a great relief. Also, through the task of addressing her role in her team's performance, she was able to release control for everything and take responsibility for that which was attributed to her.

Susan, by releasing the self-imposed pressure was able to regain her enthusiasm and role on the team as providing emotional strength. The team's first test was a tournament with several top 25 teams. Although they did not win the tournament, the team play was improved and Susan was regaining her old form. Susan continued to improve, as did the team, and the team was able to turn their season around and gain a NCAA tournament berth.

Susan's perspective of her current situation was skewed and magnified due to the pressure of the season, especially coming off an overwhelmingly successful season in which she red-shirted. Consequently, she was pressuring herself to be better than she could be at present. This caused her to doubt herself, and forced her to look outside of volleyball.

Susan returned for her junior year in great shape and expressing a positive attitude. In the words of her coach, "She is no longer just a good setter, she is a great setter.".

Discussion Questions

1. List 5 suggestions for improving communication skills for coaches and 5 suggestions for athletes.

2. Explain an exercise that could improve communication between coaches and athletes.

3. List 5 suggestions for improving listening skills.

4. Explain a technique for dealing with conflict situations.

5. How could using the Myers Briggs Inventory improve coach athlete relations?

6. What are the 3 phases of a goal-setting program?

7. List 5 reinforcement principles that can be used to modify athletic behavior.

8. Explain the DESC formula for assertiveness.

9. Were the issues addressed through intervention the critical issues? What other issues might have been addressed?

10. What is the advantage of having a discussion with the coach prior to meeting with an athlete? What possible complications may be presented by having such a preliminary discussion?

11. Where is the line drawn between reflecting thought and planting a thought?

12. Was the intervention appropriate for the problem presented in this case? What other types of interventions night have been used to bring about better results?

13. What are the possible positive and negative effects of working with a team to "accept the coach as he or she is" ?

14. Are there possible conflicts of allegiance when the sport psychology consultant is working with a team and coach simultaneously?

References

Balague, G. (1993). Case study of a 'mature' athlete: What can be learned. Paper presented at the National Sportpsych Conference, Utopia, TX.

Botterill, C. (1983). Goalsetting for athletes with examples from hockey. In G. L. Martin and D. Hyrcaiko (Eds.), Behavior modification and coaching: principles, procedures, and research. Springfield, Illinois: Thomas.

Carron, A. V. (1988). Group dynamics in sport. London, Ontario: Spodym Publishers.

Dorfman, H. A., Kuehl, K. (1989). The mental game of baseball: A guide to peak performance. South Bend, Indiana: Diamond.

Gould. D. (1998). Goal setting for peak performance. In J. M. Williams (Ed.), Applied sport psychology: Personal growth to peak performance (pp. 158-169). Mountain View, California: Mayfield Publishing Company.

Greenberg, J. S. (1990). Coping with stress: A practical guide. Dubuque, Iowa: William C. Brown.

Gunesch, M. (1992). Turning broad goals into measurable objectives. American Ski Coach, 15, 12-14.

Henschen, K. & Miner, J. (1989). Team principles for coaches. Ogden, Utah: Educational Sport Services

LeUnes, A. D. & Nation, J. R. (1989). Sport psychology: An introduction. Chicago: Nelson-Hall. Ogilvie, B. & Greene, D. (1992). Learning styles profile. Los Gatos, CA: ProMind Institute.

Ravizza & Sime (1991). Working in a team setting: Addressing coach-athlete conflict. Paper presented at the National Sportpsych Conference, Utopia, TX.

Tuffey, S. (1995). Psychological characteristics of male and female athletes and their impact on coach behaviors. Unpublished doctoral dissertation, University of North Carolina, Greensboro.

Vernacchia, R., McGuire, R., & Cook, D. (1992). Coaching mental excellence: "It does matter whether you win or lose. Dubuque, Iowa: Brown and Benchmark.

Wooten, M. (1992). Coaching basketball effectively. Champaign, Illinois: Human Kinetics.

Yambor, J. (1995). Effective Communication. In Henschen, K. F. and Straub, W. F. (Eds.) Sport psychology: An analysis of athletic behavior. Long Meadow, MA: Mouvement Publications.

CHAPTER 9

~ Team Issues and Considerations ~

Rick McGuire, University of Missouri

One of the greatest challenges facing sport leaders is to successfully mold a group of young athletes into a highly effective and competitive team. From the outside, this may appear to be a very simple task, one which is often even taken for granted. But for those of us with many years of experiences within the world of sport, we share a mutual understanding and a very real respect for the multi-dimensional, complex, often subtle, and sometimes seemingly mysterious entity known as TEAM!

Whatever the level of sport competition, from youth sport to professional sport and even the Olympic Games, the task and challenge facing coaches and sport psychology professionals is the same - to take these boys and girls, men and women, with various abilities, skill levels and capabilities, with differing temperaments, attitudes, value orientations, and motives, and to lead, guide, shape, mold, teach, influence, nurture, and sometimes 'will' them into becoming a highly focused, highly effective, highly performing and highly successful TEAM! In short, the task and challenge is to build a SYNERGY - where the production of the whole TEAM is greater than the sum of the contribution of all of its individual members!

To achieve this level of synergistic performance is magnificent and an awesomely thrilling experience for everyone involved. But it doesn't happen easily or by accident in the sport setting. In fact, it will only occur as the result of skilled leadership, displaying great knowledge and understanding, driven by empathic caring, and applied with experienced wisdom! In short, the development and maintenance of a great TEAM, requires the application of both the science and the art of coaching!

This chapter will focus on issues, considerations and cases involving the challenge of building a group of individuals into an effective team, even a great team, and those that influence the team's stability. From the beginning, we must be clear in our understanding that there is no proven formula, no secret recipe, and no blueprint for a team! We must be comfortable with the key roles of 'subtlety', 'nuance' and 'nurturing' in both understanding and shaping the team building process. We must be willing to move beyond the safety of traditional, yet proven ineffective sport models; we must move beyond the power of public opinion, and see past the folly of editorial rhetoric from our sports media; and, we must move beyond the delusions of popular sport cliche's, slogans and catchy phrases . In short, we must seek to uncover and understand the TRUTH of what really happens in the experience of each of the individuals who play on our teams, and to provide for each of them, and for all of them, in such a way as to most predictably allow for a great TEAM experience to occur!

Team Dynamics

While there is no simple recipe for building a successful team, there is a common set of dynamics, or stages, that all teams experience in the evolution of their life as a team. Tuckman (1965) has identified four stages of team development that are common to all groups working to be an effective team.

Every group or team of which you or I have ever been a member, whether in sports, 4-H, scouts, in our workplace or careers, in civic organizations or even our families, have all worked their way through these same four stages. The recognition of the reality and validity of Tuckman's model allows it to serve as an appropriate rubric or template for observing, assessing, understanding and, ultimately, shaping the team building process for any specific sport team.

The four stages of Tuckman's team development model include:
1. Forming Stage
2. Storming Stage
3. Norming Stage
4. Performing Stage

All sport teams must first 'Form'. They 'Form" with the intention to 'Perform". But on their way to 'Performing' they pass through the 'Storming' and 'Norming' stages. How quickly, easily and effectively they accomplish these transitions may impact the quality of the team performance that they eventually deliver. Many teams encounter great difficulty in moving through the stages. Some may even find themselves "stuck" along the way, and never get on to achieving great performing. Let's take a closer look at what happens in each of these team building stages.

Forming

Just as the name implies, this is the stage where the group first comes together as a team. There are many different ways in which sport teams form. Some teams form by formal try-out; others form by various methods of recruiting or invitation; some teams form by drafting or selection; and still others form by volunteering or simply registering to be a member of the team. Whatever the method of forming, this stage in the development of the team is defined by those first experiences that create the team and define its membership. Typically, the Forming Stage is an exciting and happy time in the life of the team. Team members are usually happy to have "made the team", and share in some celebration of their mutual inclusion within the team. Similarly, this stage is usually characterized by lots of enthusiasm, shared positive belief and support, hope, and anticipation of great achievements to be accomplished together as a team! In short, the Forming Stage is typically a very positive and happy time!

An analogy could be made to the marriage process of forming two people into one "family team". There is the wedding ceremony, where the bride and groom declare publicly their love and devotion to each other, and are formally and legally united in marriage; and then, the reception that follows, where everyone parties and celebrates the marriage and shares hopes and best wishes for a great and happy life together. In many cases, the couple then goes off together on a honeymoon, where they engage in more celebration and many other traditional forming activities.

But even in the very best of marriages, the honeymoon does not last forever. Every day is not a continued celebration. The family team's Forming Stage gives way to the next stage ... Storming! And so, too, it is true for sport teams. In sport, just like in families, the "honeymoon" does not last forever!

Storming

This is the stage for the give and take process that occurs naturally as people get to know and work with each other. Sometimes there are rough edges and conflicts; all doesn't go smoothly; and, there are STORMS. Some groups get stuck in this stage!

Typically, storming within a team is evidence of petty envy and jealousy. Frequently, the object of the envy is another team member's role with the team or with the coach, often measured in playing time, starting position, attention received, or relationship with the coach. Whether real of perceived, this form of envy and jealousy can plant the seeds of storms that can stymie, even debilitate, the growth and development of the team.

In sport, Storming and great Performing are not compatible. A team cannot be Performing at its very best while still mired in the throes of serious Storming! (Storming is not to be confused with teammates competing intensely with each other in practice.) No matter how well a team may perform while it is storming, its performance would have been even better if it were not. Thus, it is critical that any team that is storming move itself on to the next stage ... Norming.

Norming

This is the sign of a maturing group and team. This is the stage where people begin to know their roles and responsibilities, and feel comfortable that they fit. Norming means NAMING! A team is fully 'normed' when every member of the team can look at every other member of the team and NAME each individual's role, accept their role, like them in their role, and allow and encourage them to do their role. This, of course, includes each individual being able to name their own role, accept their own role, like their own role, and allow themselves to perform their own role to the very best of their ability! When this occurs, formally or informally, figuratively or literally, then the team is fully "NORMED', and it is now able to get on with the task of great PERFORMING!!

Some might question, 'How do players who genuinely wish to play different roles, appropriately strive for that opportunity and show their desire for such?' The answer would not be to tear down a teammate and cause "storms" that could undermine the entire team. Instead, the best way for any team member to aspire for a different role is to do their very best with the role that they currently are assigned, deliver the greatest performance possible, and encourage and support every teammate to do the same!

Norming allows for great performing. Only when a team is fully normed is it able to deliver the great PERFORMING that is intended and desired!

Performing

Now this is what all teams should be looking for - to get through the Forming, Storming and Norming stages, so that they can get on with being a GREAT PERFORMING TEAM!! In the Performing stage, teams are characterized by singleness of purpose and great focus. Players are confident and trusting of themselves and of each other. There is great energy, enthusiasm and effort! There is genuine spontaneous support for one another. Everyone makes a significant contribution! Players move out of their comfort zones, take risks, and become capable of performing better than they ever have before. Team members experience great joy, pride, satisfaction and personal fulfillment! This process becomes self regenerating, creating a "luscious cycle", where great performances lead to more great performances! This is the Performing Stage! This is what all teams should aspire to attain!

FORMING
↓
STORMING
↓
NORMING
↓
PERFORMING

Now, let's suppose that a team has worked its way through each of the stages and is now performing great! Does this mean that it will stay in the Performing Stage indefinitely - that having once achieved it, great performances are guaranteed forever? Of course, not! Remember, Tuckman's Model identifies the "dynamics" of the team building process. Dynamic means that it is ever changing. What changes might occur? Here are just a few examples to illustrate a critical understanding of the model:

- ♦ A player's family moves out of town and the player must leave the team. At what stage is the team now? It's at the FORMING STAGE, of course! It's a new team! It's not just the same old team minus one player. This team is cycling back through the Forming Stage? Predictably, what stage is coming next? Storming ... !!!
- ♦ A new player moves into town and joins the team. At what stage is the team? Forming!! What stage is just around the corner? Storming!!
- ♦ A key player gets injured and is lost for the season! What stage...? Forming!! What stage is next?? Storming!!
- ♦ A couple of players on the second team have been playing absolutely great during the past couple games. The coach rewards them by moving them to the starting team. What stage? Forming!! What's next?? Storming - maybe even pretty soon!
- ♦ Teams do not have to cycle their way through Forming to get back to Storming. For example, sometimes in the heat of an intense practice or even a competition, one team member may be openly critical of the play of another. This may result in moving directly to Storming!

The picture should be becoming quite clear. The team building process is very dynamic, constantly changing, with the team constantly moving itself into and out of the Storming Stage! All teams Storm! That's correct - ALL teams storm! Not just poor teams, not just losers, but ALL teams storm! But the mark of a great team is that when it storms, it quickly and effectively gets on with the Norming process so that it can get right back to great Performing!

The challenge for the coach and the sport psychology professional is to continually be in tune with the team, to recognize any storming that occurs, and to then nurture the team back through Norming so that it can move on to great Performing! Or, even better, the coach may anticipate where and when storming may occur, and then shape the team experience in such a way that the storming may be avoided or, at least, minimized. The sport psychology professional can prove to be a valuable resource; providing objectivity and a source of unique ideas.

Tuckman's Model provides a valid and valuable tool to recognize, understand and anticipate what is happening with a team. But it doesn't provide any guaranteed strategies to insure that every team becomes a highly performing team. What can a coach do to best assure the development of a great team?

The Role of the Coach

Kids meet sport at the coach! The coach is the definer, shaper and provider of the sport experience for the athletes of the team (Vernacchia, McGuire and Cook, 1996). The impact of the coach is portrayed and felt in many different ways within the team. It is imperative that the applied sport psychology professional understands the variety with which a coach impacts the team.

ENVIRONMENTAL ENGINEERING - The coach serves as the engineer for the sport environment. The coach defines and shapes the environment within which the athletes and team experience and play sport. This environmental engineering includes both the physical environment as well as the interpersonal and relational environment. The coach determines what goes into the environment and what is acceptable within the environment. Most notably, this would include determining and modeling which actions and behaviors are portrayed, accepted and allowed, as well as defining those actions and behaviors which are never portrayed and are not accepted and allowed. Similarly, the coach defines the language and words that are acceptable within the environment, as well as those which are not acceptable, and thus, not present. By carefully and wisely defining and engineering the environment within which the team experiences sport, the coach may impart the most intimate and impacting influence for enhancing the total team building process.

LEADING THROUGH INFLUENCE - A difficult reality for coaches and sport leaders to understand and accept is that they really have no authority over a group becoming an effective team! Authority exists only when a leader can MAKE whatever they want to have happen to become reality. It should be intuitively obvious that no coach can MAKE a group of athletes become a highly effective team. The coach just does not have authority over how individuals think, feel and relate with one another.

And, yet, coaches absolutely do desire for their groups to become highly effective and highly performing teams. Lacking authority over this, coaches must rely on their ability to INFLUENCE their athletes. This is done through what they say, what they do, and the relationships they build. This influence is also supplemented by the coaches' ability to impart influence on others who may, in turn, have influence upon the athletes (i.e. parent, peers, fans, other coaches, boyfriends and girlfriends, etc.).

The coach's role in the team building process is a nurturing role. It is a role of influence. It is a role of paying attention to the details, to the "little things" that ultimately affect and shape the course of an athlete's experience, and the collective experience of the group of athletes as they strive to become a strong team.

COMMUNICATION - Great teams are characterized by great communication within the team. Whether formal or informal, great teams evidence highly efficient and effective mechanisms for communication. Some key considerations for coaches regarding communication for enhancing the team building process would include:

1. Always communicate with those below you as you would wish to be communicated with by those from above you! This is no more than the "Golden Rule" applied to issues of communication within a team.
2. Seek to have important communications within a team be provided in a REGULAR, CONSISTENT and THOROUGH manner.
3. Always take care of the "Bottom Rung".

Obviously, the quality of communication within any group or team has a powerful impact on the quality of the effectiveness of the team. Coaches can influence the building of the team by influencing the quality of communication within the team.

LEADING THE STAFF - Nearly every team has some 'teams' within the team. One of the most significant of these is the 'staff team', including the head coach, assistant coaches and whatever other support personnel may be available (i.e. - athletic trainers, medical staff, managers, etc.). The staff team also evolves through Tuckman's Forming, Storming, Norming and Performing stages. It is the responsibility of the head coach to provide effective leadership and influence to insure that the staff team is a highly 'performing' team, supportive of one another and delivering a consistent message to the rest of the athletes and team. Anything less than this will sow the seeds of destruction, predictably undermining the overall team building effort.

"HAVE A BIG HEART"

The interpersonal dynamics of any team may be characterized by a series of concentric circles emanating from the heart of the team (See Figure A). All team members place themselves, or find themselves, somewhere along these circles, with those closer to the center being within the "heart of the team", while those farther from the center necessarily finding themselves more on the "fringe of the team".

The Heart of the Team!

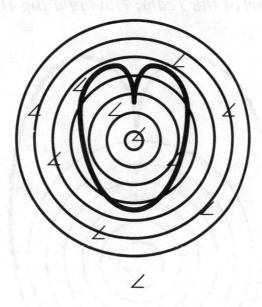

Figure A.

People could perceive or find themselves on the fringe for any number of reasons - lack of playing time, injury and being a newcomer would be among the most typical. The quality of communication and connection to the team is different within the heart of the team than it is on the fringe. In the heart of the team - where everyone is 'on the same page', excited about preparing for upcoming challenges, striving together, believing in each other, and sharing with, supporting and encouraging each other - communication is easy and highly effective! But on the fringe, where individuals do not feel included, may feel disconnected and disenfranchised, communication is typically negative, critical, and destructive.

This is obviously not good! And, it is not necessary!! The goal should be to build and lead a team with a "BIG HEART"!! Ideally, one wants a team with a heart that is so big that there is enough room in it for everyone on the team (See Figure B). And everyone can be INVITED to come into the heart, and to become a big part of the heart, and to join in a great team! Have a Big Heart!

The Heart of the Team: Having a Big Heart!!

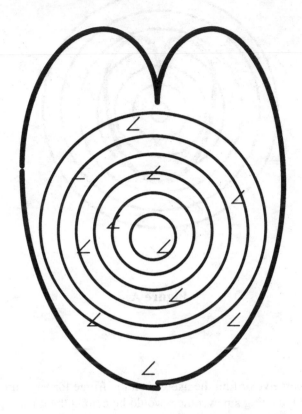

Figure B.

THERE IS NO "I" IN TEAM!

Here is one of those time honored sport cliche's which probably was once well intended, but which has ultimately contributed as much to destroying the concept of team as it has to encouraging the development of great teams. At least, the phrase serves to explode the myth of coaches being nothing more than "dumb jocks", as it clearly validates that coaches are fine spellers. There certainly is no "i" in the word, "team"!

With all due respect, the phrase was coined with the intention of portraying the value of giving of oneself for the good of the team, of sacrificing some personal glory or gain for the overall success and achievement of the team. It points our attention to the universal truth that we can do and achieve more together than any one of us can produce individually. And, that it is honorable and good to be a contributing part of a successful team! The value of teamwork is certainly an important cornerstone in the foundation of success of any team, and of our society, and this phrase was meant to capture and rivet our attention on its priority.

But through the years, this notion has been taken too far, way beyond its initial intent. That 'There is No "I" in Team' has come to mean that there is no place for consideration for the individual when it comes to team sport; that any thought of self is merely selfish, and an attitude to be scorned and despised; that the team counts for everything and that the individual counts for nothing. This attitude and approach is simply wrong and absolutely unnecessary. This approach plants the seeds of divisiveness and destructiveness into the team dynamic.

Alternatively, while there certainly is 'No "I" in Team', we seem to have overlooked that there is an "I" right in the middle of another rather important sport word - "wIn". Yes, there is an "i" in the word, win. And, there is a great big "I" right in the middle of every team 'wIn'.

This recognition should serve to remind all sport leaders that our first responsibility is to build each and every individual participant into a bigger, better person as a result of their sport participation. As each individual's self worth and self esteem is enhanced, as their pride in themselves grows and motivates them to work even harder to become more capable, and as each individual is then willing to put all that they have into the collective effort of the team, only then does the team become capable of becoming the best team that it can be!

Instead of denying and devaluing the place of the individual, the "I", within the team, sport leaders must develop the individual, that is each and every individual, FIRST! When each individual in the team feels valued, appreciated, respected and loved, they feel good about themselves. This allows them to better understand the importance of assuring that their other teammates also must be allowed to feel valued, appreciated, respected and loved, to feel good about themselves, as well. When this foundation is in place, there is little probability of prolonged destructive storming. And, there is a great probability that the individual team members will be wholly receptive to being encouraged and shown how to put their best, their biggest "I", into being the very best team that together we can possibly become!

I'm sorry, but there is a big "I", in fact, there are a lot of BIG "I's", in every great team!

Special Issues

To this point, the thoughts presented have focused primarily on issues and ideas related to what would be considered to be the typical or normal development of a team. But all of the challenges facing sport leaders in building a group into an effective team are not always normal. Sometimes we face some challenges that are absolutely abnormal.

Sometimes in our everyday life, we face some events or occurrences that absolutely SHAKE our society, our community or our family. These events include such things as the unexpected and tragic death of key individuals, natural disasters or the destructive and debilitating impact of severe weather and climatic conditions, or sharp drops in the economy, with devastating personal financial repercussions. And we have witnessed for generations our society's uncomfortable difficulty in dealing with issues related to race and gender. This is true at many levels - society, community and individual.

Abnormal challenges require abnormally strong responses. But usually, the best responses are found within the very foundation of the values, beliefs and principles which define the society, the community, the family or the individual. The best responses to abnormally difficult challenges are drawn from the reservoir of this foundation, and then delivered with abnormal and uncommon strength.

The same holds true when a team faces the challenge of dealing with abnormally difficult special issues. These could include the tragic death of a teammate(s) or coach(es), unusual restrictions of resources (i.e. budget, facilities, equipment, etc.), prolonged debilitating weather conditions, and just as with society at large, the divisiveness of difficulties related to race or gender. Any of these can pose significant additional challenges to sport leaders in attempting to build and maintain a strong, cohesive team.

And, once again, there is no special recipe, no guaranteed strategy that will assure success. Sport leaders and coaches must rely on the strength of their foundation, drawing from their reservoir of values, beliefs, principles, experiences, knowledge, understanding, and trusting their ability to apply wisdom to their efforts to provide the nurturing influence and leadership necessary to meet the challenge. This again, is the artistry of coaching and leading!

The Role of the Sport Psychology Professional

Sport psychology professionals have a unique and meaningful opportunity to assist sport leaders and teams in achieving a more successful and fulfilling team experience. They have been invited into the inner workings of the team, where they can see, hear and feel the pulse of the individuals and the team as a whole. At the same time, they are able to step back and remain outside the team and observe with detachment what is actually occurring. This distance often allows for better focus, and benefits the consultant in being able to see more clearly that which is very good, as well as that which is not so good!

The consultant is then able to discuss with the head coach that which has been observed, and to share from their own knowledge and understanding of the psycho-social dimensions of individual and team dynamics which might assist the coach in building an even stronger team.

But, sport psychology consultants must be careful to not add to, or become a part of, the "storming" or difficulties of the team. Consultants must always maintain respect for the role of, as well as the trust of, the head coach. Further involvement by the sport psychologist should occur only if the coach requests the consultant to intervene or to share with the team or individuals in some manner. Consultants should resist the urge to "fix" everything, and to become all things for all people. And, most importantly of all, the consultant should resist the urge and opportunity to take on roles and responsibilities of the head coach. Consultants should always remember that they have been asked to become the consultant, and not to become the coach!

Final Thoughts on Team Dynamics

- ♦ Kids meet sport at the coach! The coach is the definer, shaper and provider of the sport experience for each individual and for the team!

♦ The coach is an Environmental Engineer, literally building and shaping the sport environment in a way that will most predictably allow for the greatest growth and development of each individual and for the team. (There is a big "I" in TEAM!)

♦ Tuckman's model for the dynamics of team building - Forming, Storming, Norming, Performing - provides coaches, sport leaders and sport psychology consultants with a great window for observing, assessing, understanding and, ultimately, shaping the development of the team!

♦ Every team has the room for a really BIG HEART, a heart big enough that there is room for every member of the team to fit within it!

♦ The recipe for great coaching, great sport leadership and great team building are roughly one part science and three parts artistry! We all need to be responsible to have a good base of scientific knowledge, but from then on it's really all about the wise application of that knowledge. This is the artistry! Picasso!!!

♦ The sport psychology professional is only an actor in a supporting role on the athletic stage. The consultant's role is to be found backstage or off-stage, but should never become center stage!

♦ It really does matter that we win in sport, because it does matter that we WIN in the lives of every individual that we have opportunity to meet and influence in the intersection of our lives with theirs in sport! (Vernacchia, McGuire and Cook, 1996).

Case Studies of Team Dynamics

#1: College Team Facing the Ax

Introduction:

The previous spring, the Athletic Department announced that it was considering cutting a particular women's sport due to severe budget constraints throughout the department mandated by the Governor. The coach, in his 3rd year, resigned at that time; however, he reconsidered and decided to stay on despite what he considered an ongoing lack of financial commitment to the program.

In the fall, the Administration announced that a decision would be made in January regarding the continuance of the program. It was stated that the decision to keep or drop the program was in no way dependent upon the team's win/loss record: the decision would be made strictly for financial reasons. The team had four returning starters and good talent coming in. The coach (and others) thought the team could realistically challenge for the conference title.

I was new to the position and had a good working relationship with the coach and assistant coach. They were interested in having me meet with the team in preseason and on an informal basis during the season as needed.

At the first meeting with the team I stressed that I was not there due to the situation with the Administration, but rather for performance enhancement. I encouraged them to not deny the importance of the situation, but not to dwell on it either. They still had to go out and play every day, finding ways to improve, be successful, and enjoy the sport.

Media guidelines presented by the Associate Sports Information Director were very helpful in establishing the mood and attitude the coaches thought would be most productive under the circumstances. A brief discussion with athletes and coaches seemed to indicate that everyone was in agreement about what needed to be done and the best way to go about it. The focus was to be the sport, keeping outside influences outside as much as possible.

Over the next several months, the players seemed to become fully entrenched in an attitude of "us vs. the administration" - "We'll show them." The "cause" became more important than the game. The team played tight, no fun, and normal ups and downs were exaggerated. This was compounded by the head coach who was struggling with the situation himself. He tended to be very (too) understanding of what all the players were going through, which was not consistent in terms of bringing them back to focus. In other words, he "babied them." Their game suffered, the team hit a slump, frustrations built up, and normal stuff was blown out of proportion.

At this point, the consultant was not asked to work with team. The coach preferred to talk with the consultant and relay information himself. The assistant coach privately expressed frustrations, and how she would do things differently.

In February, the program and three others were cut, then reinstated a week later following a reversal by President's office when "funds became available from anonymous donors". The coach resigned at this point. The season was all downhill at that point, players just waiting to "get it over with." It was a very emotional time for staff and players.

Overview:

The outlook for this group is actually pretty positive. The assistant, a former talented collegiate player, was hired as head coach and she has brought in a young former All-American as her assistant. Three seniors (who had not been exactly positive in their influence over the course of events) have graduated. Recruiting was hurt by the turmoil in the spring but the talent present and coming in seems to be good. The coach is interested in sport psychology as she had a very positive experience with having a consultant work with her team on a regular basis when she played. She is enthusiastic about her new position and has definite ideas for positive changes in terms of past work habits, discipline and team attitude.

#2: College Baseball Player

Introduction:

The college baseball team's cohesion has, over the past three years, been the team's strongest asset. One player, though, has been a source of discord, and as he heads into his senior year, is in need of special attention.

Generally, Franklin is a minority in every sense of the word. He comes from a relatively poor background in Brooklyn and attends a wealthy, white bread college in the Northeast. Franklin is half Puerto Rican and half Black and is the only non-white player on the team. The only other black player to try out for the team was cut last fall. Many of the other players on the team attended posh prep schools in small town New England. He is thus different both ethnically and socioeconomically, and, in addition, seems to make considerable efforts to reinforce these differences (i.e., by not taking part in team cheers, by wearing a different jersey from everyone else during warm-ups, and by generally being too cool to take part in team things).

Overview:

A few private discussions with Franklin about the issue have revealed that he feels that as a non-white player he is always in the spotlight and is expected to play exceptionally well. It is very clear watching him play that he is making a concerted effort to be a cool, smooth, Latino-type of player. Although he does have some good insight and knowledge of the game, he's not close to being as good as he thinks he is. He also gets pressure from the black community at the college to not spend so much time with white, main stream guys. So he is getting it coming and going.

His performance the last three years has improved, but is still substandard. He has battled for a starting spot with one other guy, whom the coaches (and other players) think is a bit better than Franklin.

The complication comes in that the other shortstop, a white guy and popular team player isn't really that good either, only marginally out-hitting and fielding Franklin. Franklin's perception is that he is better than the other guy, and that the coach's decisions on playing time are influenced by the player's race and popular attitude. Although a freshmen is coming in that may take over the spot, Franklin will be needed to play some innings at this pivotal position. Perhaps more importantly, Franklin has also improved each year on the mound and figures to see some important innings in the coming year.

Last, but far from least, this year he will be the only non-captain senior. The players voted two seniors and, for the first time, a junior, to be this year's captains.

Desired outcomes include: Maximizing Franklin's contribution to the team and optimizing his personal experience with this baseball team; in particular, handling his status   as the only non-captain senior and as a role player.

How does the sport psychology professional address this situation and help facilitate the desired outcomes?

#3: College Women's Golf Team

Introduction:

Last year, the women's golf team had finished fourteenth at the NCAA championships. Three seniors had graduated, and three players were returning: a junior with one year starting experience, a freshman with one year starting experience, and a sophomore with no starting experience. The coach had a poor recruiting year: two freshmen with limited tournament experience, and a junior transfer student with top skills. The transfer student had tried to commit suicide at her former college and had a history of drinking and drug abuse. The team travels with five players.

Outcome:

The team started the year with a good attitude, and had a fairly successful fall season. The transfer player won two individual championship, but was very moody. When she played poorly, or if she hurt someone on the team with a sarcastic remark, she would withdraw from the team. The young players on the team took it upon themselves to "nurse her back to health." This became the pattern of the team for the spring season. The coach felt that he was caught between helping this individual, and doing what was necessary to help the team. He did not recognize what was really going on until very late in the season.

The team task performance dropped continually, and finished the season with the poorest ranking in team history. More importantly, the many fine team traditions were replaced by new traditions of relationship activities over task activities.

#4: Death of a College Basketball Player

Introduction:

In March, Cliff a University basketball star died in his sleep of a heart attack caused by an abnormal heart rhythm. He had Wolff-Parkinson-White Syndrome. His death came only two days after he led the team to the District Championship in an emotional victory over their arch rival.

As one might imagine the shock and confusion in the days following Cliff's death were at times overwhelming for the athletic department administrators and staff, team members, and coaching staff. The players were obviously the most affected since for many of them it was the first time in their lives that they had dealt with the death of someone their own age. The recognition of the fact that someone as young and vital as Cliff could be mortal stunned many of the players, it was simply unbelievable to them. Young athletes tend to think, and are taught to think, that they are invincible. The whole experience seemed to be somewhat surrealistic for us all.

Cliff was the glue of the team, the players fed off his quiet confidence and talent on the court, and off the court he was the social leader of the team-the players truly loved him. His loss was enormous for the players and coaching staff. The week following Cliff's death was emotionally confusing for the players and during this time the coaching staff, administrators, and athletic department support staff did all possible to guide the players through the grieving process.

Intervention:

At the time of his death Cliff was a student in my sport psychology class as was the team's student-athletic trainer, team manager and several other players on both the men and women's basketball teams. I made myself available to the team members and was able to provide support for team members through both informal conversations as well as in private meetings. During these meetings I explained the stages of the grieving process which they were experiencing (disbelief, denial, isolation; anger; bargaining; depression; acceptance; resignation, the Kubler-Ross model) and explored the reasons for the overwhelming and confusing emotional feelings they were feeling and expressing.

The days initially following Cliff's death attracted many *'rubberneckers,' those* people who surfaced primarily because of their curiosity regarding the situation. As you might imagine the media, fans, students, and faculty wanted the 'scoop' on Cliff's death. Dealing with these questions was effectively handled through the university sports information office. Our local newspaper was very sensitive to the situation and handled it in a very professional and tasteful manner.

The team had decided to play the semi-final game of the district tournament which was to be held only three days after Cliff died. I was asked by the head coach to meet with the coaching staff the day after the team learned of Cliff's death in order to discuss the sequence of events which would occur before the upcoming game and how to best prepare for them. I had made myself available to the head coach who had, as you would expect, taken on the role as the head of the team family.

The practice that afternoon turned out to be a media and curiosity event as much as a practice session. Players were interviewed intermittently throughout practice by newspaper and TV media persons, it seemed impossible for them to escape thinking and talking about Cliff.. I attended practice as I occasionally did throughout the season and sat off to the side of the court near the managers, trainers, and practice ball rack. Several players (6) as well as athletic trainers and team managers and coaches came by during the course of practice, sat down next to me, and talked briefly about the situation. I listened and provided what support I could. For the most part they were stunned and overwhelmed by the whole experience. I recall one comment by the coach which he made to me as practice began as he was about to explain the offensive and defensive adjustments in the team's game plan, he said, "...this is the hard part." This was the first time the reality of Cliff's death hit both the team and coaching staff.

After practice I accompanied the team to the funeral home to visit Cliff's family and to view his body. Again the reality of Cliff's death hit us all, the team was still in a state of disbelief and shock. The head coach and his wife did a marvelous job dealing with this situation by providing the spiritual and personal support for the team and Cliff's family.

Outcome:

The next evening the team played the semi-final game in a very *overemotionalized and over-memorialized* environment which in some ways was a media circus. Everyone wanted to do something to honor Cliff and show their support. This made it impossible for the team to concentrate on the game. Their dominant thoughts were on the loss of Cliff, winning was of secondary importance when it really came down to it. The players were trying too hard for Cliff. They all wanted to make the big play for Cliff and as one opposing player put it, "They played as hard as they could, but it was too much for them, they all wanted to step up and be the player." The team's co-captain stated after the game that "We were trying so hard to be awesome we couldn't do anything." The team didn't score until 7 minutes of the first half had passed and eventually lost the game 90-75.

Overview:

Looking back it seemed that the game was just too close to Cliff's death (3 days) and it would have been best to play the game later in the week after the memorial service which was conducted the day after the game by the athletic department and the university. Having the memorial service prior to the game would have brought about an emotional closure to the grieving process for the team, media, fans, and campus community and perhaps the game could have been a celebration for Cliff rather than a memorial service. I suggested this in my meeting with the coaching staff but it was impossible to do based on the scheduling. for the district and national tournaments. The team had to elect not to play or to play to the best of their ability under the circumstances. Essentially the team was grieving rather than healing when the game was played.

I also suggested that we have a reception for the team and their family members after the game, win or lose. As stated previously we did lose the game and the reception provided emotional and personal support for many of the players.

The university memorial service the following day was excellent and provided the needed impetus for the healing process to formally begin for many of us. The team also traveled to Cliff's home town to attend his funeral service.

In my work as a sport psychology professional it has become evident to me that the very best athletes play each game as though it might be their last. In some sports such as football, the best players make each play as though it were their last. I believe they truly understand the reality of sport. Cliff understood this as well as the reality of life and his mortality, this is why he was a great player and human being. Perhaps this accounted for his care-free attitude toward life which attracted his teammates to him.

It was mentioned at his memorial service that Cliff's mother had spent the week before Cliff's death with him. Cliff was an avid fisherman and during his mother's visit he had convinced her to purchase a framed print of a fisherman in a boat on a placid lake at sunset. The print was entitled, 'Going Home', and was displayed at his memorial service.

#5: Women's College Volleyball Team

Introduction:

One of the team's best players, Courtney, displayed an attitude and behavior which reflected her unwillingness to accept the team norms established by the coach and team members during the preseason. Her behavior was essentially learned helpless; she externalized her failures by blaming teammates for her inability to cope with performance situations. Courtney openly ridiculed teammates when they were unsuccessful in performance situations. She felt she was "above" team rules, norms, and standards of behavior for team members.

Courtney was also a single parent (one child) with extensive social, economic, personal, and economic responsibilities. She has never been married. Her father was a faculty member at the university and often expresses his opinions to the coach regarding the team's play as well as the performance of his daughter.

The coach is a young male, relatively inexperienced at the university level, and is in his second year as the head coach. The team was runner-up in the district last year and will contend for the district title again this year. The coach has very strong foundational beliefs regarding the educational values of the athletic experience. He is an excellent teacher and his effectiveness as a coach is demonstrated by the skill competencies his team displays in the competitive setting.

The team norms and goals were established during an extended preseason road trip which Courtney was unable to attend because of family and work responsibilities. Courtney's behavior and attitude was causing a considerable amount of intra-team tension. Her behavior was disruptive to the actualization of the norms and goals which the team had established. The team was winning but resentment was growing toward the player even though it was evident that she was largely responsible for the team's success.

Intervention:

The coach and sport psychology professional met and discussed the problem. The coach was encouraged to:
- Clarify his values and foundational beliefs
- Redefine his concept of a successful team and program
- Evaluate the effect Courtney was having on his team and himself, as well as with his relationship with the team.

The coach and the sport psychology professional discussed several strategies which could be employed to deal with the situation and problem effectively and expeditiously. The coach was also encouraged to solicit feedback from the team captains regarding Courtney's behavior and the effect it was having on the team.

The coach decided to confront Courtney, individually, and ask her to consider changing her behavior or else to leave the team. He explained the negative effect her behavior was having on the team members and that her behavior was inappropriate and counterproductive to attaining and actualizing the team and program goals and norms.

In response, Courtney decided to leave the team.

Outcome:

Team cohesion was renewed. The coach gained the respect of the team for not compromising the program's foundational beliefs and educational value orientation.
The team continued to win and enjoy the practice and performance experience. Courtney attended the matches even though she was no longer a member of the team. She eventually approached the coach and asked to be reinstated as a member of the tam. The coach left the

decision to the team. Courtney met with the team, apologized for her behavior and reassured the team the behavior would not re-occur in the future. The team accepted her apology and she became an integral part of a very successful and cohesive team.

Discussion Questions

General for any sport psychology consulting setting:
1. Who is the client? Who has invited me into this setting? How am I to serve them best?
2. What is the issue? Where did they come from? How did they get here?

Specific to the issues of Team Dynamics:
1. What is the ultimate goal? To have a "strong" team?, To win the game(s)? championship?, To "win" each individual?
2. What price is the team willing to pay for having a strong team?
3. Is the coach willing to pay attention to the psycho-social and psycho-emotional issues of building a team? Or, is the coach only willing to spend time on the X's and O's of the game? Either way, what is the consultant's role?
4. How can the sport psychology consultant nurture these understandings with coaches?
5. Am I working with a strong "staff team"? At what stage is the staff team relative to Tuckman's Model?

References

Tuckman, B.W. (1965). Developmental Sequence in Small Groups. Psychological bulletin, 63, 364-389.

Vernacchia, R.A., McGuire, R.T. and Cook, D.L. (1996). Coaching mental excellence: It does matter whether you win or lose. Warde Publishing. Portola, CA.

CHAPTER 10

~ Parent-Athlete Issues ~

David Yukelson, Penn State University

Just a Little Boy

He stands at the plate with heart pounding fast.
The bases are loaded; the die has been cast.
Mom and dad cannot help him, he stands all alone.
A hit at this moment would send the team home.
The ball meets the plate; he swings and he misses.
There is a groan from the crowd, with some boos and some hisses.
Tears fill his eyes; the game's no longer fun.
So open your heart and give him a break.
For it's moments like this, a man you can make.
Keep this in mind when you hear someone forget.
He's just a little boy and not a man yet.

- Author Unknown

This poem was given to me prior to the start of a community little league all-star season by a parent who happens to be a very successful college football coach. All too often, young athletes are confronted with pressure situations like the one listed above. The questions arise: "Where is the source of the pressure?", and "What factors undermine the young athletes motivation to want to be in that situation again?". Most kids want to have fun in sport and feel good about themselves and their sport participation. Unfortunately, sometimes adults can dampen kids enthusiasm for participation. It's tough enough for a young athlete to conjure up the courage and mental/emotional fortitude required to cope effectively during critical moments in competitive contests, however, the situation does not need to be further exacerbated by detrimental comments or actions on the part of parents or fans.

Personally and professionally, I have always been interested in competitive youth sports. In particular, the psychosocial relationships that develop between parents, coaches, and athletes. Many outstanding articles and books have been written about the subject (Brustad, 1996; Hellstedt, 1987; Horn, 1985; Martens, Christina, Harvey, & Sharkey, 1981; Rotella & Bunker, 1987; Smith, Smith, & Smoll, 1983; Smoll, 1997; Weiss, 1995). In my own personal experience as a sport psychologist, parent of three very active competitive boys, and occasional volunteer youth sport coach, I have seen the whole spectrum of parental involvement in sport. I have traveled on international trips with USA Track and Field Junior National Teams and have seen first hand over-involved parents telling national coaches how to train their kids, challenging the coaches authority, contradicting the coach, leaving the athlete caught in the middle confused and bewildered. As a spectator, I have sat in the stands and observed highly critical, overzealous parents act very silly and throw an "attitude muscle" over some unacceptable play or call they felt was unjust. Likewise, I have had the fortune of being one of those much maligned "all-star little league baseball coaches" parents love to complain about, and have experienced first hand the wrath of over-involved parents talking behind my back, attempting to undermine the philosophy and code of conduct by which the program and team was governed.

The Value of Sport

Unfortunately, many parents, coaches, and programs get caught up in the "win at all costs" mentality that is so pervasive in our society and sport culture today, and lose sight of what sport participation is supposed to be about: the personal growth and development of the participant. Sport is a wonderful vehicle to help kids feel good about themselves. As such, there are many lessons to be drawn from participation in sport. Within sport, athletes learn how to compete, set goals, take risks, control emotions, and deal with various success and failure experiences. Important values and attitudes are formed with regard to friendship, achievement, discipline, sacrifice, persistence, self-confidence, teamwork, respect for self, and respect for others. However, the potential benefits that are supposed to be derived from sport are not guaranteed based on mere participation alone. Rather, research indicates the most important factor influencing whether or not youngsters have a positive or negative competitive sport experience is the quality of adult leadership that is provided (Martens, 1990, Martens et al, 1981; Smith et al, 1983; Weiss, 1987, 1995). That is, the interactions young athletes have with parents, coaches, and other significant socializing agents, all of whom play a major role in shaping positive competitive sport experiences for the participant.

Motivations and Issues

In terms of understanding what kids want out of sport, it is important to recognize young athletes have multiple reasons and motives for participation. Typically, they want to have fun, develop skills, feel stimulated, challenged, and good about what it is they are striving to accomplish. In addition, some kids participate to get in shape, others want to affiliate with friends, or simply identify with being a member of a team. Reasons cited for discontinuation include lack of playing time, reduction of fun, lack of improvement, dislike for the coach, too much pressure, overemphasis on winning, conflict of interests, or other things to do (Gould & Petlichkoff, 1988; Weiss & Chaumeton, 1992). Common themes for dropping out seem to revolve around issues related to low levels of perceived competence and/or perceived control, dissatisfaction with adult leadership, or no longer enjoying competition. Since parents, coaches, peers and various significant others combine to play a vital role in shaping young athletes psychological development and emotional reactions to sport (Brustad, 1996; Weiss, 1995), everyone involved should be working toward enhancing young athlete's self-perceptions, self-esteem, enjoyment for sport, as well as intrinsic reasons for participating and competing.

Coaches play an important role in helping kids reach for their best. Although coaching styles and objectives vary, most kids look up to their coach for guidance, support, wisdom, and inspiration. As such, coaches should never underestimate the influence their actions and attitudes have on the kids they instruct. The goals and priorities they establish for kids, the skills and strategies they teach, the type of learning environment that is created, and the methods used to provide feedback and motivate kids are factors that combine to make the sport experience rewarding and enriching.

Coach-Parent Issues

At all levels of competition, there is a lot of pressure on coaches to win. Some of the pressure comes from within (internal standards of excellence); other sources of pressure are externally imposed (expectations from administration, parents, and/or the community). Although the demands and constraints can be quite excessive, successful coaches formulate a coaching philosophy that keeps winning in proper perspective, and their values and integrity in tact (Martens, 1990). Recognizing there is a tremendous amount of stress in coaching, I am often asked to conduct educational seminars for coaches on psychological issues that impact their coaching effectiveness. Whereas most coaches seem to have a pretty good perspective on what they are trying to achieve with their athletes and program, inevitably, the number one thing I hear from coaches that causes them undue stress and takes the fun out of coaching is parental over-involvement. In particular, pushy, manipulative, selfish parents, with hidden agendas and ulterior motives, that often attempt to sabotage and discredit a coaches reputation by talking behind their back, constantly undermining what the coach is trying to accomplish.

An innovative approach designed to minimize potential conflict that might arise between coaches and parents has been proposed by leaders at Catholic Central High School in East Lansing, Michigan (Gantert, 1997). At the beginning of the year, coaches should consider offering a parent orientation program to discuss their coaching objectives, gather support, and open up positive communication processes (Martens, 1990; Smoll, 1997). Coaches should inform parents of their coaching philosophy, goals and expectations, team rules and policies, parent roles and responsibilities, and offer suggestions as to how parents can help. Appropriate concerns for parents to discuss with the coach include treatment of their child, ways to help their child improve, specific concerns with regard to coach's philosophy and/or expectations, or observations and concerns about their child's behaviors and/or emotional reactions to the sport experience. Issues that are not appropriate to discuss with coaches include playing time, team strategy, play calling, or other athletes. Consequently, it is suggested that coaches be open to parental input, if done in a respectful and constructive manner.

Parent-Athlete Issues

Another issue to be concerned with is conflict that might arise between parent and athlete. Some parents have been known to place excessive pressure and stress on kids (Brustad, 1996; Gould, Tuffey, Udry, & Loehr, 1997; Scanlan, 1986). Overemphasis on winning or rankings, too much concern about social comparison processes, failure to meet unrealistic parental expectations, and negative demeaning comments that undermine a youngsters self-esteem are just a few problems that come to mind that are the result of negative parental influences. Along these lines, over-critical parents never seem to be truly satisfied with their child's performance. Problems arise if the youngster perceives parental love and approval being contingent on how well they perform (Smith et al, 1983; Smoll, 1997). The key word is perception. In most circumstances, over-critical parents do not see how their kids internalize their actions or comments. Children should never have to feel their performance in sport in any shape or manner will effect their relationship at home with their parents. Thus, parents should accept their kids for who they are, and be taught to give unconditional love and support regardless of outcome.

On a related topic, some parents fall into the "reversed dependency trap" where they over-identify and live vicariously through their youngsters sport experience, subsequently defining their own self-worth in terms of how successful their child is at sport (Smoll, 1997). Similarly, some parents in the heat of competition have a difficult time keeping their emotions in check. Derogatory comments directed at coaches, officials, teammates, and/or other competitors are inappropriate and often embarrassing to the athlete. Likewise, parents who constantly yell instructions from the stands may contradict a coach and confuse the child. Consequently, parents need to be exemplary role models, demonstrating appropriate sportsmanship like behaviors and comments, and emotional self-control skills.

But all fingers shouldn't be pointed at parents alone. Some conflicts that erupt between parent and athlete can be attributed to age related developmental factors. This might include hormonal changes due to biological maturation or a teenager's search for independence. For instance, well intentioned parents attempting to probe into their 15 year old son or daughters sport experience may run into unexpected roadblocks such as emotional mood swings, rebellious attitudes, communication breakdowns, or wanting more space and privacy. To compound matters further, as young athletes move toward adolescence, peer evaluations and peer comparison processes take on greater significance (Horn & Hasbrook, 1986). Hence, whereas coaches and parents play an important role in shaping young athletes early sport experiences, adolescents are more susceptible to peer influences, and somewhat less responsive to what the "old folks" have to say.

Communication

The importance of effective communication skills and positive social reinforcement techniques cannot be overstated (Gould et al, 1997; Martens et al, 1981; Smoll & Smith, 1996; Yukelson, 1997). The emotional ups and downs, joys and disappointments, trials and tribulations of competitive sport can be very trying for everyone involved. Young athletes in particular must learn how to keep winning and success in proper perspective. For instance, the outcome of a competitive contest (e.g., victory or defeat) can be the result of external factors beyond the athlete's control such as ability level of the opponent, playing conditions, poor coaching, or luck. Or it may be the result of factors within the athlete's control such as poise under pressure, executing skills effectively, and/or the amount of effort expended. By improving young athletes' understanding of why they performed the way they did, and the contingencies that underlie their performance, parents (and coaches) can instill within kids enhanced feelings of perceived competence and perceived control over their competitive athletic experience (Smith et al, 1983).

Likewise, parents need to be good mentors for their kids, providing guidance and support without pressuring and badgering (Rotella & Bunker, 1987). Parents should have open discussions with their children about the goals they are striving to achieve and what it takes to for them to excel at their sport. Active listening skills and supportive encouraging statements will go a long way in developing trust, mutual respect, confidence, and the will to move forward.

Along these lines, I have found kids to be very responsive to philosophical discussions about what it takes to be a champion (e.g., pride, belief, commitment, and perseverance), and mental training skills that might enhance their confidence, focus, and poise under pressure (e.g., relaxation and visualization techniques, pre-performance preparatory routines, energizing cues, and concentration refocusing techniques). Champions focus on targets, goals, desires, and solutions. They seek out weaknesses and work hard to eliminate them. Champions believe in themselves, expect to do well, are dedicated, determined, and driven by the desire to be the best they can possibly be. They commit themselves to excellence, and the goals they are striving to achieve, and are able to develop enough mental toughness and emotional self-control to perform well under a variety of difficult situations (Orlick, 1990).

Suggestions

Recognizing that attitude is everything, youngsters need to learn how to approach competition in a confident, focused manner. Young athletes should be taught to embrace their goals with a passion and be driven by the desire of wanting to get better. Based on one's current level of ability, success in competition should be viewed as a byproduct of the amount of preparation put into a task, the amount of effort expended, and one's willpower to stay on track (Vernacchia, McGuire, and Cook, 1992). Parents and coaches must help youngsters learn success resides in personal improvement, giving maximum effort, and striving to do one's best (Smith et al, 1983). Success then becomes a relative term based on what each individual is trying to accomplish. The gratification associated with committing oneself to a goal, and working diligently with enthusiasm and determination to reach these goals is what sport is all about.

Similarly, parents and children need to be aware of each other's goals and expectations. Since there are individual differences in what young athletes want out of sport, a premium should be placed on open and honest communication processes. Communication involves mutual sharing and mutual understanding (Yukelson, 1997). By getting things out in the open, and expressing how one truly feels, parents and athletes are in a better position to be responsive to each other's needs. Although kids have a tendency to be egocentric and think primarily of themselves, parents need to be respectful of the time, energy, commitment, and emotion kids put into their sport. Recognizing the fact that "kids will be kids", parents need to be patient, tolerant, empathetic, and understanding.

Case Studies of Parent-Athlete Issues

#1: Female Race Walker and Parental Expectations

Introduction:

Barbara was a 17 year old female race walker who was participating in the final domestic international track meet prior to the world championships. Barbara was coached by her father who is a track and field coach at the university which she was going to attend in the fall. He was not a member of the USA coaching staff for the upcoming world championships.

At the time of our first meeting, Barbara had yet to meet the world championship qualifying standard in her event, the 5,000 meter race walk. She had resigned herself to the fact that she would not qualify for the world championships and would return home after this domestic meet.

During the team meeting the night before the meet she was notified that her race, which was originally scheduled for 3,0000 meters, was now going to be moved to 5,000 meters in order to give her a last chance to qualify. She was upset by the last minute change since she had prepared mentally and physically to race 3,000 meters the next day and had resigned herself to the fact that she had not made the team.

Intervention:

I had observed that Barbara was upset as I watched her reaction to the announcements at the team meeting. I asked if she would like to talk about her feelings and thoughts regarding the situation. She appeared eager to discuss her situation and we met immediately after the team meeting. She related that her father had designed her training for a 3,000 meter race and felt unprepared both physically and mentally to race at 5,000 meters. She did not want to race the longer distance even though it would give her another opportunity to qualify for the world championships. This was an example of the following adage: " A person convinced against their will is still of the same opinion."

We talked about responding to the unexpected changes she was being asked to adapt to and the opportunities this new situation could provide for her. She cried, calmed down and appeared ready to accept the fact that she would race the longer distance. She then went to call her father to discuss the situation.

After discussing the situation with her father/coach they decided that Barbara would participate in the 5,000 meter race but only to the extent that she would race the first 3,000 meters and then drop out of the race. Barbara appeared to be torn between pleasing her father/coach and the USA coaches, particularly the coach for her event.

The day of the race Barbara asked her event coach to call her father to finalize the race plan. This occurred 20 minutes before the race began. Her father and her event coach agreed on a plan which would allow her to race the first 3,000 meters and then to use the last 2,000 meters of the race as a "cool down."

Outcome:

    Barbara executed the agreed upon race plan and did not qualify for the world. She appeared relieved to have this uncomfortable situation end.

#2: Male Junior Golfer and
The Intervention That Should Not Have Been

Introduction:

    Owen, an 18-year old, nationally ranked junior golfer had just failed completely at the State competition playing for his high school. He felt that he was very inconsistent, doing particularly bad during the first few holes. He stated that sometimes, "when it was too late: he was able to play great for the last holes. This pattern had been present for a little over one year.

Intervention:

    Initial assessment involved administration of the TAIS and a measure of self-confidence. In addition to the information from the initial interview, Owen was asked to develop a statement of goals. Owen was encouraged to participate in self-monitoring which would have to be conducted at the driving range or when playing for practice because of absence of tournaments for a few months.

    Owen attributed his poor shots to technical problems and tended to change his grip, his stance, etc. His main distractions came from within, from his own thoughts. He was often too tense at the beginning of the play. It was also evident that his life was dominated by golf and that he missed being with his friends. Owen's father was a golf pro and very invested in his career. The family had moved to Chicago two years prior and Owen stated that he missed his previous home and school.

    The interventions attempted were several - relaxation and arousal control, centering and refocusing exercises, identification of a stable pattern of thoughts and actions that avoided his making decisions under stress, he was also encouraged to cut down on golf time and engage in some other age-appropriate activities. Owen usually did not do the exercises agreed upon and always formulated some excuse.

    After the third session Owen said he was fine, he had seen his problem and could control it with relaxation and positive thinking. He agreed to continue working for a while but kept sabotaging the interventions. He did quite well on his first competition and totally lost it on the second, a more important tournament.

    At this point Owen had a very serious fight with his father and stopped golfing all together for a while. He received a golf scholarship to a college in the state he used to live and I assume he is there now.

Outcome:

    In retrospect, I think I failed by treating just as a sport performance what I now think was an adolescent father/son conflict, played out through golf when the son was getting better than the father. I don't know that they would have agreed to a more traditional psychological intervention; probably not; but I don't think that there can be improvement ignoring the underlying conflict.

#3: Female College Gymnast

Introduction:

Rachel, a 21-year old gymnast was referred by her university coach. The coach indicated that Rachel was experiencing decrements in her performance; was often moody, sullen, and temperamental ... especially when her parents were around. According to her coach Rachel has outstanding ability, a former Olympic bronze medal winner. When her parents are not around during practices she is a "leader" by example in determination, dedication, hard work, independence, and personal sacrifice. As soon as her parents show up to observe a practice she sulks, pouts in a corner, or follows the assistant coach around. The one competition where her parents were unable to attend she set a NCAA record for an all-around performance. She reportedly yells at her parents to leave the practice area and to not attend competitions. Reportedly, she appears to lose her concentration when they are around.

The coach has indicated that Rachel's parents are warm, but a bit over-protective of their daughter. They immigrated to be near their daughter. The parents run their own cafe just off of campus. Reportedly, the University students frequent the place heavily because of the exceptional food, friendly service, and LOW COST. Rachel has moved out of their house and lives with a senior medical student two blocks off campus.

Reportedly, Rachel is not doing very well during winter quarter. She indicated to her coach that she flunked her Chemistry examination and got a C- on her English paper. She maintains that she loves school but has been distracted lately........ "you know, with gymnastics in the morning and in the afternoon, working in the cafe, and trying to be with my friends..."

Intervention:

After exploring possible ways of defining and resolving issues, it was decided that a meeting with her parents followed by a meeting with all three of them might be helpful in resolving these feelings. It was suggested that perhaps the head coach could also meet with the parents to help them (parents) understand the nature of practices and performance during meets... and how their (parental expectations and behavior) presence affects outcome.

Following the meeting with her parents and the coach I met with Rachel and her parents to increase the level of mutual understanding and commitment to stated goals and objectives. This was followed by several individual meetings with Rachel to foster insight into the dynamics involving her parents and gymnastics.

Outcome:

Apparently, the series of meetings resulted in a change in Rachel's understanding of her relationship with her parents and how gymnastics "fits" into that dynamic. Her behavior during practices is much improved now that her parents are not allowed to observe practice. Her performances during meets has been outstanding. She has won all three all around titles following the two meetings with the three of them. Her parents continue to sit in the front row, but hold up signs of encouragement and support regardless of outcome.

#4: Female Youth Swimmer

Introduction:

Amanda was referred by her mother (and father) because Amanda was swimming "so poorly during meets". Amanda was brought in by her mother who introduced us then asked Amanda to wait outside in the outer office. Her mother begin to cite her "wonderful" 9-10 year old swim national records and inform me of her daughter's wonderful manners until just this year. "Now we just don't know what to do with her. She pouts, stays in her room with the door locked, talks on the phone to her girlfriends and we think that she also has a boyfriend ... now.. Some poor boy that lives on the South side of town." The mother continued to express exasperation at not being able to control her daughter the way she used to.... "I just don't know what's got into her...". After 20 minutes, I informed her that it might be most appropriate for Amanda to come in and for us to have a little chat.

Amanda presented herself as a very articulate 12 year old with a good grasp of the situation. She acknowledged that "mom is just trying to keep me her little girl., And I just want to grow up... I am almost 13 now. I am in 8th grade and know some stuff". When asked about why she is able to swim so well in practice and yet not perform during meets, she smirked with a little grin and remarked... "Its my parents, they think that I am the best and go around bragging about what a wonderful daughter they have and how that have given me the best training ... Its like they are taking all the credit. ... And sometimes I just get nervous too ... you know. Sometimes this winning is so important to everyone... I mean, I just want to do my best and have that be good enough. I know that I can be one of the best in the world even if people will just back off." At this point, Amanda became tearful and wept for a minute or so .... She suggested that I talk with her parents and get them to back off and just love her for who she is and not what she can do.

Intervention:

Subsequently, I met with her mother the following week; however, the father refused to attend. Her mother acknowledged that she had been less than loving and probably did spend too much time extolling her daughter's abilities as a swimmer at the expense of her other wonderful talents as a pianist, poet, and thespian. Her mother agreed to not mention her daughter's swimming activities for one week and praise her for her other accomplishments.

During the first few visits it became clear that Amanda needed recognition for her contributions in activities other than her swimming. She appeared to be somewhat passive aggressive at meets by consciously refusing to swim her best. While the possibility seemed to exist that she was also overly nervous because she might have believed that her status as a "loved" individual was contingent on her swimming performance. After careful interviews, her nervousness was adjudged to be within the "normal" range for competitive athletes. After the week of reprieve from constant bombardment regarding swimming, her mother reported that her daughter had really improved in her deportment around the house. She seemed happier and easier to get along with.

Outcome:

After three months of weekly visits Amanda broke the junior national record for the 100 meter back, 1000 meter free, and individual medley. She has been invited to the junior Olympics and to train for the upcoming Olympics. She reported that her mother had changed entirely and was one of her best "pals"... "We actually do things together and don't talk about swimming that much..." She even told me about the time she met dad... It was way cool !!!"

#5: The Homesick Junior National Long Jumper

Introduction:

Deborah was a 17-year-old female long jumper and member of the USA Junior National Track and Field Team which was preparing to compete in the World Championships. She was going into her senior year in high school. During training camp Deborah's coach had shared her concerns with me regarding Deborah's practice behavior. According to her coach she was detached, moody, and aloof as well as unresponsive to coaching suggestions and instructions.

After receiving this feedback I observed Deborah in both social and practice situations. My room in the training center was located close to the public telephones and I noticed that Deborah was frequently "on the phone" in her free time. One day during lunch, I observed several athletes and a trainer taking Deborah to the training room. The athletes had to pass through the lunchroom to get to the training room. Deborah was crying and appeared to be injured as a result of a training accident.

Intervention:

I approached Deborah the day after observing the lunchroom incident at the conclusion of her morning practice session. I expressed my concern for her health and asked if she was all right. Deborah said she was fine but that she was upset because it was her first time away from home for an extended period of time. She was very close to her family and was apprehensive about leaving the country to compete in the world championship meet. Her parents, especially her father, wanted her to return home because of the stress this situation was causing her.

I asked Deborah what she wanted to do. She replied that she was all right, then paused, and said that she wanted to compete at the world championships. It was during this meeting that she admitted to being homesick and relayed her parent's advice to me. She was torn between returning to the comfort of home and pursuing the reality of her athletic dreams.

Once Deborah had decided to stay on the team and travel to the world championships her practice and social behavior began to improve. We talked about how difficult it is to be away from home for the first time. In this case she was going to be far away from home as a result of the competition site for the world championships.

I suggested that she spend more time with other team members in social settings (i.e., shopping, at meals, etc.) since she had been socially isolating herself during the training camp.

We talked about the importance of having a support group and how this would make the travel, practice, and performance experience more enjoyable for her.

Outcome:

Once Deborah had made the decision to stay on the team she began to enjoy the situation she was in and performed extremely well at the world championships making the final of the long jump. More importantly she really enjoyed the social aspects of being a team member. She made several new friends and appeared to genuinely enjoy her teammates and benefited greatly from their mutual support.

#6: The Baseball Coach's Son

Introduction:

The baseball coach has voiced "lip service" for mental training for five years but just never got around to arranging to have a structured program developed. The consultant offered services to one or two individual players each year in response to their personal interest. The coach seemed oblivious to further arrangements because he felt he was already doing "mental training" as a coach.

The spring season was a bust. The summer finally came and more players began to show interest independent of the coach. The telephone rang on the 4th of July. The "coach" was calling to say that his son, Drew, a high school player (pitcher) was having problems, and he was desperate to get some help. Due to vacation schedules, I was faced with attempting to utilize two to three sessions spaced over eight days to affect change in a 17-year-old who feels the pressure of his father's image and who has lost confidence in his own ability due to his experience with high school coaches who have taken out their jealousy for the college coach on the celebrity kid. Minor "miracle number one" was to achieve rapport with an apprehensive and very skeptical young man who has size and ability but is faced with unduly high community expectations.

Intervention:

During our first meeting, we discussed why Drew was visiting with me. He acknowledged his sub-par performance and I explained what he could expect from me to handle the stress he was experiencing and implement some strategies to aid his performance. Drew outlined the situation as a "self-fulfilling prophecy" wherein he would buckle under the stress he was getting from fans, his parents, and coaches.

Drew was hoping to hear a "quick fix" solution that he knew wouldn't work any better than all the previous efforts he had put in. I decided to give him the answer out of his own repertoire for failures and this time label it accurately: "likely to fail, too." He seemed to perk up when he had permission to really blow it. "It's possible that on your next outing you could let go and really mess it up, but this time it just might be necessary to experience failure once more in a very big way before you are ready. In fact, I'm not really sure that you are going to be ready then. Only you will know whether you have gotten rid of all that whether you have blown it bad enough that you can let go."

At our next session, I asked him how he did in a recent game. He said, "Well, I don't know; I never got a chance to pitch, but I played right field and my hitting was really off again. I just can't seem to connect when I need to .... I mean I rip it in batting practice; but in the game, I just blow it.". I offered that this might be what it took for him to get it out of his system. Only he could tell for sure.

We then tried a simulation task. I gave him three "wads" of paper and asked him to throw them at a target I identified. Drew made a haphazard, sloppy effort as if he didn't care-- missed all three. I told him to watch and relax for a minute. I told him that I was going to throw three wads of paper. I told him I cared a great deal about hitting the target, but I knew that if I tried too hard, I couldn't get a clear picture of "hitting the target".

At this point, Drew asked to try again. I told him wait a minute, sit back, get some composure, take a couple of deep breaths; then create a picture of just the target. I then directed him to create a picture of the trajectory: a slow moving piece of paper which requires some arc. He was to then create a new target that allowed him to compensate for the arcing trajectory. When all this was completed, Drew was to throw the three wads of paper, figure out his error factor, calculate his compensation, then stop. He then was instructed to get composure and throw three in rapid order with a smooth motion. Just letting it happen comfortably. His task was then to figure out how this applied to his pitching and the session was over.

After one additional session in which the player became more and more intrigued, the consultation ended with substantially more "permissive" dialogue. The player was encouraged to continue "self-discovery," tempered by a sense of smooth motion, letting it happen. Make the decision .... create the image .... then go for it. Learn from each pitch; make adjustments in the target; keep the motion the same.

Outcome:

The coach came back four weeks later raving. He could not believe the difference. Drew had improved dramatically and his Dad, the coach, wanted to set up a regular plan for intervention for his son throughout his entire senior year.

What about the coach's own baseball team? Nothing mentioned - NOT A WORD. I guess we know where the priorities in life are. Perhaps, we know what is too threatening, also.

Discussion Questions

1. Was the intervention appropriate for the problem presented in each case? What other types of interventions might have been used to bring about similar or better results?

2. Discuss the phenomena of homesickness? Under what conditions/situations could you anticipate that young athletes are vulnerable to this phenomena?

3. What were the "tell tale" signs of homesickness which were displayed by the athlete in this situation?

4. What additional social strategies could be employed by coaches to help young athletes adjust to their first experiences "away from home" which involve domestic and international travel, unfamiliar living and competition situations, and a new social environment?

References

Brustad, R.J. (1996). Parental and peer influence in children's psychological development through sport. In F.L. Smoll, & R.E. Smith (Eds.). Children and youth in sport: A biopsychosocial perspective (pp. 112-124). Dubuque, IA: Brown and Benchmark.

Gantert, T. (1997). Parents vs. coaches: Competing for control. Lansing State Journal Newspaper, Tuesday, May, 6, 1997.

Gould, D., Tuffey, S., Udry, E., Loehr, J. (1997). Burnout in competitive junior tennis players: III. Individual differences in the burnout experience. The Sport Psychologist, 11, 257-276.

Gould, D., & Petlichkoff, L. (1988). Participation motivation and attrition in young athletes. In F.L. Smoll, R.J. Magill, & M.J. Ash (Eds.), Children in sport (3rd ed.) (pp. 161-178). Champaign, IL: Human Kinetics.

Hellstedt, J.C. (1987). The coach/parent/athlete relationship. The Sport Psychologist, 1, 151-160.

Horn, T.S. (1985). Coaches feedback and changes in children's perceptions of their physical competence. Journal of Educational Psychology, 77, 174-186.

Horn, T.S., & Hasbrook, C.A. (1986). Informational components underlying children's perceptions of their physical competence. In M.R. Weiss & D. Gould (Eds.), Sport for children and youths (pp. 81-88). Champaign, IL: Human Kinetics.

Martens, R. (1990). Successful coaching. Champaign, IL: Human Kinetics.

Martens, R., Christina, R.W., Harvey, J.S., & Sharkey, B.J. (1981). Coaching young athletes. Champaign, IL: Human Kinetics.

Orlick, T. (1990). In pursuit of excellence (2nd ed.). Champaign, IL: Human Kinetics.

Rotella, R.J., & Bunker, L.K. (1987). Parenting your superstar. Champaign, IL: Leisure Press.

Scanlan, T.K. (1986). Competitive stress in children. In M.R. Weiss & D. Gould (Eds.), Sport for children and youths (pp. 113-118). Champaign, IL: Human Kinetics.

Smith, N.J., Smith, R.E., & Smoll, F.L. (1983). Kidsports: A survival guide for parents. Reading, MA: Addison-Wesley.

Smoll, F.L. (1997). Improving the quality of coach-parent relationships in youth sports. In J.M. Williams (Ed.). Applied sport psychology: Personal growth to peak performance (3rd ed.) (pp. 63-73). Palo Alto, CA: Mayfield.

Smoll, F.L., & Smith, R.E. (1996). Competitive anxiety: Sources, consequences, and intervention strategies. In F.L Smoll & R. E. Smith (Eds.), Children and youth in sport: A biopsychosocial perspective (pp. 359-380). Dubuque, IA: Brown and Benchmark.

Vernacchia, R., McGuire, R., & Cook, D. (1992). Coaching mental excellence: It does matter whether you win or lose. Dubuque, IA: Brown and Benchmark.

Weiss, M. (1995). Children in sport: An educational model. In S.M. Murphy (Ed.), Sport psychology interventions (pp. 33-69). Champaign, IL: Human Kinetics.

Weiss, M. (1987). Self-esteem and achievement in children's sport and physical activity. In D. Gould & M.R. Weiss (Eds.), Advances in pediatric sport sciences (pp. 87-119). Champaign, IL: Human Kinetics.

Weiss, M., & Chaumeton, N. (1992). Motivational orientations in sport. In T.S. Horn (Ed.), Advances in sport psychology (pp. 61-99). Champaign, IL: Human Kinetics.

Yukelson, D. P. (1997). Communicating effectively. In J.M. Williams (Ed.). Applied sport psychology: Personal growth to peak performance (3rd ed.), (pp. 142-157). Palo Alto, CA: Mayfield.

CHAPTER 11

~ Mental Skills Training ~

Mark Thompson, Inner Edge

Previous case studies chapters should provide guidance for the applied sport psychologist who is asked to alleviate a defined performance issue such as an athlete lacking confidence, losing focus, "choking", or experiencing interpersonal conflict with a coach or parent. However, what about a situation in which there is no "presenting problem"? Is there relevance to analyzing case studies that address mental skills training, in general?

The answer should be an unqualified, "Yes!". Many reasons can be offered to support the necessity and value of utilizing case studies of mental skills training (MST). Foremost among these is the idea that a comprehensive mental skills training program can prevent the occurrence of potentially devastating performance problems. In other words, an ounce of prevention (mental skills training) is worth more than a pound of cure (intervention to alleviate an acute performance barrier). The title of this book, *Case Studies in Applied Sport Psychology: An Educational Approach*, was chosen to provide the potential reader with an understanding that its emphasis is on **education**, believing that education is the key to prevention and lasting change.

Similarly, **mental skills training** is being used to refer to a comprehensive educational program that seeks to "...develop, individualize, and refine mental skills...so that mental skills become an integral tool to use during a variety of pressure situations.". (Ravizza, 1988) This terminology is being used, rather than **psychological skills training** to highlight the differences between an educational approach and a more clinical, intervention approach. "MST" will be used with the exception of citing research which specifically uses the term "psychological skills training", whereby "PST" will be used.

The goal of many in the field of applied sport psychology is to develop acceptance and incorporation of mental skills training so that it becomes commonplace. The case studies in this chapter outline attempts to incorporate comprehensive MST programs for athletes and teams. The focus of this chapter will be an overview of the dynamics surrounding MST. Specific recommendations or guidelines for training program components (i.e., confidence, concentration, dealing with conflict, etc.) are covered in the other chapters, so little attempt will be made to address them in depth. This overview of MST will discuss the: rationale, common components, guidelines, limitations, and goals of training programs.

Rationale for Mental Skills Training

One argument for mental skills training programs has already been highlighted; the ability to prevent performance barriers. In addition, the rationale for incorporating MST into athletic development should be based on empirical evidence of its efficacy. However, until recently, the empirical evidence has been lacking. Until the late 1980's, practitioners had tremendous difficulty finding research that would back up their claims of MST efficacy. Few articles were published that detailed the components of such successful programs nor were there significant longitudinal findings of the utilization and effectiveness of mental skills training programs.

Greenspan and Feltz (1989) helped quantify the effectiveness of psychological skills training, when they reviewed more than 20 PST studies and concluded that educationally based psychological interventions were effective in increasing performance of college and adult athletes in competitive situations. They were unable to extend their finding beyond the college and adult populations due to the lack of studies with youth athletes. Five years later, Vealey (1994) found that nine of 12 studies testing psychological interventions demonstrated enhanced performance associated with PST.

As opposed to research investigating the impact of PST, Williams and Krane (1993) point to findings that elite athletes demonstrate higher levels of self-confidence than less-skilled athletes. Elite athletes also have more self-belief, better concentration, are less distracted/more focused, experience less anxiety, and have a greater capacity for rebounding from their mistakes. These findings may elicit "chicken vs. the egg" discussions, but the inference is that elite athletes benefit from foundational components of MST.

Increasingly, there appears to be a movement to evaluate the efficacy of "Mental Skills Packages" as opposed to more broad-based programs. These "MSP" usually involve a grouping of three or four mental skills and a specific focus on the development of these limited components. The reasons for this movement have yet to be clarified, but one may assume that the number of components are being limited in the interest of research clarity or the influence of a number of limitations discussed later in this chapter. Regardless, the incorporation of a "MSP" rather than a more comprehensive "MST" may be a viable option as an introductory vehicle for working with athletes, teams, and coaches.

Gordin and Reardon (1995) acknowledge the value of these specific components, but allude to the necessity of a more comprehensive program. They propose that more common, "popular" skills like imagery, visualization, and self-talk management are appealing because of the promise of quick results. However, they believe the ability to incorporate these skills in a high pressure atmosphere is dependent on the development of concentration, composure, and confidence abilities. These abilities are considered "fundamental" and are prerequisites to a "Flow State".

Finally, a logical argument for the value of MST, via experiential evidence. Even elite athletes acknowledge the role mental skills play in their performance. Elite athletes are likely to credit their slim margin of victory to their "mental gameplan". Whether it is through a statement that "sport is 80% mental", or a recognition that they failed because they experienced a "mental letdown", the elite athlete is acknowledging the value of MST and the amount of work they have put into the development of their mental game, in addition to their physical skills.

Common Components of Mental Skills Training

What one chooses to include as components of mental skills training programs is likely to vary, to a degree. One might assume that any MST will include "the basics" such as goal-setting, relaxation training, imagery, thought-stopping and self-talk, and concentration exercises. However, is there agreement as to what "the basics" are and if they are relevant for the given situation? This section will attempt to answer that question.

Graham and Yocom, in their book, *Mental Toughness Training for Golf* (1990), highlight components they believe essential to performance excellence in golf. Among these are: visualization, breathing exercises, relaxation, and modeling. These components are the most relevant to general MST. Loehr, in *Mental Toughness Training for Sports* (1986), encourages the use of visualization, self-motivation strategies, relaxation, breath control, activation strategies, self-talk, and focus exercises. Comparing the two, one can readily identify commonalities, but also note some differences, likely reflective of differences in ideology. This difference in ideology is likely to be reflected in a number of MST programs.

Syer and Connolly (1984), incorporate a variety of skills and exercises in their twelve-week programme. Among these are: relaxation, concentration exercises, thought-stopping, coping strategies, positive self-talk, modeling, goal-setting, and visualization. The terminology used may differ, but the concepts underlying them conform to these commonly-used components. Orlick (1986) identifies goal-setting, focus, psychological preparation, re-focusing, confidence, relaxation, and imagery as components of his "Psyching for Sport" program. Again, comparing the two programs, one can readily see similarities and differences.

The previous examples are provided to offer a glimpse of the components typically included in published psychological skills training programs. However, one might still wonder if research indicates common components for MST. Weinberg and Gould (1995) cite goal-setting, imagery, arousal regulation, concentration, and mental preparation as components of PST recommended by educational sport psychologists. Weinberg and Williams (1993) recommend the inclusion of strategies to address anxiety management, imagery, goal-setting, concentration, self-talk, thought-stopping, performance routines, and self-confidence.

Vealey (1988) branches out from the strict performance-focused orientation and recommends PST that addresses personal development in addition to performance enhancement. Components she identifies as essential to this "holistic" PST include: volition, self-awareness, self-esteem, self-confidence, physical arousal, mental arousal, attention, interpersonal skills, and lifestyle management. The incorporation of the last two components is the primary difference between Vealey's recommendations and other PST programs outlined here.

Viewing the variety of MST components, some "basics" do emerge. Relaxation/arousal management is a very common aspect, as is visualization/imagery. Goal-setting, concentration, confidence, and coping strategies are also prevalent. Consequently, the answer to the question of the existence of "the basics" for MST appears to be yes. However, situational dynamics will determine variances to these basics, such as if, and how, they will be addressed. The case studies in this chapter reflect this variety. As one reads these cases, thought should be given to why the program was structured in such a manner and are there changes that would have made the program more effective.

Guidelines for Mental Skills Training

The following are general guidelines for mental skills training programs. An acknowledgment is made in advance, recognizing the significant variance between programs dependent on the training of the sport psychology professional, the type of sport involved, the situational constraints for the program, the perception of relevant skills to be addressed, and the consulting style of the practitioner. The case studies in this chapter, to varying degrees, adhere to many of the following guidelines:

- The best time to incorporate a mental skills training program is in the off-season or during pre-season (Weinberg & Williams, 1993). This allows more time to develop necessary skills and avoids the time crunch associated with the competitive season. Case #8 in this chapter demonstrates the negative impact of inappropriately timed MST.

- The MST should be preceded by, or inclusive of an assessment of individuals' psychological skills and the relevance of the skills to the performance arena. (Weinberg & Williams, 1993) This assessment should also involve information from "informal" assessments (i.e., watching practices, game performance, conversations with the athlete, etc.). By assessing the present abilities and necessary skills, the applied sport psychologist can tailor the program to meet the needs of the athletes.

- During the beginning stages of MST, the applied sport psychology practitioner should educate the athletes and coaches about the program. This education should include an overview of the components involved, how the skills are to be developed, the importance of the skills, and the commitment necessary to derive benefit from MST. This "education" should be viewed as a "sales pitch". The practitioner needs to sell the athletes and coaches on the program to elicit the necessary initial commitment to give the program a chance. Ravizza's article "Gaining entry with athletic personnel for season-long consulting", can be a valuable resource for understanding this "selling" component. Recommendations for "Gaining Entry", as discussed in the article:

  - *Establishing respect, credibility, and trust* is identified as critical to the process. One means of establishing these elements is the development of an "individualized" program.

  - *Gaining the head coach's respect* is a recognition of the typical hierarchy of a sport setting. Failure to establish respect and trust will doom a program.

  - *Knowledge of the sport* includes knowing task-relevant demands and inherent variations in the sport. This knowledge should be developed through reading, talking with participants, and viewing actual practice and competition.

- *Become knowledgeable of coach's orientation and team dynamics* implies that an understanding the coach's and team's history with sport psychology, as well as the coach's philosophy and situational demands, will be very helpful.
- *Gain support at all levels of the organization* is a recognition of the politics and territoriality of sport. It is essential that the consultant develops as many supporters from as many levels as possible, to be able to develop programs with little resistance.
- *Clarifying the services provided* is a point that is elaborated under the proceeding primary bullet.
- *Presentation to coaching staff and athletes* should be "dynamic, somewhat entertaining, and must demonstrate knowledge about the sport". Just as with any effective presentation, one must read the audience and utilize examples with which the athletes and coaches can identify.

(Ravizza, 1988)

- The applied sport psychologist needs to, at the outset, define his or her parameters. The practitioner needs to clearly define his or her role (i.e., there as a consultant, not a coach, fan, or groupie). The practitioner should also clearly outline his or her availability and expectations of the athletes and coaches. This is a preemptive move to minimize potential conflict and misunderstanding.
- Weinberg and Gould (1995) suggest three phases be included in the PST: **Education**, **Acquisition**, and **Practice**. The *Education* phase focuses on the importance of the development of psychological skills. The *Acquisition* phase focuses on the strategies and techniques involved in learning the different skills. Finally, the *Practice* phase focuses on the preparation of psychological skills for performance situations. A fourth phase, should be considered; that of a **Performance** phase. Weinberg and Gould indicate the need to practice skills for integration into performance. However, the dynamics of competition/actual performance are sometimes so unique, that practice is not sufficient. Consequently, a fourth phase which focuses on assessing how effective an athlete is at incorporating the skills in performance is essential.
- Observing practice and competition, whenever possible, should be a priority of the applied sport psychology professional. This allows the MST administrator to assess, first-hand, how well the skills are being learned and incorporated. The observation can also provide valuable insight into how to work with specific athletes. (Gould, Tammen, Murphy, & May, 1989: Partington & Orlick, 1987)

♦ Components of MST should reflect periodized and hierarchical mental skills. An example is Gordin and Reardon's (1995) progression of mental skills, as described in this excerpt:

"As the various skills are molded into a core of fundamental abilities that are integrated into the personality style of the athlete, emphasis shifts to achievement of automaticity and a flow state in focused practice sessions. At all times, the ultimate focus is on preparation for the conditions leading to a flow experience at the competition(s) deemed most important to the athlete. Physical and psychological training cycles are focused toward a simultaneous peak, thereby providing the best opportunity for an optimal experience and peak performance."

♦ MST requires a long-term commitment from both the practitioner and the overseeing organization (i.e., professional team, US Olympic team, university athletic department, junior league). There should be a recognition of two factors associated with MST: 1) It takes time to develop and integrate psychological skills., and 2) Consistency is essential to the long-term benefit of any program.

There are undoubtedly a number of other possible guidelines to be offered. However, these general guidelines should address some of the most common issues associated with MST.

Limitations of Mental Skills Training

For many athletes, coaches, sport administrators, and even sport psychology practitioners, the idea of utilizing a sport psychology consultant for a mental skills training program may not fit their paradigm of the role of sport psychology. The preeminent paradigm is likely to be one in which the applied sport psychologist is involved if, and only if, a "problem" has surfaced and is viewed as an acute occurrence that the "shrink" can exorcise. This characterization may be a little harsh, but many athletes, coaches, etc. do not view sport psychology as something that comes in a "program". Rather, sport psychology is often viewed as the quick fix so everyone can get back to their normal business of physical and technical development.

This failure to view sport psychology as being effective, or more effective, packaged as MST, is a significant hindrance. The thinking goes, "If the potential customers don't buy into the idea of MST, how will MST ever gain acceptance and become the norm?". Historically, structured MST has not been viewed as essential to the development of athletes. Instead, many assumed that mental skills developed as physical and technical skills and abilities were honed. Time that would need to be devoted to MST would only take away from more important practice and conditioning time. To be honest, part of this limitation may stem from the inability or reluctance of sport psychology professionals to creatively develop training that would fit into the practice structure. Instead, utilizing training sessions more similar to class lectures, team meetings, or other "artificial" settings.

Moving beyond the acceptance of MST, other limitations are common. Weinberg and Williams (1993) recognize situational constraints to PST. Chief among these constraints is time. The athlete or team may be faced with a limited amount of time to learn and incorporate the psychological skills. Other constraints include: a lack of time for individual work within a team setting, verifying the actual practice of skills by the athletes, maintaining contact with the athletes during the program, receiving and maintaining time allotments from the coaching staff for PST, and the day-to-day availability of the sport psychology consultant.

Thompson (1997) identified a variety of limitations associated with MST. Similar to Weinberg and Williams, Thompson noted that time posed the greatest limitation. Coaches and athletes, often do not want to "take time away" from regular practice for MST. This problem can be exacerbated when unforeseen elements come into play (i.e., weather, illness, injuries). With the NCAA 20-hour guideline for college athletes, college coaches have possibly become even more protective of the time they are allowed with their athletes. Other limitations Thompson noted were: lack of commitment of athletes, lack of sport psychology personnel, no consequences for failure to practice skills or complete tasks, and lack of support from coaching staff.

A final limitation is the difficulty for applied sport psychology professionals to provide undeniable, indisputable evidence that MST is effective in enhancing performance or preventing performance slumps. As previously noted, sport psychology is associated more with alleviating acute performance issues than with a comprehensive mental training program. In the case of acute performance issues, it is much easier to establish the effect of sport psychology intervention. Conversely, if MST is incorporated prior to a season, with a team with new players, with unique chemistry, and revised coaching strategies, how does one unequivocally attest to the positive influence of MST, other than by athlete and coach testimonials?

Goals of Mental Skills Training

The goals of mental skills training will be dependent on the goals of three parties: 1) the practitioner, 2) the decision-making authority (i.e., coach, athletic director, parent, etc.) who endorsed the MST, and 3) the athletes who are participants in the MST. In this chapter and others, it is recommended that the practitioner operate as an objective resource for athletes and coaches. Consequently, the goals of the practitioner should be those of the athletes and coaches with whom they work. However, the applied sport psychologist can still have over-riding, philosophical goals for MST. Possible goals could be: performance enhancement, minimal conflict, generalization of skills to non-sport arenas, and general life enrichment. Vealey's (1988) proposed PST is an example of a program where the practitioner's goals extend beyond the boundaries of sport to include personal development.

One would hope that the goals of the coach, athletic director, parent, or other party that approved the MST, would be consistent with the goals of the practitioner and the athletes. However, the decision to institute MST may result from any number of factors. A college coach may be instructed by the athletic director that his or her team will participate in MST as a means of cooperating with a faculty member's research agenda. An athletic director might recommend MST to diminish negative publicity surrounding actions of the school's athletes. The parent might institute MST because the parents of a competing athlete have done so.

None of these examples are inherently bad reasons for instituting MST, but the motivation behind its institution can have significant influence on the goals for the program. Ideally, the goals of the coach, AD, parent, etc. would be that MST enhances performance in and out of the sport arena. However, there may be extenuating circumstances, similar to those mentioned, which alter these ideal goals, resulting in more self-serving or situation-specific ones.

Athletes' goals for MST should be simple, focusing on performance benefits associated with enhanced mental skills. In reality, athletes' goals probably vary little from this performance-focused orientation. Not all athletes desire to be the best, but most desire to be better. Not all athletes believe in the value of MST, but many are willing to invest part of themselves into a program with the hope of improving. Regardless of the goals of practitioners, coaches, etc., athletes' goals should be respected and athletes should be involved in establishing the goals of any MST program.

Summary

Mental skills training is not appropriate for all situations. Comprehensive programs are not applicable in circumstances where there is need for speed to assist a coach or athlete with an acute performance problem. However, MST should figure prominently in the future of applied sport psychology. Mental skills training programs should be viewed as opportunities to develop skills that will aid the athlete in avoiding potential performance pitfalls. They can also provide coaches with a greater understanding of the psychological dynamics of performance and how to train for them.

The case studies to follow will demonstrate that mental skills training programs often have common components, such as goal-setting, relaxation training, imagery, and strategies for enhancing self-talk. However, the programs are also far from being carbon copies; reflecting the training and orientation of the sport psychology professional.

The guidelines for MST previously offered are present to varying extents in the subsequent cases. However, situational dynamics influence the degree to which such guidelines can be followed. Part of the role of an applied sport psychology consultant is the professional freedom to adjust a program as is deemed necessary to achieve the goals set forth. These situational dynamics may also take the form of limitations that compromise the quality of MST and the effectiveness of the sport psychology practitioner.

Case Studies of Mental Skills Training

#1: College Crew Teams

Introduction:

Over two seasons, mandatory weekly performance enhancement sessions were conducted with the men's and women's crew teams. They included discussions of peak performance, communication, cohesiveness, arousal recognition and control, motivation, visualization, concentration, self-talk and pain management. The sessions were held in the evening in a classroom setting and lasted for the first eight weeks of the season. The student-athletes were also given the opportunity and encouraged by the coaching staff to pursue performance enhancement training. Initially, numerous student-athletes took advantage of this opportunity; however, during the middle of the season attendance dropped off drastically until about two weeks prior to the National Championships when suddenly there was a dramatic increase in participation.

A follow-up evaluation indicated that the student-athletes believed the performance enhancement sessions were valuable. However, they requested that they not be held at night and that they become more specifically applied to rowing. From the coaches' and sport psychology consultant's perspective the biggest problem was that after initially learning a number of performance enhancement skills most of the student-athletes neglected regular practice of the skills until the very end of the season immediately prior to the national championships.

Intervention:

The coaches and sport psychology consultant met on numerous occasions to discuss improvements in the performance enhancement program for the upcoming year. It was decided that in addition to the weekly performance enhancement sessions, the new program would incorporate performance enhancement into the circuit training program and also into the water workouts.

The circuit training program, conducted twice a week, would now consist of 4 x 20 minute stations: (1) Rowing Ergometer, (2) Weight Circuit, (3) Plyometrics, and (4) Performance Enhancement Training. The performance enhancement training station involved body awareness development relative to various rowing positions, tension/relaxation practice for key muscle groups, and focusing and visualization for training and competition (i.e., sit in "catch" position - tense then relax hands, neck, shoulders, face. Practice relaxed easy stroke, relaxed medium stroke, relaxed 99% effort stroke. Guided visualization of 2,000 meter race (timed 7 minutes) general comments - start, sprint, base pop-off-slide, catch a crab, wind, miss warm up, use of alternate.) The performance enhancement training station was developed by the sport psychology consultant and the coaches; however, the head coach directed the station.

Performance enhancement training was also incorporated into water practice four times a week for approximately 15 minutes. This training, although developed by the coach and sport psychology consultant, was directed by the coxswain. It included tensing and relaxing specific muscle groups while in various rowing positions. This was followed by deep breathing and visualizations. First of a rower they admired taking a perfect stroke, then themselves rowing a perfect stroke from an external perspective, then internally visualizing their perfect stroke, emphasizing the kinesthetic aspect. They then visualized the U.S. National Team boat (or a crew they looked up to) in "flow," next they externally visualized their boat in "flow" and finally from an internal perspective they visualized "flow" in their boat emphasizing the "feel." They were then guided through a visualization of their workout for the day (i.e., 6 x 4 minute pieces on 12 minutes - approach each piece positively, relaxed, and focused, giving your best effort).

Outcome:

A follow-up evaluation indicated that the student-athletes believed that the new program was extremely applied and helped them to perform better in both practices and competitions. They also reported practicing various performance enhancement skills on their own more often than last year and transferring these skills into academic and personal situations. A number of athletes noted that they felt mental training was more important because their head coach was more actively involved and also because the weekly mental training sessions were held during practice time rather than at night. The coxswains' believed that the "on the water" mental training helped them become more adept at recognizing tension in their crew and it greatly assisted them in developing rapport.

The coaches reported that daily practices were more productive, that the student-athletes demonstrated greater kinesthetic awareness and improved concentration skills. The team also performed better in competition. (All boats qualified for Nationals.) The coaches also mentioned that an additional benefit of the performance enhancement station was that it provided an opportunity to physiological recovery so that the student-athletes worked harder on the other stations in the circuit.

An improvement that will be made for next year will include securing and utilizing a room off the weight room for the performance enhancement training station. The reason for this is that the weight room was extremely noisy and frequently there were interruptions. However, after the skills have been learned, the station will be moved back into the weight room to help the student-athlete learn and practice the ability to deal with a variety of distractions.

Tapes of elite crews, shown by the coaches at the beginning of the season, will be made available to the student-athletes all year. In addition, each student-athlete and each boat will be videotaped. The student-athletes will also be asked to write out their visualizations of their perfect stroke and flow. These measures will be taken to help insure that each student-athlete's visualizations are as accurate and appropriate as possible so that they can receive the maximum benefit from their visualization practice.

#2: High School Girls' Swim Team

Introduction:

A high school girls' swim team had a highly successful season, finishing undefeated in dual meets and invitationals, finishing second in the Central District Championships by just three points (262-259) and setting three school, one state, and one National high school record. However, the season was tarnished by a very disappointing high school state championship performance. At the state meet only three of fifteen swims were a season/lifetime best for the individual or relay. This resulted in an eighth place team finish.

Intervention:

The following year the high school girls' swim team began psychological preparation for the high school championship meet on the first day of practice. The psychological intervention during the ensuing months consisted of the following:

- Weekly team meetings to teach a variety of mental skills including goal setting, cognitive restructuring (self-talk modification), relaxation training, anxiety/arousal management training, and mental imagery training.
- Completion of goal sheets by all District-qualifying swimmers, listing team, individual, and relay goals.
- Completion of the Psychological Skills Inventory for Sports (PSIS-5).
- Individual review of goal sheets and test results with focus on identification of strengths & weaknesses, and development of interventions to address the weaknesses.
- Discussion of the meet schedule with the athletes, with identification of those that would receive extra mental focus.
- Daily stressing of mental training by the coach during workouts. At least one set per practice was to utilize "concentration/focused sets." During these sets, swimmers were to focus on specific mental aspects of performance, such as mental rehearsal, self-talk monitoring, arousal rehearsal, etc.
- Post-testing using the PSIS-5, conducted one week prior to the Central District Championship Meet. This meet was the "major competition" for all non-State Meet swimmers.

The PSIS-5 is a 45 item self-report instrument derived from more than ten years of research with over 800 elite, pre-elite, and non-elite male and female athletes at world class, national, and collegiate levels. While it is still in the experimental stages, scores on each of the PSIS scales offer some relevant information regarding levels of proficiency across the skill domains represented by the scales. A 5-point Likert scale is employed to respond to each of the 45 questions, and responses are awarded a numerical value for scoring purposes. Scores on scales measuring Anxiety, Concentration, Confidence, Mental Preparation, Motivation, and Team Emphasis can be reflected as percentile scores to assess relative levels of proficiency within a given athlete.

Outcome:

Improved performance was evident at the Central District Championships where 25 of 31 swims were season or lifetime bests. (Three of the non-best times involved a swimmer who was seriously injured). The team won the Central District Championships scoring 299 points, and increase of 40 points over the previous year.

The following weekend at the State's School Championships the team scored 140 points (an increase of 84 points over the previous year), easily winning the State Championship. In the process, they set seven school records, two State records, and one National High School record. Of 34 individual and relay swims, 28 were lifetime bests. Included in this number were ten individual or relay races in which lifetime bests were achieved in the preliminaries and then further improved in the finals at night. Lifetime bests were achieved in 15 of 16 performances in the finals.

While the performances were impressive, the manner in which they were accomplished was even more interesting. Most swimmers reported much less anxiety than they had expected; they enjoyed themselves. The tempo for the meet was set with a State Record 200 Medley Relay in the first event and continued through a succession of individual life best swims to the 400 Freestyle Relay which won the event, dropping nearly seven seconds from the season's best.

Mental skills training appeared to contribute substantially to the improved performance of the high school swim team. The ability to more effectively concentrate and control anxiety through improved mental preparation skills bolstered team and individual confidence. Increased confidence reinforced greater achievement motivation and team cohesion.

Interestingly enough, there was virtually no psychological intervention formally employed at the state meet. None was necessary because all of the work had been done throughout the season. Each swimmer had "programmed" herself for success and simply had to let it happen.

Implicit in the entire psychological skills learning process was a greater sense of control and mastery over team and individual performance. This control was demonstrated by team selected low points in the season and ultimately by the peak performance achieved at the High School Championship Meet.

#3: Female College Fencer

Introduction:

Jamie first came to me four years ago. Unlike most fencers, she started her career in fencing late (high school) and competes on a perennial national championship team made up of intercollegiate fencers who were former-junior national champions. First alternate on the varsity team her sophomore year and number one fencer on JV, Jamie's initial presenting problem centered around pre-competitive anxiety and social comparison processes (i.e., doubts about her ability compared to others, desire to move up the depth chart, stop losing to people she should beat, etc.). A fast learner with good athletic ability who loves the psychological challenge of fencing, Jamie would often get frustrated with herself when things didn't go the way she expected. Recognizing she had a lot of technical things to work on (i.e., foot work, disengagement's parry-repost, proper decision making on a strip, etc.), she would often put extra pressure on herself trying too hard to impress the coaches. Jamie reports her mind would wander both in practice and at competitions; she would get sloppy on the strip and would force her actions rather than react to what is going on.

Intervention:

In order to help Jamie develop the proper mind set for both practice and competition, I introduced her to a comprehensive Mental Training Program that included Goal Setting, Anxiety Management, Pre-Performance Routines, Attentional Focus, Energy Management, Visualization Training, and Life Skill Development. She wanted to work on consistency, preparation, confidence, and relaxation on the strip. My goal was to help her feel more confident, focused, and in control of those things that she wanted to occur, both on and off the fencing strip.

First, we talked about attitude and the importance of setting Jamie's mind up for success. That is, coming to practice energetic, mentally ready to learn, committed to having a quality workout and not getting so frustrated if things don't go the way she wants. We then set up a goal setting program that focused on short term performance goals as well as long range outcome goals. We discussed the importance of staying task oriented and not getting so caught up in the end result, keeping things in perspective, and focusing on things she can control (i.e., her attitude, mental readiness to perform, level of intensity, focus of concentration, and trusting her actions). We worked extensively on relaxation and diaphragmatic breathing techniques to help her feel more relaxed, balanced, and in control on the strip. We developed systematic pre-performance routines to help improve her consistency and mental/ emotional tenacity while performing on the strip. I utilized cognitive restructuring techniques to help Jamie dispute negative self-talk, take more risks, and improve her powers of anticipation and decision making. Visualization techniques were implemented for Jamie to imagine herself performing at optimal levels while competing in tournaments. In addition, we worked on coping rehearsal techniques to help her refocus on task relevant thoughts while competing and deal with distractions more effectively.

An important part of her mental plan was her pre-performance routine. Since Jamie was susceptible to pre-competitive anxiety, I felt it was important that she had something to trust and turn to in the heat of competition that would help her feel relaxed, focused, and in control no matter what the situation. Through interviewing and observation, we came up with her mask being a good focal point to think about to trigger the desired response (i.e., she steps onto the strip, makes sure her electronic devices are hooked up correctly, goes into a knee squat s and "pops up" strong to help energize self properly, acknowledges her opponent, then the mask *comes down* and the *"ultimate competitor"* comes out). The mask signifies she is ready to compete; that is, she is focused, energized, mentally and emotionally ready to reach for her best and completely committed to the task at hand. I asked that she make a 100% commitment to her mental readiness to perform and evaluate the effectiveness of her routine accordingly.

Based on the feeling and focus she wanted to carry with her into competition, we then developed a "Script of Excellence" and subsequent audio visualization tape to help Jamie program her mind, body, and emotions for success. This mastery rehearsal tape, set to her favorite music included goals, positive affirmations, the attitude and intensity level she wanted to bring with her into competition, and energizing cues that helped her feel poised, confident, focused, and in control of her thoughts and actions. Jamie kept a mental training log/journal from which to evaluate her own performance in terms of how well she adhered to her mental plans for both training, competition, as well as things that might undermine her concentration or self esteem outside her sport (i.e., school, interpersonal relationships, etc.).

Jamie made great improvement her sophomore year. She made a strong commitment to mental training, recognized the importance of taking the time to mentally prepare for training and competition, found a focus that worked for her, and reported feeling less preoccupied with social comparison processes. She competed well, improved immensely, her frequency of negative self talk decreased, enjoyment and self-satisfaction increased, and overall, was very happy with the progress she made.

In her Junior year, opportunity presented itself for Jamie to move up the depth chart. In October, she was hit by a car while riding her bike and suffered extensive damage to her lower body (bruises, abrasions, and a cut on her leg that required more than 150 stitches). As a result of this setback, old tendencies resurfaced (i.e., unrealistic expectations, emotional instability, self imposed pressure of trying to come back too soon, lots of doubts and "what if's" regarding flexibility, strength of knee ligament, and role on the team).

My intervention focused on "One Step at a Time." We discussed things that worked the previous year, underlying reasons for the progress she made, the importance of focusing on things she can control while never losing sight of her dreams and aspirations. We then dealt directly with Jamie's feelings of anger and frustration, developed a goal setting program that was appropriate for her rehabilitation and return to her sport, worked extensively on visualization training (i.e., healing imagery, goal achieving strategies, coping rehearsal, and mastery rehearsal techniques(, listened intently to her fears and concerns, and provided counseling in the areas of stress management, responsible decision making, and life skill development (i.e., helped her balance her role as both student and athlete).

As the season progressed, Jamie's injury healed, and she returned to be a valuable asset to the team. We continued to refine her mental plans for competition, in particular, energy management for competition day, (i.e., tournaments can be very demanding, lasting as much as 12 hours a day, hence fencers must learn how to regulate their arousal and be able to turn on and off their concentration light switch when necessary), mental tenacity on the strip, breathing and relaxation techniques, and refinement of her pre-performance routine. In terms of the latter point, a teammate taught her a progressive relaxation technique (tense and relax grip pressure in her thumb and forefinger) which enabled her to get proper feel and balance of the foil in her hand. Consequently, we incorporated this into her routine prior to the mask coming down signifying it is time to compete. Jamie's coaches were very happy with her poise, aggressiveness, inner confidence, and relaxed, yet mentally tough focus. Jamie made great strides and was instrumental in leading her team into the NCAA Championships.

The final day of competition at the NCAA Tournament brought about an unusual circumstance. Jamie was having difficulty fencing. She had talked with me the day before about being ill as well as anxious about the quality of her training days leading up to the tournament. She looked tired and frustrated. Coach was about to take her out of the line up when he asked that I intervene immediately. We found a spot where we could be alone and talked about putting past matches during the day, anxieties, fears, distractions including her illness and perceived lack of quality preparation behind her. I challenged her not to succumb to these self destructive thoughts and, instead, be mentally tough, get back to trusting herself (i.e., all the hard work and preparation she has put into this moment, and most importantly, trust the basic ingredients that make up her pre-performance routine when she walks onto the strip). This hit a chord for Jamie said she found herself taking her routine for granted, going through the motions, as opposed to using her routine to help her focus properly and go out and reach for her best.

I was very proud of Jamie that day. She was fantastic. She regrouped her composure, refocused her concentration, trusted herself in the face of adversity, and was a force to be reckoned with the rest of the tournament, leading her team to a second straight national championship. After the celebration, the coach called me at home wondering what kind of miracle I did to turn her around. I told him there are no miracles, she was the one who worked hard to improve both mentally and physically the past two years; she was the one who committed herself to mental training, and she was the one who trusted herself and regained control when she needed it the most.

Outcome:

Jamie had a very successful senior year as a student-athlete both on and off the fencing strip. She was honored as a First Team All American in her sport, was an outstanding student-athlete with an exceptional GPA, was active in various honor societies and university student activities, and a pleasure to be around. Currently a fifth year senior and an undergraduate coaching assistant, her goals have changed and now Jamie has Olympic aspirations. Nationally, she is moving up the depth chart. As a result, her commitment to fencing and training has increased. She continues to come in on a regular basis, and our mental training sessions are geared toward staying mentally focused, emotionally strong, and confident in herself while competing against the best in the country. Her visualization skills have improved over the years and she reports being very good at visualizing herself successfully executing her routine and fence perfectly with fluid motion, rhythm, confidence, and feel. In addition, much of our conversations revolve around managing stress effectively and keeping things in proper perspective. A major concern is identity foreclosure (i.e., becoming engulfed in her identity as a fencer and the dream of being an Olympian, to the exclusion of having a well rounded life outside her sport).

In retrospect, Jamie attributes much of her success to her commitment to mental training. As she puts it, "it is so easy to get lost on the strip, or get caught up in who it is you are competing against. Consequently, learning how to concentrate is an important part of keeping focused." Now that she is trying to secure a spot on the 1996 Olympic Team, she has a much different understanding of what she needs from herself to be successful. According to Jamie, mental training is an ongoing process of assimilation and accommodation. Whether it is dealing appropriately with the adrenaline or nervousness prior to a match or remaining poised and controlled on the strip, there is always something new to assimilate and take care of in one's quest to be the best This past year, she has done extremely well in her major circuit events and is one step closer to achieving her Olympic dream by recently being named to the United States National Fencing Team.

#4: Male Professional Golfer

Introduction:

Lance was PGA tour player. He had been an All-American college golfer but his tour career was in the journeyman category at best. He did win one tour event but most of his years were spent struggling to stay exempt from the next year's qualifying school.

Lance was an extremely analytical, perfectionistic person who played very mechanically with very little touch or feel. He hit thousands of balls and worked very hard on his technique. However, it was very hard for him to let go of his mechanics and swing with tempo and rhythm especially in tight spots. He tended to steer or guide his shots rather than swinging through them when he was under any type of pressure. His perfectionistic attitude never let him accept anything other than a mechanically perfect swing even though the ball might end up inches from the hole.

Intervention:

Techniques and strategies which were tried with this golfer were: relaxation training, coping tapes, mastery tapes, Cybervision-type videos of his swing, pre-shot routines, goal setting, process vs. product, playing in an analytic mode vs. a self judgmental mode, visualization training, and breathing exercises. These were met with varying levels of interest and commitment. The overriding factor of Lance's perfectionism stood as an obstacle to true incorporation of many of the techniques and strategies.

Outcome:

During the next eight years the player had a modicum of success finishing second once and third once while retaining his tour card. Three years ago he lost his card, went back to tour qualifying school and regained it but never again achieved the level of success he wanted. He left the tour a year ago to coach a college golf team.

5: Elite Male Race Walker

Introduction:

Arthur was a very promising 20 Kilometer Race Walker, whose goal was to make the Summer Olympic Team. I had met Arthur a few times in Colorado at various developmental camps at the Olympic Training Center, where he expressed an interest in learning more about visualization and the mental side of his sport. In March, Arthur and I met for a prolonged period of time at a National Race Walking Event in Long Beach, California to discuss various mental plans for future competitions. In particular, he liked the idea of having his own audio visualization tape incorporating goals, positive affirmations, mental tenacity, and poise under pressure.

Intervention:

First, we assessed his goals, expectations, incentives, as well as personal and athletic strengths and weaknesses. I also had him reflect upon his best and worst races (similar to concentration skills while competing). Arthur perceives himself to be extremely gifted athletically and is confident in his ability. Personally, he draws faith and inspiration from his relationship with God and his family and is driven by a long-time desire of wanting to be a member of the Olympic Team since he was 8 years old.

Although he reports being in the best shape of his career, he says he lacks the discipline needed to work hard and train consistently. We talked about commitment to excellence and the importance of quality workouts in one's quest to be the best, how this relates to the goals he was striving to achieve (i.e., sub 1:29 for 20K, Top 5 in the US for membership on the World Cup Team and the Olympic Team), and how he can use the power of his mind and belief systems effectively to pre-program himself for success.

In the past, Arthur would get distracted and overly concerned with the setting or road course (e.g., wonder if he could handle the conditions), who it was he was competing with (e.g., certain competitors would cause him to lose his focus), or environmental conditions (e.g., heat, humidity, fluid replacements). We talked about focusing on things he can control and affirming the things that he wanted to occur. Subsequently, I had him think about the type of focuses he wanted to carry with him, both pre-event and during various phases of a 20 kilometer race, then develop a list of affirmations and energizing cues from which we could develop an appropriate script for his visualization tape.

With progressive jazz music in the background, the pre-event phase of the tape included relaxation and breathing exercises, warm-up and stretching, positive self-statements affirming the preparation, conditioning, and hard work he had put into this moment, review of his race plan, followed by a prayer at the end. Recognizing he has been working on improving this technique, cue words centered around "quick turnover," "fluid motion," "hitting the groove," "trust," and that feeling where "everything clicks." The following serves as an example of how the tape is set up:

> "Arthur, this audio visualization tape is designed to help you relax and concentrate more effectively when you compete in 20K races. Start by focusing on the rhythm of your breathing, inhale, take a nice deep breath, slow and easy, now hold the breath,...and release, let the breath go. Allow yourself to focus on the rhythm of your breathing as you inhale..... and exhale."

He would then focus on the rhythm of his breathing for a few minutes, followed by scanning his body for tension, and breathing for relaxation. Once relaxed, I would then have him visualize himself walking down a staircase to a mental training room, sitting in a lazy boy recliner overlooking a panoramic view of the beach of his choice. Once comfortable, he would project himself onto a screen in the room where he would begin to see himself arriving at the race site and focus fully and completely on the feeling he wanted to carry with him that particular day.

> "Begin to see yourself arriving at the race site. You know the course well and feel good about your preparation and race plan. Notice the crowd of people talking among themselves. As you see your competitors, you feel relaxed and confident, energized yet focused. See the starting line, hear and see all the sights and sounds of the upcoming 20K race. Use all of your senses to really feel like you are actually there. Now go over your warm-up routine, begin to stretch, slow and easy, feel relaxed and in control."

As the starting time nears, I want the athlete to become more and more focused.

> "Feel the nervous energy and butterflies in your stomach, that familiar and normal feeling you get when you are ready for a good race. Now tune into your focal point and allow that ultimate competitor to come out. Arthur, you have every reason to believe in yourself, both as a person and as a competitor. The challenge before you is going to require an all out effort, but you are fully prepared for this challenge. You have worked really hard and prepared

extremely well for this race, nothing is going to stop you today! Before the race begins, take a moment to think about the attitude and intensity you want to carry with you during various phases of your race."

Start of the race - 1 K:

"Now see yourself at the starting line, adrenaline pumping, ready to go. Hear the instructions of the starter, the race begins and you are off. You begin strong and confident, relaxed and in control. Really feel yourself pushing firmly off of the back foot and really getting up on your toes. Get into your own rhythm. Make sure you are not getting out too fast. Hold back and stick to your game plan. "Trust"!"

1K - 5K:

"Relax, stay loose in your jaw and shoulders, watch your breathing, pick up the tempo/pace. Key words include: "Set the Tone," "Quick Turnover," "Find the Groove," "Smooth it Out"."

5K - 1OK:

"Time to go for negative splits, go for it! Focus on good technique and remember to stay within yourself. Read your body, push the pace, find the groove, and smooth it out. Keys to focus on: "Relax and Drive," "Arms Square and Low"."

10K - 15K:

"Maintain the intensity from the 10K split. Build upon the strength of the first 10K. Stay relaxed, shake out the tension in your arms. Stay with the group and think about picking off the person in front of you. Keys to focus on: "turnover, Turnover, Turnover," "Arms Square and Low," "Stay Relaxed, Confident, and In Control"."

15K - 18K:

"Homestretch, time to kick it in, be mentally tough, this is my time of the race! Stay focused on good technique and quick turnover, you love that burning feeling in your calves. Key words to focus on: "Relax," "Trust," "Your whole body is working together like a tireless machine," "You are doing great, reward yourself for how great you are doing"."

Last 2K:

"Now is the time to extend yourself. You are tough to beat. Keep your focus. Kick it in and bring it home. Keys to think about: "Go for it," "No regrets, just do it," "Remember your goals for you have the ability to reach them"."

Outcome:

Mental skills, like physical skills, take practice to be perfected. An individual has to believe in what they are trying to accomplish, stay focused on their own goals and objectives, and learn how to have the courage to "act as if' they are going to be successful no matter what the circumstance. In the year that followed, Arthur worked hard at refining his mental training skills and improving upon the quality of physical workouts. As a result of his dedication and commitment to both himself and his sport, his times dropped considerably throughout the year, and he did indeed secure a spot on the Olympic Team. Although he did not do as well as he would have liked in the Olympics, he was proud to be a part of the process and fulfill a dream he has had for a lifetime.

#6: College Cross Country Team

Introduction:

When I took over the college cross country program, I had no real background in the field of sport psychology other than the common-sense approach to dealing with athletes. I would like to comment about the change that occurred in the program over those first three years and why I chose to implement various interventions to help initiate that change.

Intervention:

My first year as cross country coach was a very challenging one for me. I had been the track coach at the college for four years, so I did understand how athletics fit into the scope of the college. What I didn't know was that the next three years would be both discouraging and gratifying, all the while helping me to shape my philosophy of coaching.

I was appointed the cross country coach in April, and my first responsibility was to call a team meeting in May - a chance to meet the team and give out summer training booklets before the students left school for the summer. I was excited as the day approached, and I spent a considerable amount of time preparing the packet for them. It included the summer workout plan, results of the past season, and even a history of cross country at the college. I felt confident that the team could improve on their 5th place finish at the conference meet of the previous fall. I walked into the meeting armed with 30 booklets and was stunned to see only three runners! I hid my disappointment and launched into my prepared text for the meeting.

When I told them that I believed that they could improve to as high as third at the conference meet, they laughed! I was devastated. Later, I realized that they weren't really laughing at me as much as the fact that I thought they could improve. They believed in themselves so little that they could actually laugh at that prospect! It became painfully clear that the team's lack of belief in themselves would become the primary issue for me to deal with over the next three years.

Rationalization became my greatest enemy as the athletes used this tool to justify their poor performance. The most over-used was the belief that the academic challenge at the school simply didn't allow for athletic excellence (the average ACT score for students was 29).

What follows is a listing of the mental training interventions that were implemented:

- **Goal Setting Sessions:** Both individual and team sessions were used to plot a direction for the future. All were recorded with the athlete taking an active part in the process.
- **Relaxing the Body to Relax the Mind:** Relaxation techniques have been very important as both a way to control arousal and to "clear the screen" for visualization techniques used in the program. Progressive relaxation and variations of it have been very effective.
- **Visualization:** We visualize both as a team and as individuals. A film library of race courses and previous races help to jog the runners' memories about the courses and aid the freshmen in having a frame of reference for visualizing an upcoming race.
- **Reinforcement Techniques:** Without a doubt, the poor self-belief of the team was the greatest hurdle for me to clear when I took over the program. Fortunately, with a lot of positive encouragement and an eye for "scheduling for early success," the team began to believe. We began to implement positive self-talk as a way to "re-write" negative programming of the subconscious brain.

That first team again finished fifth at the conference meet, but were only a few points out of second as several teams were log-jammed in the final standings for 2nd-6th (the year prior we had been over a hundred points out of fourth!). The May meeting was again repeated and I again entered with 30 new booklets and a load of enthusiasm. This time there were five athletes. And when I told them that I thought they could go as high as second the following fall at the conference meet, I got only smiles. Perhaps change was occurring, albeit slowly.

Outcome:

That team did finish second, and the past three seasons have resulted in conference championships and top 20 rankings. I should also note that the team that finished second at conference was the same team of the previous year that finished fifth at conference. The same athletes and virtually the same training. What was the difference? I believe the mental training program was an invaluable catalyst.

The winning attitude of the runners now seems to have a snowball effect on the younger runners. They "Feel Successful" when they come in. I think it is very important in a program such as ours to emphasize the value of every athlete (regardless of their gene pool). They each have something to offer and are challenged to find this and offer it. It seems to be working!

#7: Female Olympic Weight Lifter

Introduction:

Jennifer is a 27 year-old female Olympic weight lifter who sought me out because she was unable to lift in competition near the weight she lifts in training. Jennifer's best lifts have happened when she was "not thinking." She tends to obsess about technique and has a particular difficult time with breaks in between lifts. Jennifer stated that she would like to control her thoughts during competition.

Intervention:

The intervention began with an assessment of Jennifer, consisting of the following:

- Sport Confidence Inventory
- Motivation Questionnaire
- Relaxation/Imagery Exercise
- Profile of Mood States
- Statement of Goals
- Self-Monitoring exercises during training
- Analysis of successful and unsuccessful competitions using videotapes.

From the initial assessment, it was determined that Jennifer has an extremely perfectionistic attitude, is highly critical of herself, and demonstrates an absence of self-praise. She is prone to negative thoughts and images (imagines self dropping weight). In an attempt to regain control, she tries different things all the time which does not allow for a stable successful routine to develop. This leads to feelings of fatigue and lack of strength developing during competition.

Jennifer is highly intelligent, articulate, motivated, persistent, and possesses a high level of self-confidence when compared to other female lifters. She is also very creative in using images and relaxes very well.

The first task was to assist Jennifer in finding a centering focus. It is observed that Jennifer must use different images for snatch and for clean and jerk. We attempted to identify thoughts that are helpful. In her case it's activity statements rather than positive thoughts. She then practiced these concentration exercises during her workouts.

The second phase was to start preparing for the nationals two months away. We implemented a relaxation and imagery training program: a) practice imagery before workout, b) focus on feelings of strength, enthusiasm and control, c) practice relaxation after workout, allowing maximum rest and recovery.

In order to identify emotional states that correlate with good performance, we decided that Jennifer would answer the POMS daily before practice for 2 weeks, and afterwards write down her impressions of the workout and rate it on a 1 - 10 scale. Negative performances occurred under two conditions mainly: tension was very low and confusion was moderately high (she described herself as physically "too loose") or when Vigor was low (sense of fatigue, negative feelings and thoughts).

We focused on increasing her sense of vigor, energy. She chose some "explosive" images. We tested the effectiveness of visualization exercise by repeating the POMS before and after the session.

Outcome:
Jennifer was very encouraged by the results of the visualization and prepared a series of images to use during the competition, some focusing on resting and recovering energy, others on feeling strong and competitive and enjoying it. She placed at the Nationals and had a PR and felt really in control of her performance.

In Jennifer's case, the combination of being highly intelligent, obsessive and needing proof that she was doing the right thing (or things the right way) made the use of tests before and after a very useful tool that allowed her to reach her potential.

#8: Male College Hammer Thrower and Inappropriate Timing of Intervention

Introduction:

This case study involves a 22 year old male hammer thrower, Charles. My first contact occurred as a result from a referral by his head coach the day prior to the conference championships. Charles was anxious about his ability to remain calm and focused during the competition. I spoke with him for about 45 minutes. He recalled feelings he had during good performances and what he did to prepare for these performances. He sometimes became distracted by others' performances during the competition.

Intervention:

We agreed on his taking a Sony Walkman to the competition and to listen to his favorite music while disregarding the others during warm-up, and competition. Charles threw a personal best of 211' and won the championships. In the subsequent few weeks as he prepared for the NCAA's and the TAC championships we worked together for several sessions both on and off the field on distraction management and stress management techniques while also incorporating these techniques into his personal life. He is married with two small children.

The main error occurred two days prior to the NCAA championships. Charles, his coach and I conducted a simulation (model) training session and Charles threw his best 6 throw series ever. No throw was less than 210' and he set a PR of 216'. He had a poor meet at the NCAA's finishing as an All-American but not meeting his performance goals. He further failed to qualify for finals at the TAC.

Outcome:

I feel he became too over-anxious and nervous about duplicating his previous best series in an important competition. Model training was not part of his mental preparation in the past. A classic case of a technique wrongly and inappropriately timed.

Discussion Questions

1. What are the "common components" of mental skills training found in the case studies?

2. Relative to the dynamics of each case, was MST the most appropriate means of enhancing performance? Why, or why not?

3. For any given case, is there evidence of: a) generalization of skills, or b) personal development extending beyond the boundaries of sport? Why, or why not?

4. To what extent are the "Guidelines for MST" adhered to in any give case?
5. How do the goals of various parties (sport psychologist, coach, athlete, parent, etc.) influence the structure and effectiveness of MST?

6. What are the primary challenges faced by an individual interested in instituting a MST?

References

Gordin, R.D., & Reardon, J.P. (1995). Achieving the zone: The study of flow in sport. In K.P. Henschen & W.F. Straub (Eds.) Sport psychology: An analysis of athlete behavior. (3rd ed.) Longmeadow, MA: Mouvement Publications.

Gould, D., Tammen, V., Murphy, S., & May, J. (1989). An examination of the U.S. Olympic sport psychology consultants and the services they provide. The Sport Psychologist, 3, 300-312.

Graham, D. & Yocom, G. (1990). Mental toughness training for golf. New York: The Stephen Greene Press/Pelham Books.

Greenspan, M.J., & Feltz, D.F. (1989). Psychological interventions with athletes in competitive situations: A review. The Sport Psychologist, 3, 219-236.

Loehr, J.E. (1986). Mental toughness training for sports. Lexington, Mass.: The Stephen Greene Press.

Orlick, T. (1986). Psyching for sport: Mental training for athletes. Champaign, IL: Leisure Press.

Partington, J., & Orlick, T. (1987). The sport psychology consultant: Olympic coaches' views. The Sport Psychologist, 1, 95-102.

Ravizza, K. (1988). Gaining entry with athletic personnel for season-long consulting. The Sport Psychologist, 2, 243-254.

Syer, J. & Connolly, C. (1984). Sporting body sporting mind: An athlete's guide to mental training. New York: Cambridge University Press.

Thompson, M.A. (1997, April 12). The realities of conducting a mid-season mental training program with college athletes. Proceedings of South-Central Student Sport Psychology Symposium, College Station, TX.

Weinberg, R.S., & Gould, D. (1995). Foundations of sport and exercise psychology. Champaign, IL: Human Kinetics.

Weinberg, R.S., & Williams, J.M., (1993). Integrating and implementing a psychological skills training program. In J.M. Williams (Ed.), Applied sport psychology: Personal growth to peak performance. pp. 274-298.

Williams, J.M., & Krane, V. (1993). Psychological characteristics of peak performance. In J.M. Williams (Ed.), Applied sport psychology: Personal growth to peak performance. pp. 137-147.

194

Vealey, R.S. (1988). Future directions in psychological skills training. The Sport Psychologist, 2, 318-336.

Vealey, R.S. (1994). Current status and prominent issues in sport psychology intervention. Medicine and Science in Sport and Exercise, 26, 495-502.

CHAPTER 12

~ Injury and Career Termination Issues ~

Wesley E. Sime, University of Nebraska-Lincoln

The human body is a wonderful machine that has tremendous capacity for adaptation to overload and for growth or development in response to challenge (e.g., weight lifting and endurance training). Differing from the most exotic technological machine however, the human body has the innate ability to repair and recover naturally from most injuries that occur during the course of training or competition within a reasonable period of time. However, in most levels of competition today, athletes are functioning so close to the edge of physiological and anatomical limits that injuries occur regularly and repeatedly while coaches, athletes and managers have minimal tolerance for a slow gradual rehabilitation process. Furthermore, in contact sports like football and ice hockey, we might say that the athlete is merely an *"injury waiting to happen"* and he better get back into action sooner rather than later. The question is not whether there will be an injury but rather when and how it will occur followed by how quickly does healing occur. Among the female gymnasts I work with, there is such a long history of micro-trauma from years and years of pounding and straining that pain and subsequent treatment for injury are a natural part of the daily routine.

Fear of Injury

The risk of injury is compounded further when athletes have a significant *"fear of injury."* Fear is one of many stress manifestations occurring as a result of serious injury (Gould, Udry, Bridges & Beck, 1997a). Of course, we must acknowledge that many sports routinely involve physical demands that create a legitimate, natural inclination toward being afraid of the worst possible outcome, i.e., injury or perhaps re-injury. For a diver, hitting the board during rotation before entry into the water is a very real possibility every time they attempt a dive in practice or competition. However it is necessary to set that fear factor aside because it obstructs performance and because it can be a paradoxical cause of injury.

Physiologically, injury may occur because the athlete braces him or herself fearfully with extra muscle tension prior to impact (guarding against the risk) thus creating extra strain on ligaments and joints (Heil, 1993a). By contrast, some individuals can withstand a terrible fall (e.g., even down a staircase) if they are very, very relaxed. Simply being *a little apprehensive* about some new task or even a routine skill may make reinjury occur more easily. The mechanism for emotional risk involving fear is that it causes a disruption in concentration and quite simply, it messes up normal execution of a skill (Heil, 1993a).

Epidemiology of Injury

It is estimated that there are about four million sport injuries in this country every year. A large body of epidemiological research has documented the risk factors for injury (Muse, 1985). These range all the way from situational factors such as weather/field conditions/sleep deprivation to various forms of emotional stress including interpersonal conflict, loss of relationships, and financial problems. To the extent that these situational factors (e.g., cold, wet conditions, sleep loss and money problems) can be avoided or controlled, we would prefer to act in advance to prevent the problem and the impending injuries. However, regarding most of the emotional factors that create increased risk of injuries, it is not easy to even recognize the symptoms much less to control the risk therein.

Most athletes (male and female) are groomed through years and years of coaching to be macho and stoic about the personal and emotional issues surrounding their sport experience. It seems as though the emotional stuff is thought to be *"unmentionable"* in practice and competition. Thus, the failure to attend to such personal issues of worry, anger, frustrations, and other emotions is very common and it may distract an athlete from attending to important warning signs that ordinarily would protect one from injury. For example, a baseball player who is very worried about losing his position if he doesn't get a hit, may be unduly tense causing slower reaction time which results in being hit by a pitched ball because he couldn't get out of the way quick enough.

Risk Factors for Injury

Much has been written about the psychological and behavioral risk factors for injury in sport (Anderson & Williams, 1993). Emotional stress and the manifestations thereof are the most prominent factors associated with performance-related injury. Some examples include recent personal history of stressful life events (e.g., loss of loved one, conflict with friends, financial problems, academic problems and absence of social support). The mechanism by which these experiences increase risk of injury might follow this pattern for the athlete who:

gets angry or upset → can't sleep well because of it → misses meals or loses appetite → misses practice or conditioning sessions → tries extra hard to make up for absence in the next session → gets worried that coaches are bothered by the change in behavior → becomes hyper-aroused, anxious, nervous, stressed out → visual field becomes narrowed, somewhat distracted → can't see or does not notice teammate or opponent coming from blind side → unexpected collision or fall resulting in unnecessary injury.

Ironically most of the athletes I talk with are completely unaware of this relationship between stress and injury. Furthermore, the medical staff and the athletic trainers do not routinely inform or educate the athletes about this phenomena. Therefore the coaches and the consultants may wish to share their insight about stress and injury in whatever discrete manner that is possible.

Special Populations at Risk

Studies on the sport of football in particular, have revealed a relationship between stressful life events and the increased likelihood of injury. It was significant in 18 out of 20 research studies on football and was also very common among 14 other sports ranging from Alpine skiing to track and field (Williams & Roepke, 1992). It is also apparent that major competitions in any sport seem to be associated with higher risk of injury primarily because of the heavy training schedule that precedes it, the stress of anticipating competition and perhaps sleep deprivation and travel problems (Kerr & Minden, 1988).

Another interesting factor regarding proneness to injury is the fact that marginal players (reserves) seem to take higher risks in order to impress coaches and secondarily they may hide their injuries so as not to lose the rare opportunity to play (Rotella & Heyman, 1986). Thus the injuries may be higher in this group but the coaches and trainers may not be aware of the number or the severity therein.

Relationship of Personality to Injury

It should also be noted that there are selected personality factors such as hardiness (Kobasa, 1979), coping skills, optimism, relaxation, and ability to concentrate (Smith, Small & Ptacek, 1990) that appear to provide protection from injury as well as to enhance performance. Surprisingly, athletes who are sensation seekers in high-risk adventure activities (i.e., rock climbing) appear to have less risk of injury than those who are not. It has been suggested that they are able to confine their daring adventuresome nature into a constructive means of experiencing exhilaration and stimulation thus protecting from injury.

While it might be tempting to make recruiting and professional draft decisions based upon selected personality variables, it is probably more productive to work toward the development of these characteristics in practice and in psychological skills training. The real benefit to knowing about personality factors and injury is that coaches and practitioners can use their gut instincts about observable behavior that seem out of the ordinary. For example, when an athlete appears to be moody, irritable, tense, fatigued, sleep deprived or lacking confidence, it would be important to explore what is going with him or her. If the athlete appears to be bothered but yet denies any problem, it might be prudent to reduce the intensity or duration of practice and consider foregoing competition until such behaviors are improved. In other words it is not necessary to find out what the life (stressor) event might be, but we do need to react appropriately to the manifestations of stress in the best interest of the athlete and the team. For example, if the athlete ignores an emotional concern and plays anyway, in the short run they may get to compete but if injured seriously because of the distraction caused by stress, it hurts the whole team in the long run by their extended absence from competition.

Psychological Effect of Injury

The impact of any significant injury upon an athlete can be devastating. Among the immediate effects of injury are pain, shock, anger, isolation, humiliation, helplessness, and the feeling of loss. (Heil, 1993a). In addition there is the possibility of more serious effects such as phobia, blame, depression, guilt, depersonalization, post-traumatic amnesia and post-traumatic stress disorder (Heil, 1993b). Some athletes suffer loss of friendship supports when injured; they become cut off from interaction with the team and get jealous by comparison with their healthy teammates (Gould, Udry, Bridges & Beck, 1997b). Psychologically they also lose their edge in readiness to perform and often become scared to go for it in routinely difficult and dangerous moves or challenges.

For most athletes an injury means more than losing an opportunity to perform, it also means a temporary loss of identity. Unfortunately most athletes have their identity (as a person) wrapped up in who they are as an athlete. As a result, throughout the rehabilitation process the athlete is constantly reminded of what he/she cannot do and that people do not adore or respect them as much when injured. In some cases the athlete may tend to brag about past accomplishments as a way of off-setting the loss of current identity.

Following injury there is often a serious loss of important social roles wherein the athlete feels left out of the action (in practice and competition) and left out of the informal interaction with their teammates as well. The impact is universally dramatic such that the need for grieving is apparent (Evans & Hardy, 1995). Initially many experience traditional reactions that include denial, anger, depression and finally resolution by acceptance of the consequences. Since many athletes have their self-esteem linked to how they perform, the injury often compromises self image and creates negative effects that carry over to life goals, and to personal values. As a result, disbelief and denial of the severity of the injury may be manifested. Regardless of the severity of the injury, athletes often perform poorly in academics and they may also have more personality conflicts in their relationships following the injury because of the negative self-esteem that prevails.

The sad irony in sports injury is that the athlete suddenly has a lot of extra time (less training and no competition or travel) thus they could be making productive use of their time, but most don't. For example, the injured athlete could be catching up on their studies, exploring future career options or developing some unique skills (related or unrelated to their sport), however, the more common reaction is that the athlete gives up on other areas of their life as well when the injury occurs because they feel so bad about not being able to perform. Thus, the paradox is that, in spite of the extra time available post-injury, academic course work may suffer and personal relationships may be strained because of the frustration and anger related to a difficult rehabilitation process. This phenomena represents an opportunity for coach or sport psychology consultant to help the athlete "reframe" a season ending injury to acknowledge one of several potential benefits, i.e., extra time to accomplish other important life goals (Udry, Gould, Bridges & Beck, 1997).

Individual Interpretation of Injury

Athletes may choose to interpret the injury in one of many different ways (Heil, 1993c): a) it could be just a challenge for me to overcome, b) it could be a tremendous relief having this injury so I do not have to live up to the expectations of others in my performance, c) it could feel like a punishment for my prior transgressions, d) it could feel like I will never be able to perform again, e) it could be a means of manipulating people to get extra attention or special accommodations, f) it could be an opportunity to get some other responsibilities taken care of during the rehab period, or g) it could be an opportunity to come back stronger and more effective than before the injury because I learned so much about physical limitations (Ievleva, 1988).

It should be noted that several of the interpretations (above) are more positive than negative. As such, putting emphasis on a positive view of the injury through cognitive restructuring (i.e., asking if one can discover any redeeming value in the rehabilitative process) may be critical to a successful outcome. Qualitative research results from injured ski racers has revealed a substantial list of benefits of injury, not ordinarily recognized (Udry, Gould, Bridges & Beck, 1997). These include such things as:

1. Gaining new perspective on life; it made me slow down and reflect more seriously.
2. Personality changes for the better; I became more mature and empathetic with others.
3. Character development; I became more patient, understanding and independent.
4. Enhanced self-determination; I now believe in my capacity to overcome and recover
5. Physiological and emotional awareness; I learned more about my body and about my emotional strengths and weaknesses

Could the Injury or Reinjury Have Been Prevented?

Most athletes would tell you that there was nothing they could do to prevent the injury. However, as a former athlete and former coach, I think that I can use my knowledge from physiology, anatomy, kinesiology and psychology together with my personal experience to predict when an athlete has begun to exceed the limits of performance and is leaning toward an injury. By contrast, there also appears to be a peculiar risk associated with playing too cautiously. Many athletes find that there is greater protection (paradoxically) from injury by going all out in the sport setting than in being tentative or conservative. One example is the football player who leaves his feet to dive over a tackler also avoids the risk of knee injury that often occurs when the body weight fixed to the ground in a awkward position during a hard tackle from the side.

I think it is possible for some athletes to become internally aware of when they are vulnerable to injury. For example, with experience one can usually tell whether they have warmed up adequately in order to tolerate powerful, explosive moves without incurring strain or injury. This is especially important for athletes who are in and out of action repeatedly. Classic examples include baseball players who sit in the dugout between innings and gymnasts who move from one apparatus to another waiting for other competitors and ultimately having very little time to warm up on each event. Self-awareness and planning ahead to allow for warm-up and staying warm during periodic delays is critically important. The mechanism behind the prevention of injury seems to be getting adequate circulation and slowly stretching vulnerable areas such as the hamstrings (Heil, 1993d).

Education of the Injured Athlete

It is important that the athlete (Heil, 1993d): a) recognizes the basic anatomy of the injury; b) understands the mechanism by which the rehabilitation works; c) uses heat and cold and other home treatment therapies as specified between visits to the training room; d) understands the purpose of medication and the side effects that might occur; e) acknowledges the limits of function they might have due to injury; f) views their rehabilitation as a challenge to overcome thus becoming mentally tougher after the experience, and g) learns self-maintenance, i.e., to know when to go all out and when to be more cautious.

In addition, it is important to set goals for treatment success and for return to competition. In order to achieve the goals in rehabilitation, it is critical to:

A. Have specific measurable goals expressed in positive language *(I can get through 3 sets of rehab exercises)*.
B. Make the goals challenging but realistic with timetable for completion *(I can regain joint flexibility 1-2 weeks before expected)*.
C. Integrate short, intermediate and long-term goals for the best outcome *(I will regain flexibility in two weeks; I will be practicing in 4 weeks; and I will be playing fully recovered in 6 weeks)*.
E. Have a specific plan for what to do every day and monitor progress *(Today I expect to complete water exercises and strength training and I will record it in my log)*.
D. Make rehabilitation success a model for other life experiences *(Now that I have overcome this injury successfully I know that I can approach school and work with the same intensity and I can expect a comparable successful outcome)*.

Mental Training Strategies Used With Injured Athletes

Many of the traditional performance enhancement training strategies are applicable for injury rehabilitation (Heil, 1993e). For example:

1. Relaxation—to be used for recovery to regain homeostasis, develop awareness of body responses, and to facilitate flow of circulation into peripheral areas such as hands and feet.
2. Mental Imagery—to envision a healthy healing process without complications and with reduction in pain symptoms.
3. Self Talk—to assert and verbally affirm the positive outcomes and confidence in the rehabilitation process while developing some dissociative strategies to divert attention away from the pain.
4. Biofeedback—using psychophysiology to provide a reflection of body responses (e.g., electromyography revealing the bracing muscle tension that interferes with

healing) and learning how to become aware of and in self-control of other autonomic mediators of the healing process).

5. Self-hypnosis—to develop a dissociative skill to enhance the intensity of attentional focus on the healing process or upon the subsequent return to competition.

6. Cognitive-behavioral Interventions—to gain a sense of thought control, to maintain focus on specific tasks and to modulate emotional reactions such as anger, frustration and anxiety (Gould, Udry, Bridges & Beck, 1997b).

In addition to the traditional mental training skills described above, I suggest the use of creative functioning to develop positive vivid rationale for the treatment, (e.g., ultrasound can be a healing glow; ice can be freezing out the pain; the pain of rehabilitation exercises can be felt as the necessary stimulation of circulation to "fix" the injury). Other pain management efforts (Wack & Turk, 1984) might include creative imagery techniques such as computer-like cut and paste technology to move the pain (thus demonstrating control) or shaping the pain by modifying the size, depth, color and/or intensity of the pain in a picture-like format. The most important issue is helping the athlete develop a sense of control over the pain, even if it means temporarily increasing it (by rehab) in order to ease the discomfort and dysfunction for tomorrow.

Dealing with Rehabilitation and Return to Competition

In regard to chronic injuries, perhaps it would be better if athletes were to expect problems (because they often occur) and then be surprised when the rehabilitation process goes better than expected. When there are complications in the recovery process, it is desirable to accept the delay while focusing on future potential. Not surprisingly, some athletes have difficulty being motivated for rehabilitation: yet some others tend to be overly compliant potentially becoming somewhat obsessed with the treatment and re-conditioning program. Modulation of these two extremes is obviously desirable.

One of the other common problems obstructing the rehabilitation plan is the paradoxical effort of the athlete to protect him or herself (McCarthy, 1989). Pain is a powerful intimidator; thus there is a natural tendency toward being guarded while bracing the surrounding muscles around the injured area. The natural instinct for the injured athlete is to protect or fight against the pain in a vulnerable area. Unfortunately this action may ultimately create more pain and greater risk of re-injury and prolonged recovery. Obviously this occurs because of the traumatic emotional effect of the injury.

The emotional trauma of the injury can also obstruct the rehabilitation process. Specifically, fear, depression, isolation, depersonalizing and post-traumatic amnesia (Maviffakalian & Barlow 1981) and can later cause the development of a phobia. That is, a single traumatic experience with injury produces dreadful thoughts and vivid imagery of the event which effectively causes re-traumatizing consequences. Obviously the athlete's ability to maintain attention to the task and focused concentration is likely to be compromised. A good treatment procedure for this problem is a relatively new therapeutic procedure called Eye Movement Desensitization and Reprocessing (EMDR). It is a non-traditional psychomotor technique used in counseling to block and ameliorate undesirable thoughts and images (Shapiro, 1995). EMDR is somewhat controversial but seems to be getting a strong following in the trauma rehabilitation field. If we acknowledge the emotional trauma of a physical injury, this simple but potent technique could have remarkable benefits. Unfortunately it requires specific clinical training and a psychology license with experience in order to utilize this technique.

The Dynamics of Return to Competition

As the rehabilitation phase nears completion, the athlete and sometimes the coach, may be overly eager to get back to competition. As such, denial may become a factor once again, wherein the athlete stops participating in the treatment plan because he or she is focused upon getting back into competition. In order to play with an injury (not completely healed), pain tolerance may become a serious matter as the athlete may begin to use or overuse medications for prolonged periods beyond the initial treatment or surgery phase. In addition, most athletes, when returning from injury, will have difficulty performing up to their usual capability. As such, coaches, fans, and the media may be hyper-critical and the athlete needs to accept the limitations and the criticism knowing that it's not a personal attack on their identity. Regardless, we must all recognize that maintaining patience and prudence about safe and effective treatment integrated with essential re-conditioning activities is very difficult for any athlete.

Personal Investment in Returning From Injury

Some athletes look for every opportunity to engage in rehab treatment (including ice, stretching and strengthening) even at home while others tend to avoid treatment almost as a way of denying that there is really any problem (Heil, 1993f). It is the athlete who keeps a positive outlook and who is patient and progressive about his or her expectations in performance who stands the best chance of fully recovering from the injury quickly. Often the injured athletes' self esteem is compromised significantly during the convalesce. By contrast, there are some benefits of an injury such as the fact that he/she may develop an extra level of mental toughness because of the need to battle through the impairment. In addition, the period of time required in rehab may allow the athlete to develop other less well developed skills or physical capabilities not present before the injury. Ultimately, it is important for the athlete to learn how to push their limits and develop stronger mental training skills during this rehabilitation time period.

Dealing with Fear of Re-Injury

The common experience among most successful elite athletes is that *fear of injury or even death* is normal but it is important to accept it realistically and move ahead as if it is not there. Fear may manifest as one of many different symptoms ranging from nervous stomach to fatigue and even sleepiness. Sometimes symptoms of fear are masked as chronic complaints of unrelated nagging aggravations simply because the athlete can not acknowledge openly that he or she is afraid. To conquer this fear it is important to identify the source of the fear as well as the realistic chance of injury; then control all possible safety factors (protective gear, spotting assistance, etc.). In addition, it is critical to adjust the training conditions in order to gradually desensitize the athlete to the event that is causing the fear. In stepwise fashion consider the following strategies to deal with fear of injury among athletes:

1. normalize this fear and give reassurance, protection, safety etc.;
2. build confidence through preparations(strengthening, support systems, etc.);
3. recognize and accept anxious thoughts and feelings (nervous, fidgety, etc.);
4. reframe the nervous reactions to appear as extra energy to get the job done; and
5. train with control strategies (relaxation, breathing, and self affirmation)

Regarding previous injuries it may be desirable to clarify injury status with the athletic trainer noting the progress in recovery and the realistic expectations for the present stage of healing. Always reassure the athlete about the fact that pain is simply a natural part of the healing process and that he/she can use this uncomfortable experience to develop even greater levels of concentration while continuing to re-condition toward full competition once again.

Career Ending Injuries

There are many more severe psychological problems associated with career-ending injuries than those where athletes return to active competition (Svoboda & Danek, 1982). Athletes need very strong social support and additional coping resources as soon as it is determined that it may be a "career-threatening" injury. One of the primary issues is the threat to loss of identity they once had. There is a common saying about identity, "when who you are is what you do (as an athlete) . . . then what happens to who you are when you can't do what you do (as an athlete) any more?"

Often athletes who experience career-threatening injuries go through all or nothing thinking. That is, if they can't compete to fulfill their role and identity, they tend to blow off everything else in life as well. Thus, school, friends, former teammates, and coaches become constant reminders of what the athlete can no longer do.

"The Case of Lyn"

This is a case example of one female athlete who experienced a classic career-ending injury. Lyn was a 21 year old "phenom" volleyball competitor at a NCAA Division I school. In her junior year, she was an integral part of the team that won the National Championship in her sport. She was an emotional leader on the team. Her enthusiasm for competition and her fervor on the court following a score was contagious for the rest of her teammates and for the crowd which delighted in her success as well as that of the team. When she went down with injury, there was a noticeable decrease in the overall performance of the team.

Historically, Lyn began having back pains her freshman year in College, but she played through this discomfort as a necessary part of competition. Over the next two years she developed a complicated series of inter-related injuries. First she blew out her knee (ruptured ACL with surgery) and then had two herniated disks, brought on by the years of pounding on genetically vulnerable tissues (she has a family history of back problems). Not long after her knee was rehabilitated, she needed to have another surgery to repair one of the herniated disks.

After a long arduous period of painful and frustrating rehabilitation, Lyn again began training for competition in the sport that she loved so much. Unfortunately, the delicate balance between treatment and reconditioning was compromised because the pain from each of the post-injury surgeries prevented her from properly strengthening and conditioning the rest of her body during the recovery. In the end, she suffered a re-injury to her back and though she was cleared by physicians to play, she choose to retire from the sport. Knowing that she would have to live with constant pain to continue to compete and with the prospect that she could have a more severe injury with possible disability, caused her to make a difficult but prudent decision to stop competing. In retrospect she stated that, "It was simply too painful (emotionally) sitting around and watching the rest of the team play without her."

The reason that she participated in the sport was because she loved to compete; she enjoyed the camaraderie of the team; the structure of the coaching/training format; and she needed the scholarship to pay for her education. When asked about identity, Lyn announced proudly that she was Lyn the volleyball player. She confirmed an identity issue when she stated that, "I didn't know who I was anymore . . . after quitting the sport. Who I had been (as an athlete) was always on my mind and it crushed me not have that recognition from others anymore." Her friends on the team would tell her that they admired her personality and that they missed her smile and joviality (as much as her athleticism) on the court. However that reinforcement was not as meaningful to her as the public recognition of how well she played the game.

Another theme was "*loss of control*" and that devastated her. She said, "that is why I quit; because sitting and watching others practice and play was just another reminder that I can't do anything; it was emotionally draining to just be around my teammates."

The rehabilitation experience for Lyn was even more complicated, because the injuries in her knee and in her back restricted her from any heavy training or conditioning sessions. As a result, she never knew exactly what her teammates thought about her. For example she said, "I wished I had a cast or a big rash that reflected how much pain I experienced so that people would know and understand how frustrating it was for me and to confirm that I was not able to work out or compete." One day she could practice and play and the next she couldn't even walk because of the pain, which of course was not visible to others.

The emotional response was nearly overwhelming. She cried often and found it extremely painful emotionally to watch the team play in competition. It caused her to become seriously depressed. She denied it to herself for a long time. Finally she left school, and went home to her family (out-of-state). Ironically she discovered that family members showed a deeper level of support than she had ever experienced previously. She said, "I think they kind of took my athletic ability for granted and allowed me to thrive on the public acclaim, not recognizing me as a person." After her injury, the family became empathetic in a way that showed her a new level of intimacy and appreciation.

During rehabilitation Lyn used many mental skills. In particular, when she turned to family and friends for social support, it was like she couldn't get through anything by herself. She learned a deeper level of perseverance in the recovery process. She discovered reframing and cognitive restructuring which appeared in self-statements such as "look how much worse it could be." She also set realistic goals, learned to be patient and how to deal with setbacks and frustration.

The effect of the career ending injury was devastating at the time she made the decision. She fell behind in school and it set her back more than a year. She made many bad decisions. She said, "I couldn't think straight. I had been an athlete so long that I had become dependent on structure associated with being on the team." In other words, the coach dictated when to study, when to practice, when to sleep, etc. She didn't have to make any decisions about routine daily functions. When her career was over, her social support system fell apart and she felt like she was entering college once again as a freshman with very little structure in her life. She felt estranged from old friends, teammates and coaches. It seemed as though they didn't want anything to do with her. Lyn said, "I interpreted that to mean they must be thinking I didn't really have a serious injury and that I was malingering." In retrospect, she felt that was the most devastating effect of the injury. Now it is two years since the decision to quit playing because of injury, and this young woman is still in and out of therapy for depression related to the effects of her competitive experience. I think it is very important to recognize these long term hazards of sport (and injury therein) and to be available to athletes especially when they are recovering from injury and after career termination.

Conclusion

It is important, when working with athletes who have career-ending injuries, to help the person recognize the trauma, acknowledge the loss (physical and emotional) and to re-orient to other alternative options. In addition, we need to help the athlete understand the meaningfulness of the injury with all of it's benefits as well as liabilities. For example, the athlete can also use their sport injury experience to build upon other life skills such as developing good problem-solving skills and identifying other vocations (not previously considered). For example, Lyn discovered that she wanted to become a physical therapist after having endured the agonies of her injury. Finally, it is important for the athlete, the coach and the sport psychology consultant to think of the career-ending injury as a positive turning point as if it were merely a career change, not retirement or disability.

Unfortunately for Lyn, it took her a long time to accept the career-ending injury; she lost a year of eligibility and missed a full year of school during the post- injury grieving process. Fortunately she is back on track and will be finishing school very soon looking forward to her next career transition as a physical therapist specializing in sport injuries.

Case Studies of Injury & Career Termination

The first eight case studies reflect a qualitative research design utilizing a case study methodology used to investigate the psychological and emotional responses that occurred during injury rehabilitation. The research involved gathering data from an interview, questionnaire, and survey to develop a comprehensive case profile. The first case is presented in greater detail, including the results of the survey. Those that follow are abbreviated. These first eight cases do not revolve around an intervention, but instead detail the psychological, physical, and emotional aspects of injury rehabilitation.

#1: Female College Basketball Player - Back Strain

Overview:

Shawna was a 19 year old female collegiate basketball player. She had played two years at the collegiate level, and had been recognized as honorable mention all-region, and all-tournament teams for two separate tournaments. She suffered a lower lumbar strain in a game situation prior to the season and was out of sport for two months. Due to the nature of her injury she was very limited in what she could do (i.e. no bending , no lifting etc.).

Shawna's main reasons for participating in sport were for competition, pursuit of excellence, fitness, personal improvement and for outlet of aggression. On a scale of 1-6, from 1 = "not at all" to 6 = "absolutely", asking her if she would describe herself as an athlete, she marked herself at six. Her goals had been to play basketball at the collegiate level and she "wanted to be really good", and "make an impact and go from there which is what I have done". When asked whether her goals changed after the injury she replied "in fact if they've changed at all I think I'm going to be better than I thought I was going to be, better than I wanted to be .... I was brought back to life ..... I feel you have to play for that day, not the next day or the next day, but if you play for that moment you are going to give it all you have, and then some."

She said that she would like to be a disc jockey for a radio station. She expressed several interests outside of basketball including soccer, biking, hiking running and spending time with her friends and family. Consequently, sports were important to her at the time in her life yet they were not her whole life.

She had support from her family concerning her participation in athletics and viewed their level of involvement as just right. During her injury experience her teammates were quite helpful, "my teammates were really supportive, you know I had some that boosted my self-esteem probably more than they should have".

Over the course of her rehabilitation her behaviors and self-talk varied. At the time of the physician diagnosis she had little effort and very pessimistic self-talk. In early rehabilitation she was attending but was still putting forth little effort, her self talk at this point involved significant self doubt. In mid-rehabilitation she was putting out about 75% effort and her self-talk was more confident. In late rehabilitation she had all out effort and her self-talk was positive and optimistic. Lastly, when returning to play she had all out effort and had very positive self-talk For Shawna her self talk and effort seemed to correlate across the span of rehabilitation.

Shawna's physical experience was a roller coaster. She encountered predictable ups and downs physically, and experienced pain throughout her rehabilitation. Emotionally she started out very positive.

She said that being unable to play and having to watch was very difficult at first. She didn't want to go to practice. She attributed this in part to being selfish "like I was so good, on the cocky side, cause I felt like I was such a big part of the team". She said that early on to deal with the impairment of daily activities as well as not participating that she turned to drinking more "I partied a lot too, for a little while, what you 're not supposed to do, it's one of the worst things..."

Throughout her rehabilitation Shawna noticed that her emotions had physiological ramifications. She noticed tight muscles (feeling tense), weakness, and sleeplessness at different periods during rehabilitation. At first Shawna did not believe in her trainers and what they were telling her to do, which was basically nothing. She had thoughts like, they just don't want me to do anything, and you're just mean, I don't think you know what you are doing. "I didn't believe in them for a while." Her attitude changed though, which seemed to be related to an increase in what they were allowing her to do and their continued support of her. "They were just so positive, supportive, don't worry you'll be back and then they slowly got me started doing what I could do..." "after awhile I was like this isn't so bad it could be worse ... so after awhile I was like OK what do you want me to do now". As her rehabilitation progressed she sought them out for advice and suggestions.

Shawna stated that one thing that helped her the most during her rehabilitation was knowing it could be worse and knowing that she would get better. Another thing that she felt was helpful was her change in attitude "my positive attitude changed around, because in truth I did a lot of things outside of sport, and going from cocky to confident, I had a bit of over confidence when I got here, I think that came with all the excitement and nervousness and something to cover it up, but looking back I think that was the greatest thing."

The main thing that Shawna felt hindered her experience was the fact that it was a back and not an ankle "it was an injury that effects your entire life, and also effects what you do outside of sport, I think that was one of the most tough things." She spoke often of the effects of the injury in all areas of her life and how that made it more difficult and frustrating to deal with.

Shawna did not use much in the way of mental skills during rehabilitation. She claims she hates imagery even though she has tried it with all her heart. She does like goal setting and did use it some in her rehabilitation. She admitted that she mainly set very broad goals like just to get back and be stronger than I started out, which could have been in any area. The one goal she said she did set was to run, actually run, in three weeks. She was unable to do this. She said she likes to write goals down where she can see them but she doesn't tell people about her goals or what they are. If she does not meet them she may be in a bad mood for a day but just adjusts them saying, "No one needs to know, I just made it for fun, I'll be ready to go when I'm ready to go, I cared but I didn't care. I wanted to get better quickly but I didn't care if it took me awhile because I have so much further to go, I have so many more years to do whatever"." She ended up realizing that being out two months was better than six or seven "that's what my attitude ended up being along with goal setting".

Survey Results

First injured - shock, disbelief, no way, frustrated, helpless, in pain

Doctor diagnosis - shock, disbelief, no way, devastated, not real, angry, frustrated, reluctant acceptance, helpless, discouraged, in pain

Early rehabilitation - disbelief, no way, depressed, sad, angry, frustrated, reluctant acceptance, lonely/isolated, irritable, bored, restless, helpless, discouraged, in pain

Mid-rehabilitation - no way, depressed, frustrated, changed my perspective, lonely, isolated, discouraged, in pain, and towards the end-optimistic

Late rehabilitation - frustrated, changed my perspective, relieved, optimistic, in pain, happy

Return to play - changed my perspective, total acceptance, relieved, restless, optimistic, in pain, happy

Now - frustrated, changed my perspective, its a chance you take, bad luck, total acceptance, anxious/tense, restless, fear, optimistic, in pain, happy (current negative emotions are due to recurrences of her injury type symptoms)

Summary:

In summary Shawna is a collegiate basketball player who enjoys the sport, the competition and the pursuit of excellence and personal betterment. She had some difficult times early on in her rehabilitation with negative self talk, negative rehabilitation behaviors, not wanting to attend practices, as well as an increase in negative social behaviors. She came then to enjoy the time off and view it in a different light. She viewed it more as a chance to do things she normally did not have time for and was able to see her friends and family more. She also got a new perspective of her team and turned sifting out into a more positive venture. She returned to sport with a little fear of re-injury but also knowing that it is easy to re-injure and that she will have to live with some discomfort for her whole career for she knows it will not feel great until she is no longer playing at such a high intensity. She also returned with a new perspective as to her role on her team and with a new view of her teammates, she returned with more feelings of competence and confidence instead of cockiness. Although quite tough at times and painful she views her injury experience in a rather positive light and feels it has impacted her in a positive way.

As one can see Shawna's progression was from negative to positive throughout her rehabilitation experience until her return to play. Her current negative emotions she attributed to her recurrence of symptoms that are similar to those incurred with her past injury. Her progression was basically as follows: Shock & disbelief → anger & loneliness → depression, sadness & reluctant acceptance → new perspective → optimistic → relieved happy → total acceptance & happy

There were several things which were constant throughout her rehabilitation and this was feelings of frustration and pain. Her feelings of helplessness and discouragement were present for her until the midway point in her rehabilitation and seemed to vanish once optimism came in as well as relief during the late rehabilitation period.

#2: College Football Player - Career Ending Broken Foot

Overview:

Phil is a 22 year old football player. He experienced a broken foot during a practice session. At first it was thought that he would return to play so he approached rehabilitation in this manner, it was then discovered that his foot did not heal correctly and that this would be a career ending injury.

Phil's main reasons for participating in sport were pursuit of excellence, competition, personal improvement, fitness. On a scale of 1-6 (1-not at all, 6-absolutely) he marked five as describing himself as an athlete. His goals, which had been to be on the starting offensive line, have changed to focus more on school and his fiancé. He would like to stay in the game as a coach. He said if there was anything in life he could be he would want to be a healthier athlete. He has been plagued with many injuries over his whole football career and said he would have liked to see how far he could have gone if he were healthy.

It took some time before Phil sought help for his injury. He believed, as in the past that the pain would go away. Essentially for him it was his poor performance and not pain that brought him to seek help. Early in rehabilitation he set himself apart from the team. He still went to every game though and sat up in the stands. He did not separate himself from his coaches, however, he wanted them to know he was still there. After finding out he was going to be unable to play he was able to keep his locker for the remainder of the year and do workouts with the team.

Phil had good social support throughout his injury experience. He said the coaches were pretty good about it and especially the head offensive line coach would take the time to ask him how he was doing and have an open door for him. His family was important as were his fiancé and close friends. He said at first it was very difficult to ask or receive help for things he was unable to do. With their insistence and support he was finally able to accept and even ask for help if needed.

After Phil found out he would be unable to play he was tested. Phil feels that what helped him to come out of feeling down was leaving town. That way, he was able to get away and not think about it. There were no sports, no coaches, no team, just Phil, his fiancé, a good buddy and a family atmosphere and a good time. It helped him to put things back into perspective.

Physically he thought things were fine even though he was always in pain. Then he found out that the surgery was unsuccessful. He was more frustrated with not being able to play throughout his whole rehabilitation than with the constant pain. Physiologically his emotional states had some effects on him. He experienced weakness and sleeplessness which he attributed being due to worry and frustration.

When he found out that things did not heal right even though he tried to do things right was very frustrating to him. He dealt with it by talking to his fiancé. He said he still has negative feelings but they come and go and are not a constant for him. He says he is still sometimes depressed and discouraged by it all but appears to be moving on with his life and finding new ways to be involved with sports and activities he enjoys.

Phil said that what helped him most throughout this experience was finally getting the girl he had loved for years. "I had something else besides football, it was a big thing in my life to be with her and be happy, it was very good timing, it came about perfect."

When asked what he would do differently looking back he said "probably try to do less than I did, follow the Doctor's orders more thoroughly. That's probably what I would change just to see if those couple extra things I tried to do were the main cause that it didn't heal right, that's what I'd do." He said if or when he has the surgery to his foot again that next time he will take more time off, be a little gentler with it and baby it a bit more. He says he will have surgery on it again but does not know when he will do that. It still causes him pain on a daily basis but he says he is so used to it that it does not bother him.

Concerning mental training during rehabilitation he said mostly it was imagery that he used, picturing himself playing again, in certain game situations etc. He also used goal setting in his rehabilitation with his lifting. He did not set goals on time frames for he felt it would be too frustrating. He said "once I found out how bad it was I threw all concepts of time out the window and everything they said was what I went by". So he went by what the physician and trainers told him were appropriate time frames for such an injury and not by past injuries he had experienced.

Summary:

Phil was a collegiate football player who had experienced a broken foot and subsequent surgery. At first he was told he had good chances to return to sport. So for the beginning of his rehabilitation his biggest challenges were dealing with the inability to do daily tasks and not playing football. He also worried about what others in the football environment thought of him and his abilities. His desire to play as well as good social support helped him to reach a positive state in his rehabilitation. When he found out the surgery had been unsuccessful and he would not be able to return to sport at that level he was devastated. He attributes his coming out of depression and coming to terms with his injury to finding a new perspective on life and what's important in it also on his hopes of staying in the game as a coach so he can pass on his love of the game to others.

In Phil's case his survey data shows that he went from mostly negative emotional states to positive then back to negative and on to positive again as his rehabilitation went on and with the realization that this was a career ending injury.

His progression followed the following pattern: emotions of shock, not real, anger and frustration → depressed, sad, helpless and discouraged → fear → shock, disbelief → unfair, devastated, not real, depressed, sad, angry, changed my perspective, discouraged → optimistic and happy.

Phil had some emotions that he felt were consistent throughout his injury experience. These were frustration, irritability, restlessness and pain. He always also believed that it was a chance you take and marked having total acceptance throughout his rehabilitation.

#3: Female College Basketball Player - Foot Stress Fracture

Overview:

Hannah is a 21 year old female collegiate basketball player. She experienced a moderate stress fracture in her foot in the early season. She was out of play for 2-3 weeks. Her preferred sport or activity is basketball but also enjoys other sports and recreational activities. Her main reasons for participating in sport are for personal improvement, fun, physical fitness and competition. She places herself at a 3 on a scale of 1-6 (1-not at all, 6-absolutely) describing herself as an athlete.

Her goal is to be a great player, a dominant player. She sees herself as being on the low side of average at this point and wonders if her goals are unrealistic. After the injury her goals did not really change but she said that she feels a little more positive about them now. Her main goal in life and all she wants to do is to make people happy and to help people. She is not sure what would do that however and is still trying to figure it out.

Hannah did not have too many fears when she returned to sport. This was alleviated because the physician told her it was unlikely that her injury would reoccur. Her fears were more concentrated on her performance. That she would regress to where she had started, lose the gains she had made. When she returned to sport her confidence in her abilities were not present at first. She said that this wasn't a new feeling or a new thing to deal with having come in as a red shirt and feeling like she wasn't on their level to begin with but it did affect her feelings about the progress she had made to catch up.

She did have some social support during her injury experience. She does view some of the support she receives in sport as pressure. Later she said that she had fairly strong support during rehabilitation. She said she had some support from her coach and her teammates.

Sitting out of play was difficult for her. This was due to the fact that she had had a red shirt year where she had gotten used to sitting out. Then the next season she got used to playing and being in practice, then it happened again where she had to sit out. She felt restless but that going to watch practice also helped her by giving her more knowledge on things to watch rather than just fumble through.

Physically her rehabilitation was pretty smooth, no real setbacks. She did notice effects on her physiologically in response to her emotional states. She felt tense, weakness, sleeplessness, less alert, and a decrease in appetite. She noticed these most with feelings of depression and frustration.

She felt certain about being able to return to play about a half to three-quarters of the way through her rehabilitation. She felt positive and accepting of her injury about a half to three-quarters of the way through her rehabilitation as well. She felt positive and happy about her rehabilitation program about three-quarters of the way through rehabilitation.

Her behaviors varied over the course of her rehabilitation. At the time of the injury she still tried to give all out effort. At the time of physician diagnosis she felt shock but obeyed instructions. In early rehabilitation she had good effort and was focused on rehabilitation. At the mid rehabilitation point she stated she had fair effort and at the late rehabilitation point good effort. At return to play she tried to rebound from being out quickly, but that did not happen quickly.

Her self talk was negative for every period of her rehabilitation, including return to play, with just a little bit of positive self-talk in late rehabilitation. She used some goal setting but no other form of mental training during rehabilitation. She believes that talking to someone who had experienced a similar injury would definitely be helpful to her and anyone experiencing an injury.

Her answers as to how she is feeling now because of the injury show that she is still feeling quite negative. She is feeling depressed, discouraged, frustrated, helpless, tense, shocked, frightened etc. Optimism, at peace and relief were also expressed but to a much lesser degree.

Hannah stated that her parents and a few friends and feelings of support from them were what helped her the most during this experience. She said that what would have helped looking back was her attitude, and just knowing that it wouldn't come right back to her, that it's normal for any person coming off an injury to not bounce right back.

Summary:

Hannah is a female basketball player at the collegiate level. After taking 3 weeks off due to a slight fracture in her foot she was able to return to play. During the course of her rehabilitation she experienced depression and negative self talk. These emotional and psychological factors effected her physiologically as well as behaviorally during her rehabilitation. Her fears focused on her abilities once she returned to play and she was disappointed when her skill did not come back as quickly upon return as she had anticipated. Social support from her family and friends helped her through her rehabilitation process and her vacillating moods influenced how she was feeling during rehabilitation as they do at all times.

Hannah's emotion's progressed as follows: shock, disbelief, unfair, not real, anger, depression, sadness, sobering, fear, helplessness, and discouraged → changed my perspective, its a chance you take, lonely/isolated → irritable, restless → relieved → changed my perspective → total acceptance, relieved, optimistic, happy.

Although Hannah moved progressively towards more positive emotional states it is noted that she reported negative emotions throughout her rehabilitation experience. It is also noted that she reported only minor changes in affect over the course of her rehabilitation.

#4: Male College Basketball Player - Head & Facial Injuries

Overview:

Fred is a 22 year old male basketball player at the collegiate level. He suffered head and facial injuries in a game situation and was out of play for two days. His athletic accomplishments include all-league honorable mention and all tournament team. His goals are to be a good player and to be able to play overseas in basketball. His injury had no effect on his goals. If he could be anything he wanted to be in life he would be a record producer.

His main reasons for participating in sport are for competition, fun, self- discipline and fitness. Other reasons that rank lower are outlet of aggression and personal improvement. He said he would absolutely ,yes, (6 on a 1-6 scale) describe himself as an athlete.

Upon return to play Fred had no fears. He said he felt no sense of loss of control over his life or situation. He said he didn't care about having to sit out, citing the need for rest after a summer of play that left his legs tired. Later he said the only concern he had about sitting out concerned his teammates, because to him his injury didn't seem that bad but he said his teammates understood. When he returned to sport he said he was just as aggressive, but he did have some fears of people elbowing him.

He said he does have social support and encouragement in sport but also that he sees this support as pressure. He felt he had good support from his team and coach during his time out.

He immediately felt certain about his ability to return to play, felt positive about his rehabilitation and accepting of his injury. He went to practice each day he was out and watched. His behavior essentially centered around letting his body heal through sleep and rest.

He has a strong belief in himself and trust in his body and its ability to heal fast. His belief in the trainers varies. Believing they know what they are talking about, but also thinking that they should listen to people more about their own bodies.

He thinks sitting out and resting those few days were what helped him the most. He feels that the headaches he experienced were a hindrance to him and his recovery. He used no mental training, saying, "I don't use it, I just play and do that's all you can do now a days, I just want to play that's basically it."

Emotionally now he is at peace with his injury and the experience. During his injury experience he did experience shock at first and some anger but was also happy with the Doctor diagnosis and was a little restless during his time off.

Summary:

Fred is a male collegiate basketball player who experienced a head and facial injury in the course of a game situation. He only missed two days of practice and one practice game as a result of his injury. He believes he heals very quickly and that this helped him recover from his injury and to retain his confidence. His fears were centered on what his teammates might think of his sitting out, and he feels injuries are just a chance you take when you play a sport. His teammates and coach were supportive of him, so he was not very bothered by sitting out and was relieved to get the rest he felt his body needed. He experienced a few different negative emotions as a result of his injury which were quickly alleviated due to the nature of the injury. This brought about relief, he was happy to return to play so quickly.

Being a mild injury Fred's rehabilitation and reactions were much more brief in nature and progressed as follows: shock, pain → reluctant acceptance, happy → angry, restless → it's a chance you take, happy → total acceptance, happy.

Again we see that his initial reaction is that of shock His early happiness came when he heard it was only a mild injury and that he would return quickly back to sport. He did experience anger and restlessness during his time out of play but reported happiness upon return to play and now.

#5: Male College Soccer Player - Torn Lateral Cruciate Ligament

Overview:

Hector is a twenty year old collegiate male soccer player. He suffered a lateral cruciate ligament (LCL) tear in a soccer practice at the beginning of the season and was out of play for 8 weeks. His main reasons for participating in sport are for competition, pursuit of excellence, personal improvement, and fun. On a scale of 1-6 he describes himself as a 6, absolutely describing himself as an athlete. His goals have been to play collegiate soccer and to finish out his eligibility. He would like to continue on in soccer once his college career is over now that there are more professional opportunities in this sport. If he could be anything he wanted to be in life it would probably be a wildlife photographer.

Hector had several fears during his rehabilitation and upon return to sport. "Right when it happened I had fears about never being able to play again, but after I talked to my Doctor he said that wasn't really going to be a problem. I had fears of more of what I was going to do if I didn't end up playing anymore." Hector was at a crossroads at this point because he was either going to continue to play in college or he wasn't, "so I didn't know exactly what I as going to do if I didn't play, so that was a big fear."

Another fear he had concerned what he considered normal fears after surgery. Wondering if his body was going to hold up to what it used to do. He was also fearful of reinjury after returning to sport. On overcoming this fear he spoke of initial fear, but growing comfort as he returned to playing, developing confidence in himself, physically, and, gradually, not thinking about the injury. He spoke of realizing when he started to play how his leg was still out of shape after coming back, which brought it to the forefront of his mind.

He did not really feel like an active participant in the planning or implementing of his rehabilitation program. He always felt like doing more than what he was told to do by his therapist, because he felt pretty good. He believes they were waiting and just letting nature heal it, but he wanted to move faster and they wouldn't let him. That was frustrating for him. But, in retrospect, he believes he was too anxious because after his first two games in one week, he had to lay off for a month because of soreness. He did feel a sense of loss of control, he felt like it wasn't fair and then when he realized there was nothing he could do he just kind of accepted it and worked on getting back.

Hector had good social support from his therapist, trainers, family, and friends. He found their support to be very beneficial to him during this trying time. Hector had faith in his therapist. Hector also had a strong belief in himself even though, physically, he had ups and downs throughout his rehabilitation experience.

He said his mood when he went into therapy definitely affected how it went and how he did in therapy affected his mood coming out. He said he was unprepared for the loss of strength coming out of surgery and that the physician did not prepare him for that. It was not until he saw his therapist two weeks later that they spoke of the ups and downs of therapy. Another setback physically was in range of motion and how it would vary from measurement to measurement. That was frustrating for him.

He feels that therapy and rehabilitation are just something you have to deal with, saying "…for the most part I think its something you have to deal with yourself. It's kind of a personal demon, getting in there and logging hours, its tough…. it's just a personal demon you have to tackle by yourself, …its really the level you do it (rehabilitation) that's going to decide whether or not you are going to succeed or not… because the more you do now the better you'll be later." He feels this attitude helped get him through his rehabilitation, even during the down times.

The thing that hindered him the most was that it happened on the first day of try outs and then it took two weeks of fumbling around to figure out what was wrong with it. So he spent two weeks trying to rehabilitate a strained ilio-tibial (I-T) band. Consequently, he already felt like he was set back two weeks. He feels that a positive attitude is important but even more important is the realization of where one is going and that the more done now the less to do later. He said he did not use any mental training techniques but that it was pretty mentally taxing. He believes peer counseling would be a good idea.

Summary:

Hector is a varsity collegiate male soccer player. He incurred an LCL tear in a practice session at the beginning of the season. Over the course of his eight weeks out of play he experienced many ups and downs both physically and emotionally. His attitude and his family, teammates/friends and coach helped him through this experience. He had a strong belief in those on his rehabilitation team as well as in himself. His fears concerned his ability to come back and what would he do if he did not. He also had fears of reinjury upon his return and feels he still makes adaptations in his running style to account for his knee. He feels that other events in ones life that are going on at the same time as the recovery from the injury effects the recovery process and how one does in therapy.

Hector's progression of emotions throughout his rehabilitation was: anger, bad luck, anxious/tense, irritable, restless → shock, disbelief, no way, unfair, depressed, frustrated, helpless, discouraged → sobering → changed my perspective, optimistic → reluctant acceptance → total acceptance, happy. For Hector, the accurate diagnosis of his injury took more time which affected his response, resulting in anger came before his shock, disbelief and other negative emotions. Hector reported optimism with a change in perspective. He also moved from negative to positive emotional states over the course of his rehabilitation with the majority of his negative reactions coming at the time of the physician's diagnosis.

#6: Male College Basketball Player - Torn ACL

Overview:

Terrence is a 22 year old male collegiate basketball player. He tore his anterior cruciate ligament (ACL) in a basketball game which was a season ending injury for him. He is now in the off season but is back to playing. His main reasons for participating in sport are for competition, personal improvement, pursuit of excellence and fun. He places himself at 6 on a scale of 1-6 in describing himself as an athlete.

His goals are to play semi-pro, free agent basketball overseas. He has already had a couple of offers to play in Australia and overseas in Europe and he is scheduled to play in China in two months. He says his injury has not changed his goals at all. He says that basketball has been his life. His fears center mostly on the sense that it could happen again. He said he feels better about it not happening again because of all the hard work he has put in.

He said he basically played a small part in the planning and implementing of his rehabilitation program. He went on to say that with his knowledge of training he also knew what he had to do and that added to what the physicians and trainers were telling him. Terrence stated that he felt a loss of control over his life and situation during his rehabilitation. He also talked of the difficulty of going to the gym right after his surgery.

Terrence says he had complete confidence and belief in his doctor. Part of this came from knowing the previous job the physician had done with another athlete and how successful that had been. He also felt very comfortable with the trainers and felt they were competent people. Having this past rapport and relationship with them was beneficial for him with this injury.

Terrence felt he had good social support in sport and for his injury. His family was very influential as well as his coach. He also had good support from his teammates. He said his father had gone through injuries as an athlete and that his understanding and interest in him has been very helpful.

He discussed the early phase of his injury prior to surgery and just past as being very difficult for him and laden with many fears. He waited two months to have surgery simply because of school and other demands. He said the time between the injury and the surgery were very hard Emotionally he had a difficult time with this injury. He said for a short time his depression alleviated after the surgery, but it was more just progressively seeing himself getting better, that he has progressed. He went on to say though that even that did not rid him of the depression because of uncertainties that were still present.

He said it was difficult for him to accept his injury because he did not want to accept it. He also said that after the injury it was just very frustrating and that he was extremely disheartened. He says that his strong goals and plans, his attitude, time and physical progression are what will help in him reach a higher level of positive emotional states and that he is definitely more to positive now than in the early phases of his rehabilitation.

He did not feel certain and without a doubt about being able to return to play until at the end of his rehabilitation. He also did not feel positive or accept his injury until the end of his rehabilitation experience. He felt confident and happy about his rehabilitation program immediately.

Physically he has had no setbacks and feels physically he has rehabilitated very well and quicker than was expected. The only physiological effect he felt related to his emotional states was weakness (less strength).

What Terrence feels helped him the most during his injury experience was the support he received from his dad. Also the support from the rest of his family and his coach played a big part. Terrence also thinks that his hard work and a belief that nothing is going to hold him back helped him through this experience. He feels that talking to others who have gone through a similar injury is very beneficial.

As far as mental training skills used during his injury rehabilitation experience he said he did use them and that he is pretty mentally tough. He used some imagery as well as goal setting for this experience.

Summary:

Terrence is a collegiate varsity basketball player who suffered a season ending ACL tear. He experienced serious negative emotions as a result of his injury and now that he is returning to play he is becoming more positive. He had many fears and mostly uncertainties concerning his injury and the effects it would have. The physician, trainers, and others he talked to with a similar experience helped to alleviate his fears and concerns. Physically he had a successful rehabilitation. He felt quite a sense of loss of control over his life and situation mostly due to the fact that he could not do what he had always done on a daily basis. At one point, early on, he did turn to alcohol, but stopped as rehabilitation progressed. His family, friends, and coach were instrumental support for him. He is able to play and will play competitively again soon.

Terrence left some periods of his rehabilitation blank on his survey so the following pattern is from the brief information he did report. It is interesting to note that his attitudes and emotions even prior to being injured were ones of disbelief, unfairness, and fear: Shock, devastated, not real, sobering depressed, sad, angry, frustrated, bored, discouraged → changed perspective, reluctant acceptance, lonely/isolated, helpless, optimistic → anxious/tense → relieved → total acceptance.

Terrence followed a pattern of intense negative emotional reactions gravitating toward more positive emotions as rehabilitation progressed. Also, as other athletes have reported, optimism follows a change in perspective.

#7: College Football Player - Shoulder Separation

Overview:

Drake is a 20 year old male collegiate football player. He suffered several shoulder separations in a short period of time prompting reconstructive shoulder surgery. He has been out of play for 10 months, this was a season ending injury. Drake's main reasons for participating in sport are for competition, fun, and pursuit of excellence. He rates himself a 6 on a scale of 1-6, describing himself as an athlete.

His goals are to take football as far as he can. He said his goals initially changed with the injury, but as rehabilitation progressed, returned to the former goals. When asked if he could be anything in life he said he would love to be in the NFL either as a player or a coach.

Drake says he did have some fears during rehabilitation and returning to play. He said that during training to come back he did a lot of mental stuff, focusing and trying to get it back to where he was totally comfortable in it.

Drake also had some fears regarding his performance upon returning to sport. He said that when watching he got a new perspective of the game and realized how fast it is and how things are coming at you. He said that being in spring ball has given him confidence, that he is faster than that player, bigger than this player as opposed to when he was standing on the side lines thinking how fast these players were.

He feels he had just the right amount of social support for sport and during his injury experience. He said his teammates and coaches offered him much support. He also felt that his friends and dad were real instrumental in his life at this time.

Drake felt like an active participant in the planning and implementing of his rehabilitation. He said much of the programming for his rehabilitation he did on his own. He also said that many of the exercises he would do, he would do it and then a couple of weeks later the trainers would tell him he could do it. So he tried to train smart and do what he felt his body said was OK to do and what were proper exercises for him. He was determined to come back faster than the time they had given him and felt that if he worked harder than what they were saying then it would help him to get back faster. He felt it was better and that by doing this it gave him a sense of control. He also liked that he started rehabilitation quickly after the surgery.

He had a pretty good belief in his trainers and physician. He felt that he believed in himself more in the sense that he always took everything a step higher than they took it. He would ask the trainers and physician how he was doing and as long as they said fine he continued to work hard and do more than what they would say, without telling them.

Physically he had many ups and downs and plateaus. To deal with these situations he would work harder, switch exercises etc. Emotionally he has also experienced ups and downs during his injury experience. Prior to seeking help he said he did not seek help due to the disbelief that anything could be wrong with him.

Drake had been participating in two a day practices when he separated his shoulder three times in eight practices. When it happened it was more of a shock, then it was more of a pain. He said he had no choice but to be positive about the surgery. In his mind, he had to take a chance no matter how slim it might have been that the surgery would work because without it he had no chance at all.

He stated that emotionally he thought it went pretty well throughout his rehabilitation. He attributed this to knowing that plateaus would come and along with them peaks and valleys so when he hit a peak he wouldn't get too high and when he hit the valleys he wouldn't get too low, he felt it was pretty constant the whole way through.

The difficult times emotionally came in regards to watching practice and games. He said it was tough even to go to practice even though everyone was still pressing that he was still part of the team. He would go to practice a couple times a week to prove that he was still there and to say hi to his teammates and show them support. He said if they had not been so supportive of him that he probably would not have cared about going out and saying hi. He said when it came to game day though that it was too tough to be out there. He was also glad that it happened early in his college career; having a red shirt year available to him helped relieve stress about having to sit out a year.

He said that in dealing with not doing something he so strongly identified with forced him to put all his energy into the rehabilitation. Currently Drake has feelings of frustration, optimism and still pain because of the injury.

Drake said he immediately felt certain and without a doubt about being able to return to play and felt positive and reached the point of acceptance about his injury. He said he was never confident in and happy about his rehabilitation program. His behavior throughout his rehabilitation program has remained quite consistent with him puffing all out effort throughout. His self-talk was also consistent throughout which was, God's in control and do more than anyone expects you to do.

Drake feels that what helped him the most was the belief that he was going to be back and actually the missing of the season.. He said that all his life he has played a sport and that going to school while everyone was at practice drove him nuts.

When asked what if anything hindered his experience he said the biggest regret he has is not getting it checked out sooner. Looking back on his rehabilitation he says there is nothing he would change, that it has gone on schedule if not way ahead of schedule.

Summary:

Drake is a collegiate varsity football player who had major reconstruction surgery done on his shoulder. His rehabilitation was successful but he did have problems sitting out of play. He had a few fears concerning re-injury and his performance upon return to sport. Early in rehabilitation he was worried about whether he would be able to return to sport. He dealt with these fears by "thinking" through them, and by participating in no contact practice sessions in order to regain his confidence. He had good support from his teammates, friends, coaches and family. He attributes his success in rehabilitation to his attitude and belief in himself as well as to the new perspective he gained by having to sit out. He currently is still at times frustrated and in pain but is optimistic about the upcoming season.

Drake had no reports of depression, sadness or anger in his survey results. He progressed through the following pattern of responses: shock, disbelief, no way, not real, frustrated, changed perspective, total acceptance, lonely/isolated, fear, helpless → optimistic → relieved, anxious/tense, happy.

Drake reported fairly consistent emotional reactions throughout his rehabilitation experience. He said he was quite optimistic and happy throughout yet did experience negative emotional reactions early on with his injury. For Drake his negative emotions abated somewhat rapidly except for feelings of anxiousness and feeling tense. It is again noted that pain was marked throughout the survey.

#8: College Football Player - Pulled Hamstring

Overview:

Elliott is a 23 year old male collegiate football player. He suffered a pulled hamstring in the first scrimmage of the year and was out of play for five weeks. Among his athletic accomplishments are second team all-conference, after his sophomore season, co-captain and honorable mention his senior season. His main reasons for participating in sport are for competition, pursuit of excellence, personal improvement, and fun. He also participates for fitness, fun, and socialization. On a scale of 1-6 he describes himself as an athlete at about a 5.

Elliott's goals now that he has maxed out his eligibility are to coach and pass on some of the things that he's learned and deal with little kids. He also wouldn't mind coaching at the college level because he enjoys the commitment. He says he does not have any hopes of playing professional. He said that his goals really did change as a result of his injury. This had been his second year of being injured and he had been working very hard to get back to where he was before with his performance. When asked if he could be anything in life he said he would like to be a jet fighter pilot.

Elliott said he really did have fears. His fears were mostly centered on re-injury and performance upon his return. He said that at certain times during his injury experience that he had no confidence in his hamstring at all. Prior to his return to play he had to deal with his fear of re-injury. After five years of football, establishing himself and being co-captain, he felt significant stress to get back and help the team that way, this also helped him to feel more comfortable with telling the coaches what he needed.

Elliott was also worried about what his teammates would think. He said he finally had to do what was best for him if he ever wanted to play again that year. He said one of the most difficult things had to do with the fact that with this particular injury no one could just look at him and say, oh he's injured, so it concerned him that people might judge his performance without taking the injury into account.

Elliott's previous knee injury had a significant effect on him and how he viewed this injury. He had fears concerning re-injury and his performance and what others would think of him, would they consider the injury, that he had been out, and would they believe he was injured. In the beginning of his rehabilitation Elliott did not feel like an active participant in the planning or implementing of his program. This was tied to his feeling of belief in those working with him and feelings of control he had over the situation. He said that when you're injured you just want to try anything and anything different, you don't know if it's going to work but you just want to try something different, to exhaust all possibilities. He finally took it into his own hands and talked to a track coach who took him to a local physical therapy clinic. In essence Elliott sought out a second opinion concerning his injury at which point he decided to stay with those individuals where he then felt in better control of the situation and had a stronger belief in the individuals and program they were setting him up with.

As far as believing in himself he said he didn't think he ever had any doubts in himself. He said at times especially coming back from his knee surgery that he may have had some doubts but that he just needed to get back into it to prove to himself that he could do it.
Elliott said that he had good social support. He had good support from his family as well as from his close friends. Physically and emotionally Elliott had many ups and downs. He went through a 4 cycle of: injury, play, re-injury before his final diagnosis and out of play for 4 weeks, which contributed to his frustration and ups and downs.

Elliott also noticed his emotional states to have an effect on him physiologically.   He experienced sleeplessness, and weakness. He attributed this to it being his senior season, and 2nd season in a row of missing time. He experienced trouble sleeping because of frustration and worrying about the end being near. The loss of strength resulted from all the time and energy being put into one part of his body.

Elliott said he was pretty depressed about the injury. He said that when the two different opinions both told him he would have to sit out for four weeks was the lowest he'd ever felt. He said because at first when the physicians told him it wasn't that bad and he'd be back in a day, he still had optimism. It concerned him that he was a co-captain and was not going to be able to lead by example, that he would have to be more of a talker, a social leader, which he did not want to be.

Prior to his hamstring injury Elliott was confident that he was going to attain his pre knee injury playing capabilities. When this did not seem possible, he felt great disappointment and depression. Emotionally many of his feelings seemed related to his thoughts and beliefs about what kind of player he was and could have been and what these injuries had done to that. He did say that he had a lot of fun the last five weeks that he did get to practice. He said that he cherished every one and looked forward to them, "Because I knew they were my last 5 weeks of football or ever playing a competitive team sport at that level, so it made it really fun."

Currently Elliott is still experiencing some negative emotions concerning his injury. He often feels helpless, angry, and frustrated and also sometimes frightened, tense, shocked depressed and discouraged.

What Elliott said helped most physically was the PT clinic and the people there. Mentally he became quite interested in the mental aspect of things after what had happened to him the year before with his knee. He specifically enrolled in a sport psychology class where he learned many different things which were helpful to him. Also that this opportunity allowed him to seek out a knowledgeable individual in sport psychology who he felt comfortable with talking about his experience.

Elliott used mental training during his rehabilitation period. This consisted of mental imagery to develop scenarios of action. Because his practice time was limited, he thought maybe that could make up for some of the practice time that he missed. He really tried to focus through his blocking skills and his catching skills. He thought that the visual imagery might make up the difference.

Elliott also said that these injuries changed his perspective about sport. He says he does not feel his new perspective has carried over to other areas of his life because it is his belief that life has more guarantees than sport.

Summary:

Elliott experienced numerous negative emotional reactions when he incurred his injury which mostly continued until mid-rehabilitation. His pattern of responses were as follows: shock, disbelief, no way, unfair, devastated, sobering, depressed, sad, angry, frustrated, changed perspective, bad luck, anxious/tense, lonely/isolated, irritable, restless, fear, helpless, discouraged → not real → depressed, sad → reluctant acceptance, optimistic → its a chance you take, bad luck → disbelief, total acceptance, happy.

Elliott experienced numerous negative emotions as a result of his injury. These did finally diminish with total acceptance and happiness occurring after his return to play and more time passing. When his optimism returned his negative emotions were diminishing, of course it can not be said which came first.

#9: Retirement of an Elite Endurance Athlete

Introduction:

Cliff is an elite endurance athlete, now retired from his primary sport where he was a prominent top-ten competitor for over seven years. During his career, he won more than a half-dozen major international events and was able to maintain a modest but adequate income from sponsorship, clinics, and prize money to make the sport his full time business. Cliff is a dedicated student of human performance, which brought him to seek sport psychology support in his quest for excellence. We developed an outstanding working relationship and focused primarily on performance enhancement skills over the last five years of his career. During periods of our association we had regular weekly meetings, but our contacts ranged from just checking in occasionally over the phone to multiple intensive sessions during a single week.

It became apparent after a few years work that we would need to address some plans for retirement from the sport. Cliff was in his early thirties, and he suffered several severe injuries that threatened his ability to continue competing at the professional level. There was concern that his life was entirely designed around being an elite athlete, from his income to his overall lifestyle. Despite having a university degree, Cliff expressed a highly negative reaction to the normal office jobs that might present themselves based on his qualifications. Eventually, the injuries forced him into retirement. Cliff was faced with a dilemma encountered by most professional athletes—how to move forward in life after sport.

Intervention:

Over the course of our work on performance enhancement, we had developed some significant philosophical approaches to training and competition. Cliff took it upon himself to become totally immersed in the mastery of performance in his event. With that as the basis, we explored a broader perspective to take in not only his sport, but his life in general. The objective was for Cliff to develop a greater understanding of himself and his values for living. I anticipated that such a process would provide a foundation that he could easily carry beyond professional sport on into the next phase of his life. Importantly, this approach was expected to facilitate training and performance in the short term, as well as career transition in the long term. That is, we did not view this work as strictly beneficial to retirement. On the contrary, it was developed as a method for enhancing professional sporting achievements and other life pursuits.

Cliff was asked to keep notes on what aspects of his life he particularly enjoyed, past and present, sport and non-sport. He also reflected on what things he might wish to do in his life and the type of person he would like to be. Over the course of a year, we discussed his notes and gradually developed an understanding of what he valued and where he found meaning for his life. We examined why he enjoyed certain situations and activities, and challenged what he might really need in his life to be happy. From these discussions, we identified strong positive motivations that brought meaning to his activities and energy to their pursuit. We also were able to release some unrealistic or irrelevant expectations that had induced stress in the past, but proved to hold little value to Cliff. Through this process we developed a perspective that he could live from, regardless of whether he was a professional athlete or doing something else. Career transition now would only be a shift from one focus to a new one, rather than the shock loss of a profession and a lifestyle.

Cliff discovered a central philosophy that he could apply to nearly anything he might do. He determined that enjoying his life was a matter of 'Living Each Day Fully.' This has become his personal slogan. He found that the essence of his enjoyment in past activities was based on physical and mental challenges. Although he thrived on elite competition, he discovered that being professional and winning were only surface aspects of a greater love for exploration and adventure. Furthermore, it became clear how much he valued interactions with people. Meeting new people, sharing ideas, and pursuing activities with others were all deeply meaningful to him. Cliff realized how much he enjoyed teaching and promoting a healthy, active lifestyle. All of these rewarding elements he had been able to secure through his professional career. However, it became clear that it was not necessary to be a professional athlete for him to obtain these meaningful life experiences. Any lifestyle that would allow Cliff to Live Each Day Fully, find physical and mental challenges, interact with people, and teach and promote healthy living would be enjoyable and rewarding to him.

Outcome:

As a result of our work, Cliff began to look at his activities from a broader perspective. Still training full time, he put more effort into doing clinics and establishing connections for potential work after retirement. He arranged with a friend to co-write a book on training, and developed some additional responsibilities in public relations with one of his sponsors. Without detracting from his sport participation, Cliff began to Live Each Day Fully in a more diverse sense than before.

Approximately one year after we had established Cliff's philosophical perspective, he made a final attempt at a World Championship endurance event. Honest to his principles and dedicated to his objectives, he trained hard in the face of his injuries. Unless his performance was outstanding, he knew that it would likely be his last professional competition. Despite the pressure that a last chance effort might produce, Cliff approached it with as much enthusiasm and enjoyment as ever. He viewed training and racing as opportunities to take on challenges and Live Each Day Fully. He gathered with him a few of his close friends and supporters from over the years, and we journeyed with him to the competition to share the event.

Cliff's body simply was not up to matching the top field in the grueling event. He persevered to complete the competition, still among the professionals, but far back from his form of years' past. Although there was little external reason for him to put himself through the painful physical ordeal of the entire race, Cliff felt it was important to close that chapter of his life with a sense of completion. Despite the potential for disappointment and a sense of loss, we celebrated a great career and adventures yet to come.

Cliff has moved on from professional competition, but the philosophy he developed continues to give him direction and enjoyment. He continues to be physically active and take on challenges of new sports and activities. He has co-written a book and continues to do clinics and work for his former sponsor. No matter what the future brings, Cliff can rely on a valuable personal perspective for what he values doing and who he wants to be.

#10: College Quarterback - Multiple Injuries

Introduction:

Jake was a heralded college quarterback who sustained significant injuries to his sternum, ribs, abdomen, knee, and foot throughout an opening-season football game. Consequently, his performance deteriorated throughout the game, completing 10 of 31 passes for 169 yards. He also threw two interceptions and coughed up two fumbles. During the game the head coach called him a derogatory term in front of his teammates because of his hesitancy to "get back in the game".

A few days after the game, upon the advice of the team athletic trainer (without the head coach's knowledge), Jake met with me for sport psychology consultation. He was deemed to be emotionally and physically beat-up, but wanted to regain favor with his coach. Compounding the problem, the back-up quarterback directed the team down the field for the winning score. The once-backup is now the starter. Jake began pondering how to regain his confidence, composure, physical health, and status of starter.

Intervention:

First, Jake was asked to express all his profound fears relating to his immediate concern - "empty his bucket". This established what we could work on together. Next, we investigated Jake's perception of reestablishing trust in his physical rehabilitation and the athletic trainer. I believed that the physical aspect of his injuries could be addressed in Jake's attempt to regain his health as part of regaining his confidence.

Jake was viewed as a true leader on the team, and I reflected this to him. Consequently, we established that he did not need to prove his veracity or role as a team leader, simply because he felt his teammates trusted him.

Cognitive restructuring was used in review of his performance at critical points of play. This aided Jake in identifying his competence level and acknowledging the realistic role any physical injury actually played. I then introduced some simple negative thought-stopping strategies and positive self-talk in working through the past performance and directed him in use of these techniques to the present and future.

After a couple of meetings he shared with me that he felt comfortable with this "positive" approach, so we took it a step further. Together we developed a coping-rehearsal performance script put to his choice of music for motivation. It was based closely on Ravizza and Osborne's Three-R Principles: Ready, Respond, and Refocus. This assisted Jake in building confidence in rehabilitation and strengthened his intent in returning to play. The tape was played daily before practice and at night because there was a relaxation component on it. I really impressed upon him to use the word "Trust" throughout the script to reinforce his passing attempts as well as his total rehabilitation physically and mentally.

Outcome:

In Jake's next game, he completed 14 of 20 passes for 200+ yards, with one interception and no fumbles. Consequently, he was quickly reinstated as the starting quarterback. Throughout the season Jake continued to cope well with the injuries and mentally mend. Jake finished the season successfully, with a passing completion rate of nearly 60%.

Discussion Questions

1. Describe the epidemiology and the risk factors for injury. Give examples of how factors such as fear, stress, conflict, and anger may contribute to the risk of injury.

2. Identify specific injuries that might be more likely to occur among different types of sport categories (e.g., contact sports, water sports, winter sports).

3. Describe several examples wherein personality variables may be associated with either lower or higher risk of injury. Consider mood, confidence, sensation-seeking, etc.

4. Identify several variations in the psychological impact of an injury. Give examples of both positive and negative reactions to an injury rehabilitation experience.

5. Discuss whether you feel it is possible to prevent some injuries from happening. What might be done specifically to prevent injury in selected high risk sports?

6. In working with athletes who have recently experienced a serious injury, what mental training strategies would you consider using with them? Consider goal-setting principles that can apply to rehabilitation as well as performance.

7. Identify several common problems that occur during rehabilitation and in transition back to competition. Consider fear of reinjury and the possibility that the injury is a cause for termination of a career in that sport.

8. Select one of the case studies that is most relevant to your sport or your past injury. Describe the mental training strategies you would recommend using based upon the content presented in this chapter.

References

Anderson, M. B., & Williams, J. M. (1993). Psychological risk factors and injury prevention. In J. Heil (Ed.), Psychology of sport injury. Champaign, IL: Human Kinetics Press.

Evans, L., & Hardy, L. (1995). Sport injury and grief responses: A review. Journal of Sport and Exercise Psychology, 17, 227-245.

Gould, D., Udry, E., Bridges, D., & Beck, L. (1997a). Stress sources encountered when rehabilitating from season-ending ski injuries. The Sport Psychologist, 11, 361-378.

Gould, D., Udry, E, Bridges, D., & Beck, L. (1997b). Coping with season-ending injuries. The Sport Psychologist, 11, 379-399.

Heil, J. (1993a). A framework for psychological assessment. In J. Heil (Ed.), Psychology of sport Injury. Champaign, IL: Human Kinetics Press.

Heil, J. (1993b). Diagnostic methods and measures. In J. Heil (Ed.), Psychology of sport injury. Champaign, IL: Human Kinetics Press.

Heil, J. (1993c). A comprehensive approach to injury management. In J. Heil (Ed.), Psychology of sport injury. Champaign, IL: Human Kinetics Press.

Heil, J. (1993d). Mental training in injury management. In J. Heil (Ed.), Psychology of sport injury. Champaign, IL: Human Kinetics Press.

Heil, J. (1993e). Sport psychology, the athlete at risk, and the sports medicine team. In J. Heil (Ed.), Psychology of sport injury. Champaign, IL: Human Kinetics Press.

Heil, J. (1993f). A psychologist's view of the personal challenge of injury. In J. Heil (Ed.), Psychology of sport injury. Champaign, IL: Human Kinetics Press.

Ievleva, L. (1988). Psychological factors in knee and ankle injury recovery: An exploratory study. Unpublished masters thesis, University of Ottawa, Ottawa, Ontario.

Kerr, G., & Minden, H. (1988). Psychological factors related to occurrence of athletic injuries. Journal of Sport and Exercise Psychology, 10, 167-173.

Kobasa, S. C. (1979). Stressful life events, personality and health: An inquiry into hardiness. Journal of Personality and Social Psychology, 37, 111.

Maviffakalian, M., & Barlow, D. (Eds.). (1981). Phobia: Psychological and pharmacological treatment. New York: Guilford Press.

McCarthy, T. (1989). Managing bursitis in the athlete: An overview. The Physician and Sports Medicine, 17, 115-125.

Muse, M. (1985). Stress related, post-traumatic chronic pain syndrome pain: Criteria for diagnosis and preliminary report on prevalence. Journal of International Association for the Study of Pain, 23, 295-300.

Rotella, R. J., & Heyman, S. R. (1986). Stress and injury and the psychological rehabilitation of athletes. In J. M. Williams (Ed.), Applied sports psychology: Personal growth to peek performance. Palo Alto, CA: Mayfield.

Shapiro, F. (1995). Eye movement desensitization and reprocessing: Basic principles, protocols, and procedures. New York: Guilford Press.

Smith, R., Smoll, F., & Ptacek, J. (1990). Conjunctive moderator variables in vulnerability and resiliency: Lifestress, social support and coping skills and adolescent sport injuries. Journal of Personality and Social Psychology, 58, 360-370.

Svoboda, B., & Danek, M. (1982). Retirement from high level competition. In P. Orlick, J. Partington, & J. Salmela (Eds.), Mental training for coaches and athletes. Ottawa, Ontario: Sport in Perspective.

Udry, E., Gould, D. Bridges, D., & Beck, L. (1997). Down but not out: Athlete responses to season-ending injuries. Journal of Sport and Exercise Psychology, 19, 229-248.

Wack, J. T., & Turk, D. C. (1984). Latent structures in strategies for coping with pain. Health Psychology, 3, 27-43.

Williams, J., & Roepke, N. (1992). Psychology of injury and injury rehabilitation. In R. N. Singer, M. Murphey, & L. K. Tennant (Eds.), Handbook of research on sports psychology. New York: Macmillan.

CHAPTER 13

~ Case Studies of a Clinical Nature ~

Gloria Balague, University of Illinois at Chicago
Jim Reardon, Columbus Traumatic Stress Center

Performance Problems: Not Always Performance Related

Sometimes an athlete consults for a specific performance problem. The sport psychologist recommends a specific intervention, but the intervention does not seem to work effectively. Either the athlete does not seem to incorporate or practice the techniques or exercises suggested (as has been demonstrated in some of the previous examples [i.e. Parent-Athlete Case #2]), or the interventions are practiced faithfully, but still there is no improvement.

Regardless of how clear the performance issues seem or how appropriate an intervention appears to be for an issue, it is essential to keep in mind that the **whole person** is engaged in the activity, and before making an intervention decision, the assessment must include all important areas of the athlete's life. In general, the more dedicated the athlete (e.g., elite level), the more sport performance means to him/her in terms of identity. Therefore, life and personal issues will have more of an impact and be harder to separate from sport performance. Also, the fewer roles the person has beyond that of being an athlete, the more likely again that issues will be mixed and interdependent.

The fact that some performance issues are actually clinical in nature does not necessarily imply "pathological". It just means that other "life issues" need to be addressed before the athlete can fully devote his or her energy to the sport. On occasions, athletes consult apparently for a sport performance issue, but it may just be a socially acceptable way to seek help; a way to be able to start talking about something that is bothering him or her. Sometimes athletes feel they can only talk about sport related issues with the sport psychologist, so they bring up an issue to justify talking to the sport psychologist. Finally, other times the athlete only sees the performance related issue and genuinely believes that other problems are not going to impact on it. In the next several sections, examples of situations where performance problems were actually related to other life issues will be discussed. The first situation is when the performance problem is due to the athlete trying to avoid thinking about other relevant life issues.

Trying to Block Other Major Issues

Scenario #1:

An athlete had just finished competing in a major world championships competition and felt that his performance had been below what everyone including himself had expected of his capabilities. He approached the sport psychologist and indicated that he had a difficult time focusing his attention and felt like he had no energy. Soon thereafter, during conversations with the sport psychologist, he revealed that his girlfriend had been attacked and sexually assaulted a few weeks before the championships. He admitted that he had tried to put that thought aside until after the competition, but in retrospect he obviously found that it took too much energy to fend off the intrusive thoughts. His performance decreased because he tried too hard to "not think about it". At that moment he needed to talk about both his disappointing performance and the bottled up feelings he had about his girlfriend's attack.

If he would have approached the sport psychologist before the competition, several strategies could have been tried, depending on the amount of time available prior to his performance:

♦ If there was enough time to process and discuss his feelings, that may have been useful.

♦ If there was not enough time for procession and discussion, then he could have benefited from an intervention of: 1) having one session talking about it, 2) acknowledging that the assault had already happened and he could not prevent it, and 3) agreeing on a time afterwards when all of these issues would be examined, but making them more concrete and therefore less overwhelming.

♦ It is possible that, regardless of the available time, he could not have been able to delay examining his thoughts and feelings. In such a case, he would have to start allowing himself to feel the range of emotions, but increasing the awareness that he could control some of the flow of feelings and acknowledging that he did not need to allow the intrusive thoughts to stay on his mind all the time. However, he could acknowledge them and talk about them at certain moments during the day. Meanwhile, he could also use the emotional energy as just that, "energy".

Scenario #2:

A female athlete approached the sport psychologist before a major competition. She reported that her grandfather had passed away a few weeks before. He had been a very important figure in her life, very supportive of her athletic performance, always attending competitions whenever he could. She felt that it would be better to try to avoid thinking about him before the competition so as not to be distracted. As the competition approached, she felt unmotivated, had a hard time concentrating. She approached the sport psychologist and together they decided that avoiding the thoughts totally was not working for her so it was mutually agreed that she would find some time to think about her grandfather, remember the support that he gave her, and take that feeling with her into the competition. After the competition she would again think about him, and find a way to keep her emotional connection to him. This approach worked well for her, and seemed to free her energies so she was able to concentrate on the competition, in some ways emotionally dedicate her performance to her grandfather, and yet know that she could carry on with the grieving process after the competition was finished. In the interview it was determined that it was not a pathological grief case, just a normal reaction to the loss experienced that became more evident as the first competition without him approached.

Romantic Relationships

Problems in romantic relationships often are a great source of stress and they tend to interfere with performance. Particularly, major competitions are situations where an athlete's partner may want to be present as a show of support. Unfortunately, his/her presence often develops into a source of distraction, with the athlete having the worry about the partner at a time when they need most of their energy to focus on the upcoming event. Several variations of this scenario have presented themselves over the years:

Relationship Scenario:

Both partners are involved in the same major competition (i.e., they both made the Olympic or National Team). The stress of a major competition, added to the travel and fatigue issues, may just create temporary problems for a couple, who should find a way to have some individual time when they need it. More common, and often more disturbing, is the situation where one of the partners is having a good competition and the other one is not. The one who is doing well may not feel it is right to "enjoy" the success because the partner is doing poorly. The other one may feel he or she should not complain or discuss negative feelings so as to not "rain on the other's parade". The result is often an increase in distractions, irritability, sleep disturbances, etc. which are likely to interfere with good performance and result in diminished support for both of them.

Occasionally the couple consists of an athlete and a coach. The stress of the coach, seeing his or her professional competence as depending on the athlete's performance and also wishing that the athlete were to perform as well as possible, may result in increased pressure, less support, and a more negative interaction at a time when the athlete needs the exact opposite, more support and encouragement.

The emotional intensity often results in break ups or big emotional crises. They may be temporary (the relationship may survive), but its negative effect on the performance, sometimes in a unique situation such as the Olympics, cannot be erased.

Ideally, these issues should be prevented. That is, both partners would need to know their needs during a major competition and negotiate times for their preparation and times as a couple. If one partner does not stay with the other habitually during competitions, it is probably not a good idea to start doing so at a major competition, such as Nationals or Olympic Trials.

Clinical Depression

On occasion a performance problem masks more serious issues, such as clinical depression or anxiety. The following example illustrates such a situation:

Clinical Depression Scenario:

A male athlete attended a brief elite training camp and sought out the sport psychologist by recommendation of his coach. He reported feelings of lack of energy, low motivation to perform and several recurring injuries as his main symptoms. When asked to describe the chronological evolution of these symptoms, he reported a good performance at Nationals the year before and a steady downhill decline ever since. He kept his responses very "sport focused" and appeared surprised at the question: "What else has been going on in your life?". As if given permission to talk about it, he started to cry and discussed the sudden death of his mother several months prior, his feelings of depression and his behavioral responses of isolating himself, cutting himself off from his friends and feeling like a part of himself had also died. He had suicidal feelings in the past and had not sought treatment for a variety of reasons, including financial.

We discussed the dynamics of depression and its symptoms. He agreed not to make a major decision, such as quitting sport, while he was feeling so bad. He had been very negative and irritable with everyone, so he was finding himself alone quite often, unable to share his feelings or let his friends help. He agreed to see a counselor in his home town to deal with his feelings about his mother's death and to keep in touch with the sport psychologist to explore, if he decided to stay in the sport, how to go about regaining his motivation. Part of the compounding problem was the fact that he was extremely critical of himself, very perfectionistic, unable to enjoy partial improvements or accomplishments.

After his work with a counselor he decided he was not finished with his sport, and the specific sport psychology intervention was carried out, emphasizing cognitive restructuring of his negative thoughts, reframing his "should" statements and helping him notice his daily improvements by setting specific, achievable goals for practice. When the first competition approached he was encouraged to talk about the fact that his mother would not be there this time and he thought of a ritual that would allow him to continue a successful career without feeling he was being disloyal to his mother's memory.

Importance of Good History Taking

When assessing a sport psychology referral for possible counseling/clinical issues it is extremely important to take a thorough history of that individual's present circumstances and historical background. Following is an outline of the components of a comprehensive history:

I. General Mental Status
A. General Description
- Appearance
- Behavior and psychomotor activity
- Attitude towards sport psychologist

B. Speech
C. Sensorium
D. Affect
- Mood
- Emotional Expression

E. Anxiety
- Patient's description
- Clinical observations

F. Stream of thought/content of thought
G. Orientation
H. Judgment
- Insight

II. History
A. Family
- Parents
- Siblings
- Family of origin description
- Spouse and/or children

B. Medical
C. Psychological/Psychiatric
D. Scholastic/Athletic
- High school
- College or University
- Post collegiate

E. Nutritional Status
F. General observations
- Sleep
- Appetite
- Interpersonal/Sexual functioning

G. Medication/"recreational" substance use

Knowing One's Limitations

In working as a sport psychologist it is important to both know one's limitations, and be aware when a situation is beginning to develop beyond one's level of training and capability. For a sports science trained sport psychologist it is important to have some basic knowledge of clinical assessment. This is important because at least some of the time, individuals will be appropriately referred to a sports science trained sport psychologist for performance problems, but the sports science trained sport psychologist may recognize that there are clinical or counseling issues that are either the cause of or significantly contribute to some of the performance problems.

In circumstances like this, while it may be appropriate for the sports science trained person to address the performance enhancement issues, it is also important for the sport psychologist to refer to a counseling or clinical psychologist for personality assessment, and possible psychotherapy. Depending upon the nature of the problems, if they appear to be depression-related or anxiety- related at a clinical level, then it may be appropriate to either refer the individual to a family physician or internist or to a psychiatrist for some type of anti-depressant or anti-anxiety medication. If the circumstances involve issues of abuse history or of potential eating disorder problems then a referral to an appropriate support group or psychotherapy group may be the appropriate measure.

It is important for the sports science trained sport psychologist to develop a referral network of clinical or counseling trained psychologists or physicians to whom they can refer and work cooperatively with to address both performance related issues and counseling or clinical issues. A big part of developing this referral network is also taking the time to develop a cooperative working relationship with these other mental health and/or medical professionals. A good place to start may be by exploring possibilities with local sports medicine clinics. Often times physicians working with sports medicine clinics may be willing to handle medication issues related to anti-depressants or anti-anxiety medications.

It also might be helpful to network with counseling or clinical psychology trained sport psychologists who are more knowledgeable about performance enhancement issues, but could also handle clinical or counseling issues at the same time that the sport psychologist continues to handle the performance related issues on a primary basis. It is also recommended that one attempt to network with health psychology professionals and physical therapists so that, should the need for one of these specialty areas arise, the sport psychologist has a network of professionals to whom they can refer, in whom they can rely on, and with whom they will share a cooperative relationship.

Renegotiating Treatment Goals In the Event of Emergence of Clinical or Counseling Issues

In the event that clinical and/or counseling issues arise in the course of sport psychology intervention, it is important and, in fact, imperative that the sport psychologist renegotiates the treatment goals that may have been set by both the athlete and sport psychology professional. Ultimately, the athlete has the right to make decisions regarding their willingness to address clinical issues that the sport psychology consultant has helped them to identify. However, the sport psychology professional also has an ethical responsibility to not engage in a collusion of denial or to minimize or ignore clinical/counseling issues when they are clearly a factor in impaired performance.

The sport psychology professional should address in a very straight forward manner any reservations they have about continuing, while at the same time ignoring the clinical counseling issues. They also should offer some estimation of the probability of effectively addressing the performance enhancement issue while ignoring the clinical/counseling issue. If the athlete still chooses to set aside the counseling/clinical issue for the moment, and the sport psychology professional has informed them in a clear and direct manner of any reservations about the effectiveness of performance enhancement strategies in view of the additional issues then the sport psychologist can proceed to address those issues related to performance on which the athlete has elected to work.

Confidentiality Issues: Sharing Information With Other Professionals

It is recommended that when clinical/counseling issues do emerge in the course of a sport psychology intervention, necessitating referral to other medical or psychology professionals, that formal release of information forms be used. These release of information forms should clearly spell out the limitations of confidentiality, the specific nature of the information to be disclosed, the specific parties to whom the information is being disclosed, and the reason or necessity for disclosure of this information.

This particular issue becomes especially "thorny" when it also involves maintaining working relationships with coaches and parents, while at the same time respecting confidentiality boundaries. When issues that are initially thought to be performance enhancement issues become clinical or counseling related, then many of the legal boundaries that pertain to clinical or counseling psychology interventions or medical interventions become pertinent. One of those, which may be most important for a sport psychologist to maintain an awareness of, pertains to issues of privilege and confidentiality with minors (under age eighteen). The privilege or confidentiality in a clinical or counseling psychological/medical sense resides with the parent and not with the child. In other words, regarding a performance enhancement issue, it may be legally acceptable for a sport psychology professional to make decisions about specifically how much detail will be discussed with parents in terms of the interventions that are used. However, when the situation pertains to clinical or counseling psychology or medical issues, the right of confidentiality does not reside with the minor child/athlete, but rather with the parent. Therefore, the professional is legally obligated to share any and all information requested by the parent with the parent. By the same token, in such circumstances, only the parent can authorize the sport psychologist or clinical/counseling psychologist or medical professional to share information with a coach.

Summary

Too often, the field of applied sport psychology has served as a battle ground between clinically trained sport psychologists and sport psychology professionals trained in the sports sciences. What should be apparent is the need for and strengths of both groups. In the scenarios outlined previously in this chapter and the case studies to follow, students and professionals should recognize the necessity for individuals with specialized training to address such issues as eating disorders, clinical depression, mood disorders, obsessive/compulsive disorders, psychosomatic issues, contemplation of suicide, and a variety of other clinical and counseling issues.

It should be recognized that these types of issues fall outside the scope of many professionals trained in the sports sciences. Consequently, it is imperative for every professional to establish a comprehensive network of professionals to whom referrals can be made with the assumption of quality care and confidentiality. By doing so, the professional, regardless of his/her training, is able to offer the best and most appropriate services available to the athletes and coaches with whom they work.

All professionals are encouraged to maintain a policy of operating with open eyes, ears, and minds. People stand to gain so much from the sharing of ideas, insight, and experiences of others. The content of this book, including the case studies, stands as testimony to the value of sharing such information. These cases were initially shared as a means of mutual learning and professional development. They served to foster a deeper understanding of clinical, counseling, and sport science approaches to applied sport psychology interventions. They helped to identify limitations based on training and experiences, and stimulated development of new ideas and approaches to benefit athletes and coaches.

Case Studies of Clinical Issues

#1: The Professional Baseball Prospect

Introduction:

Charles was 17½ years old when he was drafted in the early rounds by a Major League Club as a major "prospect". Charles had been a high school "Star" first baseman; a very good hitter. Three weeks after the draft he was diagnosed with "bone cancer" in his right arm. Charles had a speedy recovery following surgery to repair his arm. He was cleared for baseball again by mid-June with the minor league team and had a reasonably good season hitting well, fielding just OK. Suddenly, he was dropped by the organization, then picked up by another club. Charles was hitting .600 in spring training when he was cut again. Thereafter several coaches, scouts and agents made promises of tryouts, winter leagues, and other great signing expectancies.

Nothing came of all the promises for another chance and Charles became irrational, taking all of the frustration and disappointment very hard. Charles moved in with his father and stepmother and proceeded to "vegetate". He had trouble relating to his stepmother and became totally dysfunctional. He was referred to me to help resolve his issues.

Intervention:

The initial interview revealed that Charles would like to get back into baseball, but no one had called him, so he was discouraged. One course of action chosen was to contact an agent, scouts, and coaches to try again for a tryout. Charles was resistant, lethargic and increasingly hostile toward his family. Family intervention revealed Charles's anger toward his father for the past divorce and toward his stepmother for breaking up his family. Charles showed more anger and despondency of a serious nature. Subsequent consultation with a medical psychologist revealed Charles is depressed.

Medication plus further counseling controlled Charles's depression and he started an intense conditioning program for either baseball or football. A local college coach evaluated Charles's baseball potential and reported that he had the fastest, most powerful batting swing he'd ever seen. Disillusioned by baseball, Charles decided he wanted to play football despite the greater potential in baseball.

Charles mentioned that he had symptoms similar to those which he first saw described in a documentary on "obsessive/compulsive disorder" featuring a prominent football player who had successfully overcome it. Further evaluation revealed that Charles had a combined anxiety/depression problem and obsessive/compulsive disorder which required more extensive clinical follow-up before dealing with sport psychology issues. As the sport psychology professional, I was facing a serious dilemma regarding prioritizing the intervention steps and separating logic from the athlete's best interest.

Charles went back home to visit his mother and her family for six weeks and returned with renewed zeal having made a decision to play football at a junior college and to give up baseball entirely. Charles stayed on his medication for depression at least two more months during which time he was seen at regular intervals to monitor and treat the obsessive/ compulsive disorder.

A strategy was devised in which Charles was instructed to carry out a prioritized sequence of steps to interrupt the obsessive thoughts. The first step was "Action-Oriented Solution" (i.e., if you can do something about the thought problem, then get in there and do it). The second step was "Rational Approach" (i.e., if there is nothing you can do about it then let go of the problem for now). In this case Charles had a strong spiritual belief system, thus the statement, "Let Go, Let God" made a lot of sense to him. The third step was "Relax" if possible using a systematic breathing sequence with or without an audiotape. If relaxation did not work then Charles was instructed to engage some new thought or new activity which superseded the obsessive thought.

Outcome:

Charles has reasonably good prospects to be successful in football. It will be important to keep his successes in perspective, as he continues to feel a great deal of bitterness and resentment toward the world of baseball which, at one time, was clearly the "love of his life". Charles will continue in consultation with the sport psychologist for both performance and personal conflict issues. It is expected to be an on-going problem.

Issues related to the intervention:

♦ What would have happened if this athlete had <u>not</u> gotten some medical attention in addition to problem-solving and sport psychology interventions?

♦ How does the family conflict over a divorce impact the athlete's performance and his/her adjustment to other life stressors?

♦ When the athlete appears to be making a bad decision how hard do you push him to consider the other alternatives ?

♦ How do you help an athlete deal with unresolved anger without losing rapport and developing more conflict ?

♦ What if the parents' expectations differ greatly from the athlete and there is an unwillingness to communicate openly with the athlete ?

#2: Female High School Swimmer

Introduction:

Anna was a 16 year old high school sophomore who joined the high school swim team in midyear. Anna swam for a relatively small school and club program in a northern state, doing well in the high school state meet. She was a top swimmer on her team.

When Anna joined the team, shortly after tapering for the State Meet, she was immediately the fastest breaststroker by nearly three seconds and also the fastest in individual Medley. However, there were several swimmers in both strokes to challenge her and several other Junior National caliber and one Senior National caliber swimmers. At the Central District Championships a year earlier, Anna swam a personal best time of 2:15.02 in the individual Medley, but finished third behind two teammates. Anna won the 100 Breaststroke and swam a personal best of 1:08.22, but beat one of her teammates by only .08 seconds. The following weekend at the State High School Meet, Anna did not qualify for either championship or consolation final, but her teammate, who beat her for the first time, made the consolation final. This teammate then beat her again in both the preliminaries and finals of the state Age Group Championship several weeks later.

Anna entered the summer Long Course (50 meter) season apprehensive since she preferred Short Course (25 yard pool). Her doubts quickly became confirmed and her performances got slower and slower. At the same time, her <u>teammate</u> continued to improve. By the end of Long Course season, there was nearly a five second difference between them in the 100 Breaststroke race.

Intervention:

Because of the "mental barrier" that she appeared to have, Anna was seen individually by a sports psychologist when the high school season began in November. Pre-testing with the PSIS-5 confirmed the devastating toll on her self-confidence. Anna appeared to be experiencing a crisis of self-confidence which markedly disrupted her concentration and elevated anxiety to disruptive proportions. Since breaststroke is the most technically complex stroke, it is also the stroke most severely impaired by anxiety.

A "self-confidence" rehabilitation program was initiated in late November which included cognitive restructuring, relaxation training, and imagery rehearsal focusing on process not outcome. In mid-December, the coach was approached by several team members expressing concern over Anna's eating habits and preoccupation with weight loss. During the "off-season" (August-September), she had gained weight and started the season at 137 pounds (5'4"). Christmas break disrupted any intervention from December to early January. By early January, Anna weighed approximately 118 pounds, a loss of nearly twenty pounds in eight to ten weeks. She was also reported to be experiencing amenorrhea since October.

Anna's failure to respond to the intervention, as well as the possibility of an eating disorder, and signs of a mood disorder prompted a decision to recommend that formal counseling be undertaken. Concerns were expressed to Anna's parents and treatment was initiated in mid-January. Psychological testing was administered, specifically the Tennessee Self-Concept Scale and Minnesota Multiphasic Personality Inventory (MMPI).

Psychological testing results indicated a generally lowered Total Self Concept (28th percentile) as well as an extremely poor Physical Self-Concept (10th percentile). Anna was extremely unsure of herself as 85 percent of her responses were qualified reflecting insecurity and a lack of confidence generally. MMPI testing indicated the presence of a clinically significant depressive disorder.

These results were discussed with Anna and her parents, and the issue of a possible eating disorder was addressed as well. Anna also took the Eating Disorders Inventory shortly thereafter. At her third session, Anna pronounced herself cured, denied any eating disorder problems and withdrew from treatment. One further session was scheduled with her and her parents at the therapist's insistence but the parents stated that she "did seem like her old self" and treatment was terminated.

Anna's Eating Disorder Inventory profile was a non-interpretable "denial" profile. She did not even report a fraction of the concern which one would expect from an adolescent female her age. As evidenced from her post-test scores on the PSIS-5, she was in a total state of denial generally. Her Anxiety scale score went from 30% to 95% and her Confidence from 19% to 100%. Those were the most prominent examples of the extreme defensiveness and denial she displayed. Not surprisingly, her swimming times did not change from in-season times.

Outcome:

Anna was a case where the failure to recognize the seriousness of the self-concept/depressive disorder, initially manifest in drastically impaired athletic performance, resulted in delayed intervention which allowed the self-concept damage to become more extended. The fragile psychological state that she was in became fertile ground for a budding eating disorder. Since Anna was overwhelmed by her inability to change/control her swimming, she seemed to refocus all of her energy into dieting, at which she was successful.

Anna had apparently accommodated herself cognitively by changing her self-concept from "fast swimmer" to "swimmer" and re-directing her ego investment into eating/dieting. This enabled her to resolve the dissonance between her self-concept and reality when she found herself in a situation where she was not the best. The therapy, especially when the issue of the eating disorder was approached, represented a threat to this newly achieved "balance." The resulting "flight into health" (i.e. 100% Confidence) enabled her to justify termination of therapy. Unfortunately, her parents were willing partners in this illusion.

Anna's relay splits, which were up .7 seconds (50 Breaststroke) from the previous year, are a clear indication that the inability to approach her previous year's 100 Breaststroke time was not physical/technical. The continued performance impairment is also evidence that test results and self-report notwithstanding, the same problem of damaged self-esteem prevails.

#3: High School Tennis Player

Introduction:

Robert was referred by his mother who had heard that "sport psychologists" could help athletes who were not performing up to their potential. She asked if she could bring her son Robert in for a visit. She volunteered that Robert was a "wonderful young man" that has great ability in tennis, but is just now beginning to lose matches to boys that he had beaten for years ... all throughout his age group tennis involvement (from the age of 7).

She reported that he was despondent, moody, and sullen especially following a match he had lost. She said, "When I asked him why he played so poorly he would just walk away from me and go to his room and began playing his stereo loud. Sometimes he wouldn't come out for several hours. What's wrong with this boy?". She also reported that Robert has complained of recurring lower back pain that (he says) interferes with his performance; however, "We have had the best physicians in the area check him out and they find nothing wrong with his back ... he has had MRI, X-Rays, massages... he has had every examination and 'nothing'".

Intervention:

During the initial interview while his mother was present, Robert was quiet and sat passively. After his mother left, Robert expressed disappointment that his mother would bring him in. He stated, "What's the big deal!?" In visiting with Robert he reported that he was indeed losing to guys that he used to beat all the time in junior tennis. He reported feelings of fear and dread when tournaments were approaching. He reported that these feelings were often so intense at the beginnings of a match that he could hardly move "...and my back has been hurting so much lately. I just want to quit playing tennis. This just isn't worth it..." He reported love for his family, but wished that they wouldn't "…make this tennis thing such a big deal". He stated that he thought that his mother loved him whether he won or lost, but seemed to be happier when he would win.

Robert described his father as a successful international businessman who traveled extensively. His father was also a former Olympic athlete who made the national team with a broken leg. He attended the Olympics but was unable to participated because of the leg. Consequently, his father doesn't understand why Robert complains about pain or forfeits matches when his back bothers him.

Robert described his mother as a homemaker and Chief Referee for all regional tennis tournaments. She has scheduled his lessons, hitting instructors, and tournaments from early-on. She is proud of her son's accomplishments and is very caring.

When asked about his back pain, Robert suggested that he might have pulled some muscles because he was so "tight" at the beginning of his matches. He though it was on the mend, but he still couldn't hit overheads or serves hard. Upon introspection, he noted that when it was a big point or match, that his back would start to stiffen and begin hurting. When questioned about tennis, he responded with some conviction and enthusiasm, saying, "I really love tennis...I just wish that my back wouldn't hurt.".

Robert was given several tests to take home and complete after his practice session immediately following our interview: the POMS, the abbreviated TAIS, the EPQ, and a modified Achievement Motivation Survey.

The POMS results seemed to indicate that Robert's affect was bordering on "burn-out"; however, he reported that he was coming off a bad practice session, reinjuring his back. A second administration of the POMS demonstrated a dramatically different picture: reduced tension, depression, anger, fatigue, and confusion, combined with a significant rise in vigor.

Scores from the Achievement Motivation Test indicated Robert was success-oriented. His State-Trait Anxiety scores indicated that in critical situations, he may experience high anxiety. The TAIS indicated that Robert may experience internal overload and excessive narrowing.

The EPQ revealed no particular abnormality other than Robert probably was presenting his best self rather than completing the inventory candidly. The Tennessee Self-Concept test suggested that Robert had a healthy self-concept, an aversion for self-criticism, and viewed his physical self less than optimal.

The problem could have been defined from a behavioristic perspective: When Robert is placed in a highly competitive situation, he quits, gives up, or plays with less than full commitment. The problem also could have been defined clinically: Robert's anxiety and subsequent poor performance in competitive tennis seemed to be linked to perceived familial expectations of successful outcome, conditional acceptance, and threats to self-identity.

The choice was to a behavioristic intervention. Therefore, Robert's behavior of quitting, resigning, or playing without conviction was accepted as the target behavior. The goal was to refocus Robert's attention from worry about loss and failure toward positive or productive foci. More specifically, Robert was instructed in and participated in setting practice and competitive focus/refocus plans. With regard to his back problems, when he felt his back beginning to tense, he would utilize Nideffer's technique of clearing the mind of worry or fear by focusing on an innocuous or neutral object (Nideffer suggested a ball, Robert couldn't imagine the ball so he used his dream car), then inserting a positive image (Robert imaged his car's heater blowing warm air onto his back to relax the muscles). With regard to a concentration break or technical mistake, Robert would picture the car, then "see" and/or "feel" the desired serve, return, or winner.

During the two and one half weeks prior to the tournament, his hitting instructors, coaches, and parents reported that he was doing much better. He was hitting harder, and was moving quicker.

Three days prior to the tournament, Robert's mother and father complained about his attitude at home. They agreed to meet with me about the problems. They reported that Robert was moody and sullen. Upon further inquiry the parents reported that Robert had stated that... "There was no use (in him) going... he would just lose.". Then a few minutes latter he reportedly stated, "I just want to go (to the tournament) by myself.". The parents were reassured that some anxiety and sullen behavior was normal for athletes about to compete.

Upon further exploration, it was discovered that Robert really wanted to go by himself, or not at all. My instincts were screaming that this might be a manifestation of his desire to "declare his independence" and/or to rid himself of familial pressure to be the "star tennis-player-son", but I decided to proceed with the behavioral plan. The parents subsequently compromised with Robert by agreeing to send him with one of his coaches to the tournament.

Three days prior to the tournament I met with Robert prior to a hitting session. Robert's affect was positive, he rehearsed his refocus plans for both his back and technical let-downs. He committed to perform his best regardless of outcome. He committed to play through minor pain in his back... to continue on.

Friday and Saturday he won both his matches, but in the quarter finals, playing against a talented opponent he lost a break point to make it 4-2 instead of 3-3, he then lost the next two sets 6-1, 6-0. Not knowing what the outcome had been, I called the mother. She reported that after the match he had called home, cried, stated that his back hurt, and threatened suicide. I called Robert immediately at his hotel. He expressed no suicidal ideation, reiterated that his back hurt, but added that he had played his best until his back began to hurt, saying, "I couldn't bend over, I couldn't move It just hurt.".

He had told his mother that he was not going to play the consolation match on Sunday. His mother reportedly told him, "If you don't play don't come home.". His mother also stated that his father talked to him from England after the match and had called him a "wimp" rehearsing his Olympic war story. Robert committed to play on Sunday, but lost 6-3, 6-0.

Upon returning from the tournament, per request, Robert called and reported that he was glad that he had competed Sunday. He stated that he was playing well ... "I was ahead 3-0 then my back began to hurt and I lost the rest of the games ... it was a player that I knew that I could bet easily ... then my back begin to hurt... I know now that it is not just in my mind.".

Given the apparent failure of the pure behavioristic plan of intervention (and with consultation with colleagues) a more clinical approach was implemented in hopes of ameliorating the difficulty. It was reasoned that given the psychological correlate of hypochondriacal lower back pain as "avoidance" and his late entry into puberty, it was reasoned that Robert's back might improve if he was given an escape route, an opportunity to experience and explore independence and responsibility.

Both parents had stated that they were not going to force tennis on Robert so they were asked if they were willing to grant Robert greater independence and allow him to schedule his own court times, hitting instructors, and even which tournaments he would attend. Reasoning that if Robert really loved tennis and wanted to play that he would schedule his own court times and request instructional sessions. Reluctantly, the parents agreed. Further, Robert's parents were asked if they were willing to focus on performance rather than outcome. Again, they agreed.

The parents asked what they should do if Robert complained about his back. They were advised to change the topic or redirect the focus of the conversation to an educational focus (i.e., what he learned from practice, or his match) and to be reassuring. That is, they should try to demonstrate love and support unconditionally without regard to tennis.

Outcome:

It appeared that a pure behavioristic approach (performance enhancement) was ineffectual in ameliorating this talented athlete's problems. Further, it appeared, at least in this case, that athletic performance was linked to emotional maturation and familial linkages, and that by addressing behavioral symptomology at the expense of more influential factors, hypochondriacal hysteria was exacerbated.

#4: College Football Prospect: Anabolic Steroids and Depression

Introduction:

Michael was an eighteen year old white male who was self-referred, and referred by his parents for "self confidence" intervention to help him prepare for Division I scholarship football. Michael was a recent high school graduate, and had attended classes at a local junior college. He was 6'4, 255 lbs., and had done extensive weight training.

Although Michael was referred for his parents initially for self-concept improvement as well as other sports psychology interventions he fairly quickly confided in the sport psychologist that he was having a real problem with the use of anabolic steroids. Michael was a very polite, soft spoken young man who was cooperative with treatment. He had graduated from a private high school with a 3.2 GPA. He had, however, since beginning junior college, failed all three courses in which he had enrolled.

He admitted that in addition to confidence with regard to academics and athletics that he was "out of control" because of the use of anabolic steroids. Michael reported that he had never really used alcohol or any kind of recreational drugs in high school, but reported that when he started using anabolic steroids, and "hanging around" with guys at the gym that he also began to go to bars and drink on a more regular basis. He reported the use of alcohol one to two times per week, drinking six to eight beers at a time. Michael estimated getting "drunk" about once a month.

Michael shared that in high school he had never been in any kind of trouble or in any fights, but that he had been in probably a dozen fights during the six months since beginning junior college. He reported that he had not had any official arrests although he said he was pretty lucky in order to have avoided that. Michael reported the following information with regard to the progression of his lifting workouts:

Pre-use of anabolic steroids
Bench press - 340 lbs.
Hipsled - 1050 lbs. x 10 repetitions
Squat - 400 lbs. x 1 repetition
Body weight - 275 lbs.

First cycle of anabolic steroid use
Bench press - 395 lbs.
Hipsled - 1050 lbs. x 15 repetitions
Squat - 405 lbs. x 5 repetitions

During this first cycle of anabolic steroids, Michael reported using Dianabol orally approximately 20 mgs a day for eight weeks.

At time of intervention
Bench press - 405 lbs. x 6 repetitions
Hipsled - 1050 lbs. x 20 repetitions
Squat - 405 lbs. x 10 repetitions

During these more recent "cycles" of anabolic steroids Michael admitted that he was using Dianabol approximately 20 mgs a day plus approximately 600 mgs per week of Testosterone in both short acting and long acting forms.

Intervention:

Because of the difficulties that Michael was experiencing, several psychological tests were administered to assess his current level of functioning. The Minnesota Multi-phasic Personality Inventory was administered to him in order to assess his personality. He approached the test in an extremely guarded manner, and ordinarily the profile would be of questionable validity. Despite this questionable approach to the test, scales that measured "Depression" and "Impulsiveness" were nearly significantly elevated. Also, a scale that measured "Over-Controlled Hostility" was extremely elevated at the 95th percentile.

These scores are significant especially when his approach to completing the test is taken into account. These results suggested that, given that he had no emotional or behavioral problems that were evident prior to beginning anabolic steroid use, it was likely that many of the elevations were related to his steroid use. Specifically, the depression and impulsiveness may be related to mood swings caused by both his use of anabolic steroids and his adjustment during periods of time when he was "between cycles". Also, the "Over Controlled Hostility Scale" is clearly consistent with the impulsiveness and the habitual conflict-seeking behavior and fighting that he had engaged in more recently in the past six months during his use of steroids.

The Tennessee Self Concept Scale was administered to Michael to assess his overall self concept. While his total self concept was average (50th percentile), his physical self concept was at approximately the 20th percentile, and his moral ethical self concept was at the 10th percentile. These scores likely reflect almost a "reverse anorexia phenomena" as well as a situation where no matter how big he gets he will continue to perceive himself as not being very acceptable, physically. Also, apparently his behavioral acting out has diminished his perception of himself from a moral, ethical, and behavioral point of view.

Therapy with Michael involved utilization of not only sport psychology principles and performance enhancement principles, but also referral for anti-depressant medication, and rebuilding his ego strength. Michael's use of anabolic steroids was an attempt to over-compensate for his lack of self-confidence even though he had a very successful high school career. He was seen with diminishing regularity over a period of approximately six months while he continued to train and slowly wean himself off of anabolic steroids. In addition to dealing with the depressive manifestations he was exhibiting, it was necessary to help him learn more effective training principles so that he could make decent gains in physical strength without the use of anabolic steroids. Finally, it was imperative to help him reinforce his own self-confidence and his trust in himself rather than believing in or relying on the anabolic agents in order to "prop up" both his self esteem and his physical prowess.

Outcome:

Michael is a good example of someone who succumbed to the pressure of anabolic steroid use in order to improve his chances of playing Division I college football. What he did not count on was the resulting damage to his self concept as well as his psychological functioning. While blood or urine testing was not undertaken in order to assess absolutely the presence or absence of anabolic agents, what can be confirmed was reported both by Michael and his parents independently. Both he and his parents reported that his academic performance once again began to improve and became consistent with that which he had exhibited in high school. Also, both his drinking behavior and fighting behavior appeared to diminish as his use of anabolic agents diminished.

He was successful at obtaining a Division I college scholarship, though perhaps not to the same level of school that he might have aspired to at one point. He did, however, participate in football, and actually played extensively, starting his final two years in college. He graduated and, to the best of my knowledge, has "gotten on with his life" in an adaptive fashion.

Discussion Questions

1. While many athletes attempt to "block out" distractions to performance, what are more effective ways of addressing these potential distracting issues?

2. If performance issues are not always "performance related", what are some other factors that may interfere with an athlete's ability to perform?

3. Why is it important in a situation where the sport psychology consultant suspects "clinical" or "counseling" issues to take a thorough history? What are the major areas to be addressed in this history?

4. Provide several examples of circumstances in which it would be appropriate for the sport psychology consultant to refer to another professional, and identify the types of professionals that might be utilized under these circumstances.

5. In each of the cases, what were the pivotal issues or dynamics that necessitated the involvement of a professional with training beyond that typically received in an exercise science graduate program?

6. What are the principal factors leading to the development of eating disorders in athletes, particularly for females?

7. Are there sports more prone to have participants develop eating disorders? If so, what are they, and why?

8. Are there sports more prone to have participants abuse performance enhancing substances, such as steroids? If so, what are they, and why?

9. How does one differentiate between a mood disorder and normal mood swings?

10. What would be your response to an athlete who says, "I would love to stop using steroids (or some other illegal, performance-enhancing drug), but what can you provide me that will be equally effective in assisting me in reaching my goals?".

PART III

Recommendations

In Part III, two chapters address topics that are rarely broached: Failure, and a Charge of Responsibility. The *Value of Failure* chapter is included to stretch the typical paradigms of the applied sport psychology student and professional. Failure is approached head-on with insight into reasons for failure and implications of not achieving success. The final chapter is *A Charge* of responsibilities for applied sport psychology professionals. Readers are encouraged to compare their perspectives to those provided here, and determine if the recommendations carry merit and should be followed. The hope is to contribute to the development of applied sport psychology into a field that is respected and utilized for its positive contributions and concern for the athletes and coaches whose lives are touched by its practitioners.

CHAPTER 14

~ The Value of Failure ~

Mark A. Thompson, Inner Edge
Kenneth Ravizza, California State University - Fullerton

> "I have failed over, and over, and over again. That is why I succeed."
> - Michael Jordan, Nike commercial

> "Failure is a wholly necessary part of the process, the stuff of heroes and legends. … Unfortunately, we haven't yet discovered an alternative route to the top."
> - Michael Johnson, *Slaying the Dragon* (p. 73)

Yes, failure helps us learn; teaching us valuable lessons on the long journey of life. But do we have to like or accept it? The obvious answer is no. However, failure should not, by any means, be dismissed or ignored. This chapter takes an in-depth look at the dynamics surrounding perceived failure by the applied sport psychologist. Yes, one can perform poorly and "win", just as one can perform well and "lose". Failure, in this instance, is to be taken at face value; a reflection that one "failed" in their own eyes or in the eyes of others.

In the world of applied sport psychology, failure is a pariah that practitioners commit themselves to exorcising from those with whom they work. Athletes and coaches can pay dearly for failures. Athletes can lose position, scholarship status, money, acceptance, and self-esteem. Similarly, coaches can lose jobs, security, recruits, and self-esteem. As such, it is a priority for the sport psychology practitioner to aid the athlete and coach in succeeding. The issue is not simple; not all interventions will result in success. Even traditional means of enhancing performance (i.e., goal-setting, imagery training, relaxation techniques, etc.) can be insufficient or ineffective.

In the real world, athletes fail, coaches fail, and sport psychologists fail. A commonly stated axiom is "We learn from our mistakes."; however, there is a general belief that more is to be gained from studying success than in understanding failure. When was the last time a book entitled, *How to Lose in Business Without Really Trying* made the list of best sellers? While it is advisable to study success to understand the factors that contribute, failure should not be lightly discarded as being unworthy of exploration. Failure occurs because certain dynamics dictate the failure. These dynamics of failure can also hold the keys to success.

This chapter will discuss factors that inhibit various mental training interventions and discuss the specific manner in which they impact performance. The implications of failed interventions will be discussed with respect to the applied sport psychology practitioner. Finally, the authors will offer the premise that with success comes trappings that can prove detrimental.

The purpose is to challenge the prevalent paradigms of failed interventions and, hopefully, foster new thinking relative to "failure".

Why Interventions Fail

Medical doctors prescribe medication that can remedy illness. Computer programmers can re-program a faulty string of commands to ensure accurate execution. Financial advisors can map out a budget that, if followed correctly, can enable people to stay afloat and reach financial goals. However, what is the sport psychologist to do if an athlete consistently comes up short in competition? The answer is not nearly so evident. The answer might lie in altering the athlete's attentional focus, ability to re-focus, self-talk, self-concept, clarity of thought/mindset, or any of a multitude of contributing factors.

The preceding chapters provide insight into the issues influencing performance and the variety of approaches that are employed to enhance such. The majority of the cases culminate with positive outcomes, but cases of negative outcomes are also included. There is method to this madness, as this mixture of successes and failures should be reflective of the experiences of the average (or above average) practitioner. Not all endeavors will be met with unqualified, positive outcomes, regardless of the practitioner or the situation. This uncertainty that is inherent in sport competition is what makes it so exciting.

In even one-to-one (athlete and sport psychologist) situations, the number of factors is challenging. The combination of performance issues, intervention approaches, and personalities of athletes and practitioners is incalculably complex. It may be difficult to believe, but sometimes the answer to performance enhancement does not involve a sport psychologist. Athletic performance is multi-faceted; incorporating nutrition, conditioning, strategy, training, and equipment as critical performance factors. As such, the "total picture" must be recognized and considered. For example:

> A golfer begins shooting abnormally high scores during tournament play, her swing doesn't look right or feel right which is coinciding with a lack of confidence. She cannot seem to correct the problem on her own so she opts for one of two possible courses of action:
> 1. She works with her swing coach who corrects some mechanics in her swing. The swing improves, her confidence returns, and she starts shooting lower tournament scores.
> 2. She works with a sport psychologist who helps her reestablish perspective and develop positive self-talk. This aids her in regaining confidence in her game and leads to her finding her former effective swing, resulting in lower tournament scores.

As the example demonstrates, an answer to a performance issue may be found via more than one route. Performance stems from the interaction of the mind and the body. They are functionally intertwined and, as such, effect each other to aid or hinder performance. Consequently, the applied sport psychology professional must possess a wealth of psychological and physiological knowledge to help the athlete or coach, or be able to recognize warning signs and make a necessary referral.

Specific Factors Contributing to Failure

In a perfect world, applied sport psychology is effective. In a perfect world, the athlete or coach derives benefit from the applied sport psychologist. This is not a perfect world. At times, the interventions will fail and little or no benefit will be derived from the applied sport psychologist. The following are overviews of specific factors that may contribute to failure for the applied sport psychology professional:

Personality - Some applied sport psychologists will not be effective with an athlete, team, or coach because of personality characteristics. Sometimes, one is just not "right" for a situation simply due to his/her personality and/or the quality of the interpersonal relationships. Personality is a factor in every other facet of human existence and sport is no different. Attempting to alter or "take on" a different personality is greatly discouraged.

Delivery - "Laid-back", "Aggressive", "Charismatic", "Business-like", and "Friendly" all might describe various styles of delivery of applied sport psychology. No delivery style will be effective for everybody. Some failed interventions occur due to an inappropriate delivery style for a given situation. Some givens, however, are: 1) avoid a delivery style which makes the athletes feel like they are in a "class", 2) repetition is a key to understanding, and 3) bring passion to the delivery.

Setting - Some interventions will be more effective if they are conducted in the performance environment (i.e. field, court, gymnasium), while others may benefit from being away from the performance area (i.e. office, home, outdoors). Other setting factors might include noise level, number of distractions, comfort-level of the athlete, and comfort-level of the practitioner.

Mis-Application of Skills - Skills, such as relaxation training and thought-stopping, might be ineffective due to faulty application. The skills must be taught and developed for application to "real-life, practical" situations that will be conducive to generalization to performance. Often the athlete is given too much to work with; it is critical in the pressure situation to "keep it simple". We believe that the need for simplicity mandates that psychological skills be integrated into task-relevant cues (i.e., Relaxation is used by breathing before one begins a pre-shot routine in basketball). Failure to do so will compromise the value of the skills training.

Perception of Practitioner's Allegiance - With whom the applied sport psychologist is perceived to be aligned (i.e. coach, general manager, parent, athletic director, or athlete) can have significant impact on the effectiveness of his or her actions. Simply put, if the practitioner is believed to be aligned with a coach, general manager, etc.... whom an athlete does not trust, the practitioner will likely share the same distrust. The sport psychologist may be viewed as an extension of management rather than an impartial resource utilized to enhance performance. It is essential, for all parties, to have the role of the applied sport psychologist clarified, with a general understanding of what he/she can and cannot do.

Lack of Sport Knowledge - One must understand the dynamics and terminology of a sport to be truly effective as an applied sport psychologist. This does not mean that one must be proficient in all sports, or any sport. However, one must be able to interact with participants in a sport through "speaking their language" and understanding the unique dynamics of the sport. For example, if one is working with volleyball players, one should readily understand "bump", "set", "spike", "dig", "block", "side-out" as well as the designation of player responsibilities (setter, middle blocker, outside hitter) and the physical nature of the game (prominence of shoulder, knee, and back injuries). Knowledge goes a long way toward establishing one's respect and credibility.

Inaccurate Assessment of Presenting Problem or Issue - The athlete and the sport psychologist may work effectively toward addressing a problem or issue, but miss the mark because the identified problem was not really a problem at all. The athlete might be masking the "real" issue or the practitioner might simply not be able to identify the critical performance issue. This factor is discussed in detail in the chapter on "The Issue Behind the Issue".

Translation Difficulty - Attempting to explain relaxation and concentration to an eight year old baseball player is often a difficult task. Translating "academic" applied sport psychology into lay terms for athletes, coaches, parents, and administrators of all ages can serve as a road-block to effective working relationships. The sport psychology professional should attempt to relate on the level of the recipient. This may prove difficult and more time-consuming, but the benefits are worth the extra effort.

Athlete's Investment - "Why are you here?", might be a good question to ask any athlete who is on the receiving end of sport psychology training. The athlete may be there because a coach or a parent insisted, or as a means of truly working to improve his or her performance. In order for applied sport psychology to be effective, the recipient must believe in what is being addressed and be committed to working and growing. With younger athletes, the practitioner may make the mistake of discussing the mental skills program without truly explaining the rationale behind why mental skills are so important. It is essential that this "education" takes place to heighten the athlete's investment.

Sabotage - In basketball, one sometimes hears a comment implying that it would be easier to compete with the opponent if they only had five players on the court, rather than seven (indicating a belief that the officiating is one-sided). Not unlike this scenario, the sport psychology practitioner may experience difficulty getting positive results with an athlete due to the negative influence of others (i.e. coaches, athletic trainer, parents, teammates). This sabotage may be as covert as the coach not reinforcing the mental skills in practice or not incorporating time for mental skills in practice; or the sabotage might be as overt as a coach openly questioning the value of the mental skills training. Whether the sabotage is conducted knowingly or unknowingly, it can prove to be an insurmountable obstacle to progress.

Avoiding the Real Issue - The sport psychology practitioner may be able to readily identify the "real" issue, but, for various reasons, avoid addressing it. A possible scenario is a situation in which the coach brings the sport psychologist in to work with the team on positive self-talk and concentration skills, when, in actuality the real issue is the negative nature of the coach and the coach serving as a distraction to the players. Wanting to work with a team, the practitioner may do what the coach requests rather than address the coach-related issues since it might jeopardize the opportunity for a long-term working relationship. The irony of this situation is that if the critical issues aren't addressed, the program will not be effective.

Following One's Own Agenda - The practitioner may have a "standard" program that is applied to all situations, regardless of the dynamics of that unique situation. Also, the practitioner may be so focused on his/her immediate reaction to the situation that he or she ignores blatant evidence that other factors need to be addressed. Needless to say, similar to the earlier factor of inaccurate assessment, following one's own agenda or demonstrating a lack of flexibility can prove detrimental.

Everything & the Kitchen Sink (Shotgun Approach) - It is possible to overwhelm athletes and coaches. In his or her fervor to impress those with whom he or she works, the practitioner may fault on the side of excess; involving the athletes or coaches in a multitude of strategies and skills training and hoping that something sticks. There is a tendency for the recipient to "turn off" the practitioner due to the overwhelming amount being presented. The athletes and coaches may also interpret this approach as a disregard for the uniqueness of the situation.

Gender - The gender-mix of practitioners and athletes or coaches should not be problematic, but, at times, it is. The situation might be the football team that doesn't give a female sport psychology practitioner a chance because of a belief that "Women don't know football.", or the female softball team that does not respond to a male practitioner because "he just doesn't understand the female perspective". Regardless, gender is an issue that can be resolved by earning the coaches' and athletes' trust and respect. This trust and respect is earned by demonstrating a knowledge of the sport, respect for the athletes and coaches, and an understanding of the unique sub-culture.

Race - Similar to gender, race should not be a factor. However, just as with gender, race comes with biases, preconceived notions, and cultural nuances that can be problematic. Race can be a very charged issue. Unintentional slights, inappropriate comments, or blatant discrimination all may be experienced by the practitioner or the athlete; negating the goal of enhanced mental training.

This compilation of factors should be considered comprehensive, but not exhaustive. Failure can result from factors not outlined here. By understanding those highlighted and fostering an awareness of how they impact the individual practitioner, one may reduce their impact. Advice on how to deal with each of the identified factors, specifically, is not included. It is inconceivable to believe that one could provide such guidance for a large and disparate reading audience. However, general advice is offered for minimizing the impact of these factors:

- ◆ Know oneself - know one's training, limitations, delivery style, goals, biases, tendencies, level of commitment, time available, etc.
- ◆ Know the field - be as well-informed and knowledgeable about the field of applied sport psychology as possible. Know the mental skills that are to be taught to others, inside and out.
- ◆ Know the sport - know the language, rules, expectations, challenges, and requirements of the sport. More importantly, know the "culture" of the sport and its participants.

♦ Know the client - communicate a clear knowledge of the client, not just as an athlete, but as a multi-faceted person. Know the client's dreams, ambitions, motivations, fears, etc. By knowing the client, the practitioner is being responsible to the client.

♦ Be prepared to break through limiting or dysfunctional paradigms relative to race and gender.

Implications of Failure

Who is responsible for failure? The athlete is responsible for failure. So, too, is the sport psychologist, coach, environment, parent, timing, etc.. Actually, no one is "responsible" for failure; failure happens. Failure occurs because each situation involves humans dealing with humans on human issues. The same can be said of success. Success occurs due to the "mixture" of human qualities and the specifics of a situation. It is a fine line between success and failure that the applied sport psychologist often operates.

The field of applied sport psychology is not unique in its focus on success and the ramifications of failure. Visit any bookstore and look up the number of "How to Succeed in ..." books that purport to possess the keys to success in business, relationships, art, and sports. This will provide an idea of how oriented our society is on success and how little patience there is to wait for it. The sport psychologist, similarly, is often faced with a real or perceived narrow "window of opportunity." Succeed now, or lose your opportunity.

The world of competitive athletics is often very closed, with access to athletes closely guarded. As such, many sport psychologists believe they may have one "shot" to succeed, and if success does not result, he or she may not be afforded another opportunity. An example is depicted in the following scenario:

> Rick is a basketball coach who is somewhat skeptical of sport psychology, but is at wits end with a situation. He calls on a sport psychologist, Terri, to work with his starting point guard, Chris. Chris is making too many mental mistakes and has difficulty focusing. Terri knows Rick's reputation for guarding access to his athletes, but is excited about the opportunity to work with this respected coach's point guard. Terri works with the point guard on focusing cues, thought-stopping, and self-talk issues. She believes that the player has made some strides in his mental game, but the coach does not see the improvement on the court. Rick decides that it was a mistake to ask for Terri's assistance and does not call on her again.

Whether or not one has experienced this scenario as a sport psychologist, it is likely that it has been imagined as a possible scenario by every new professional in the field. Whether the pressure to "succeed" is real or not, the professional who is attempting to make a foray into a new territory is concerned with the ramifications of being perceived as failing or being ineffective.

The real issue is not whether the sport psychologist succeeds or fails; the issue is whether or not the athlete derives benefit from working with the sport psychologist. However, we have yet to come up with a more acceptable means of evaluating the effectiveness of a sport psychologist than judging it by the on-field performance of those with whom they work. This issue must be clarified at the beginning of the working relationship. The practitioner should not *promise* results because of the role so many other factors play in the process. What can be promised is that the involvement of the applied sport psychologist can increase the athlete's opportunity for success.

The established sport psychologist is not as concerned with the issue of how they are perceived. Interested parties will seek them out because of their history of effective consultation. They realize that the issue is the athlete's performance and well-being and maintain such a focus. The new practitioner must realize that effective work as an applied sport psychologist develops with time, experience, and learning from successes and failures. The young sport psychology professional should avoid comparing themselves to the established person, since they do not have the wealth of consulting experience. There is something to be said for "paying one's dues" in establishing oneself in any field of expertise. Applied sport psychology is no different.

Trappings of Success

> "Success tends to distort reality and make everybody, ..., forget their shortcomings and exaggerate their contributions. Soon they begin to lose sight of what made them successful in the first place:..."
> - Phil Jackson (1995, p. 156)

Be careful what you wish for, because you just may get it. This axiom alludes to hidden or unforeseen aspects that come with the fulfillment of long-held dreams and goals. The successful applied sport psychology practitioner may encounter such trappings and be characterized as one or more of the following:

- The Graduate
- The One-Trick Pony
- Karnac The Magnificent
- The Prodigy

The Graduate depicts the applied practitioner who concludes that success is indicative of a mastery of the field. Consequently, one possesses all the necessary answers and is not compelled to look outside of one's own paradigm to continue the learning process. This results in complacency and, ultimately, ineffectiveness. *The Graduate* might also be characterized as the individual with book knowledge, but is lacking real-life experience (i.e., The novice practitioner may be concerned with whether the athlete uses internal as compared to external imagery; whereas, the established professional is just delighted to see the athlete doing any kind of imagery.). The practitioner must understand that in order to continue to be effective, one must constantly be open to learning; searching out opportunities to expand one's knowledge and experiential base. Sources for such professional growth include: 1) Remaining up-to-date with research, 2) Attending workshops and professional conferences, and 3) Interacting with colleagues. The consequences of not doing so will be short-lived applied sport psychology success. As "they" say, the only thing constant about change is that change is constant.

The One-Trick Pony approach portrays the practitioner who has experienced success utilizing a specific regimen or program believed applicable to all people in all situations. The practitioner, regardless of the situation, approaches intervention as if they were reading from a cook book recipe. The same ingredients, mixed in the same amounts, result in success for the athletes, because they are all humans. However, individual differences of athletes will predispose this approach to ultimately fail. Individual differences are extremely diverse and dynamic. Consequently, one approach will not be effective in all settings with all people. Also, no two performances are the same as we are in a constant state of flux. "You never cross the same river twice." *The One-Trick Pony* will quickly find out that athletes, like rivers, constantly change.

Karnac The Magnificent represents the "all-knowing, all-seeing" practitioner who believes he or she possesses all the answers. Beyond the obvious observation that no one has all the answers, there is a second danger to this orientation. If a practitioner, indeed, believes he or she is "all-knowing", then whatever failure might occur will, undoubtedly, be perceived as the fault of another party. The infallibility of the *Karnac the Magnificent* practitioner shifts blame to the athletes, coaches, parents, or administrators (i.e., "It can't be me, it must be the athlete who isn't doing what is needed."). Any one other than the practitioner.

The Prodigy differs from the previous characterizations due to the influence of external forces. The Prodigy is the practitioner who experiences tremendous success early and often. This, in turn, leads to more opportunities with more at stake. In essence, The Prodigy may be thrust into a situation for which he or she lacks the necessary experience. Not unlike the high school pitching phenom who one week after graduation is on the mound for a major league club. Regardless of the skill level, the potential for failure is substantial. Again, The Prodigy tends to be at the mercy of others extending very tempting opportunities. The applied sport psychology professional must exercise good judgment to determine situations for which he/she is ready. This benefits not only the practitioner, but athletes and coaches, as well. Contrary to popular belief, opportunity tends to knock more than once. If The Prodigy is patient, the appropriate combination of ability and opportunity will arise.

These "trappings of success" are manageable. To avoid such, the practitioner should adhere to the following: know what you don't know, maintain perspective, focus on the true goal, stay in the present, and utilize good judgment. If the applied sport psychology professional would simply honor the "practice what you preach" philosophy, he or she would avoid most trappings of success.

Conclusion

Failure is painful. Failure is also unavoidable. Accepting these two points is the beginning to understanding the necessity to study the dynamics of failure. Any applied sport psychology consultant will experience a lack of success at some point during a career. This occurrence should be faced head-on, because failure is positive feedback. Applied sport psychologists tend to encourage athletes and coaches to look straight into failure's eyes and stand up to the possible consequences. Practitioners should do likewise, and learn from their mistakes. Failure often precedes the greatest strides, even though the lessons learned may take days, weeks, or months to process.

Failure is not to be feared. When failure is perceived, it is likely that focus and perspective will be lost. Resultant behavior will usually be directed toward something other than the present goal (i.e. playing not to lose, stepping out rather than stepping up). Be prepared to accept the failure and be honest enough to persevere through the arduous task of self-critiquing. This process of honest self-critiquing may elicit some pain, but the benefits far outweigh the potential negatives.

Upon failure, the applied sport psychologist may experience an initial loss of confidence, self-doubt, and self-pity, but should realize this is part of the process. Just as athletes are encouraged, the sport psychology professional must, at some point, let go of the frustration, learn from the failure, and get back to the task.

The complexity of human interaction mixed with athletic competition dictate that the cure for failure will never be found. However, there are prominent factors that are common to failure for the applied sport psychology consultant. An understanding of these in combination with being aware of the implications of failure can provide valuable assistance in minimizing such experiences.

Discussion Questions

1. Is the perspective regarding failure, as expressed in this chapter, accurate? Why, or why not?

2. Are there factors in addition to those listed that contribute to failure for the applied sport psychologist? What are they and how do they contribute?

3. Discuss the benefits of "paying one's dues". Is it relevant to today's fast-paced, "want-it-now" society?

4. Are there really "trappings of success"? Why, or why not?

5. Given any case study presented, what are the critical factors determining whether the intervention by the applied sport psychology consultant was considered a success or a failure? Could this outcome have been changed? If so, how?

6. How significant are race and gender issues to applied sport psychology work? How significant are sexual orientation issues?

7. Does strong religious conviction serve as a catalyst, a barrier, or a non-issue for applied sport psychology? Explain your perspective and the rationale behind your beliefs.

References

Jackson, P. & Delehanty, H. (1995). Sacred hoops. New York: Hyperion.
Johnson, M. (1996). Slaying the dragon. New York: Regan Books.

CHAPTER 15

~ A Charge ~

Mark A. Thompson, Inner Edge

A charge? What's a charge? Why include a charge? According to *The American Heritage Dictionary* (Morris, 1980) "charge" is defined as, "To...entrust with a duty, responsibility, task, or obligation.". In other words, to serve as a steward for a specified purpose. The charge for the readers of this compilation of case studies is to serve as stewards for the delivery of applied sport psychology services to athletes, coaches, parents, and assorted other clientele. As stewards, practitioners must accept the responsibility of developing the field and operating from a sense of ethics and ownership. To honor this stewardship, the following are recommendations for the applied sport psychology professional to consider:

- ◆ Remember that applied sport psychology exists for the participants, not the practitioners. The delivery of applied sport psychology services should be selfless and devoid of practitioner ego. By so doing, the practitioner will provide the best professional service he or she can offer.

- ◆ Remain aware of one's limitations. Readily acknowledge that any practitioner does not have all the answers. Consequently, it is essential to seek advice from other colleagues who might possess more relevant experience, and to utilize a referral network of qualified professionals to provide the most appropriate services available.

- ◆ Keep the field "apolitical". The field of applied sport psychology is stronger because of the influence of both those who come from an "educational - physical education" background as well as those who come from a "clinical/counseling - psychology" background. The field's best chance at sustained growth is through the collaboration of these different orientations and a mutual sharing of the inherent strengths. This can only increase the quality of services that are provided.

- ◆ Demand self-excellence, then demand it of others. Each applied sport psychology professional should meet a self-imposed standard of excellence prior to expecting the same level from others.

- ◆ Be visionaries for the field of applied sport psychology. For the field to remain dynamic and vibrant, students and practitioners must continually venture on a voyage of discovery. Excellence in sport is an on-going process which requires constant compensation and adjustments. The type of voyage should be one typified by the following quote:

> "The voyage of discovery is not in seeking new landscapes, but in having new eyes."
>
> - Marcel Proust

♦ Help to define the parameters of applied sport psychology. Each professional is encouraged to be an active participant in defining the mission of applied sport psychology and monitoring its commitment to the stated mission. This is not a call to put blinders on that constrict the field, but rather a recognition that applied sport psychology can not and should not be all things to all people. There is room for development of other fields (i.e. exercise psychology, health behavior, etc....) outside the mission for applied sport psychology. A field runs the risk of becoming "watered down" by not defining and committing to its mission.

♦ Walk the talk. The strategies and interventions that have been highlighted here have tremendous applicability to everyday life. By internalizing and utilizing the same elements that are taught to athletes and coaches, the practitioner gains increased familiarity and is able to speak from a position of experience. This also allows the practitioner to serve as a role model for the athletes and coaches.

♦ Never lose sight of the uniqueness of the individual. Applied sport psychology should never be "packaged" to the extent that it ignores the needs of the individual. Certain aspects may be fairly universal, but by servicing the individual within the group, the group will ultimately benefit.

♦ Assist others in maintaining perspective. One common hazard is that individuals become swept up in the importance today's society places on sport and successful performance. Applied sport psychology professionals should serve as objective patrons of sport that help to balance this emphasis on success with the necessity for the health and well-being of its participants.

♦ Be an active advocate for the sport participant. The role of applied sport psychology professional is very special and intimate. Often the athlete or coach may be placed in unfair circumstances. It is the responsibility of the applied sport psychology professional to provide objective support for those in need.

♦ Accept the challenge of working in applied sport psychology to meet the unique needs and demands of the individual and/or team. The practitioner must learn to work in a variety of situations that offer a certain context in which one must develop and implement a program.

The world of sport is a truly unique and special place in society. Sport serves many purposes as: an arena for self-exploration; an opportunity to test one's abilities; an outlet for self-expression; an avenue to "get ahead in the world"; an origination for life-long friendships; a safety net for unattached youths; a foundation for the development of character; a school that teaches discipline, responsibility, interdependence, a work-ethic, and self-sacrifice; and a platform to influence greater society. The applied sport psychology professional is an integral, yet tangential part of this world. As such, the sport psychologist can be a part of a very special community.

With this role comes duty, responsibility - the "Charge". We ask each current and future professional to honor such a charge for the benefit of the field of applied sport psychology, as well as the benefit of athletes, coaches, parents, and other members of the "sport family". This "Charge" is eloquently delineated in the following excerpt:

"In working with many athletes at the university level, I am convinced that we as sport psychology professionals are doing ourselves, our coaches, and our athletes a great disservice if our main focus is solely performance enhancement. In fact, I feel this is a very small part of my job. I remember one afternoon prior to an important game, we had a tremendous discussion on what the team wanted to accomplish that evening and how they were going to go about doing it (i.e. play with poise, confidence, enthusiasm, and controlled intensity). I left the meeting feeling very good about what had just taken place, confident that they were mentally ready to reach for their best. Result - they came out tight, non-competitive, out of control, thoroughly stunk up the arena right from the start.

"The point is, we can talk until we are blue in the face about mental preparation strategies for peak performance, and what we as sport psychology professionals can do to improve a particular individual or team's performance, but unless the athlete or team is truly willing to COMMIT themselves to mental skills training and are competitive enough to transfer what is learned in counseling sessions or through educational workshops into practice or onto the playing fields, I philosophically question how effective we really are in terms of performance enhancement training. Sure we can help them strive to gain a sense of control, feel more confident, concentrate more effectively, work with more determination and quality effort, but we must also teach them that sport is not and should not be the only avenue in which they derive a sense of self-worth. Furthermore, we must help them recognize that psychological skills goes beyond the athletic field and skills such as goal setting, concentration , stress management, time management, and communication skills, are skills that transfer to other aspects of their lives as well.

"Consequently, I truly believe we should detach ourselves from our own egos and broaden our perspective beyond the narrow performance enhancement model of intervention and adopt a more holistic mode of intervention that focuses on the total growth and personal development of the people with whom we work. This means to be there as a resource they can trust, turn to, and count on for support and direction, when "THE GARBAGE HITS THE FAN," whether it be personally, socially, academically or athletically." (Yukelson, 1991)

If we are just present to improve sport skills, that is a rather superficial goal. But if we can emphasize the importance of using the mental skills to enhance an athlete's performance in all aspects of his or her life, then the carry-over value is limitless.

References

Morris, W. (Ed.). (1980). The American heritage dictionary of the English language. Boston, MA: Houghton Mifflin Company.

Yukelson, D. (1991, May). Case studies of elite athletes in a college setting. Paper presented at the National Sportpsych Conference, Utopia, TX.

Index to Case Studies

Page Parent-Athlete Case Studies

Mental Skills Training Case Studies

Injury & Career Termination Case Studies

Case Studies, by Sport